ACCLAIM FOR *RIDING TI*

"Good advice for CEOs in how to ensure that a company deploys Information Technology effectively."

Paul Bassett, author of Framing Software Reuse: Lessons from the Real World *and Senior Vice-President,* **Netron Inc.**

"Very readable ... It identifies the changes and potential changes in the way business operates; that everything will change as a result of global computing and communications — an exciting picture."

Alan Brans, Vice-President, Information Systems, **Borden Food Corporation**

"[A] one-minute manager approach to projects."

Robert Cavanagh, Director, Systems Support Branch, **Ontario Ministry of Health**

"Why there is more to using computers than computers."

Peter de Jager, President, **de Jager & Co.**

"A solid guide to delivering successful projects, with useful insights on key elements that really influence outcomes."

Michael Duffy, Manager, Information Systems, **GE Canada**

"[I] liked the emphasis on business focus and commitment of senior management as keystones for success; full cost of ownership [of IT projects] as key to no-surprises business acceptance of a project, keeping timetables and communications; the emphasis on the human infrastructure as key to success."

Ivor Faithfull, Director, Information Systems & Automation, **Philips Electronics Ltd.**

"Before you start working with your Information Technology group, read this book."

Tom Gove, Director, Corporate Affairs (Ret.), **Procter & Gamble Canada**

"Lots of good thoughts on the ingredients for successful projects; also examples of project pitfalls.... I liked the emphasis on people vs. technology."

Liz Grigg, Director of Information Services, **Cadbury Chocolate Canada**

"[A] management view of the things that need to be considered to effectively manage IT projects ... hits all the right points."

*Bob Minge, Manager of PC Options and PC Integration, **IBM Canada***

"A recipe for planning, executing and improvement with emphasis on being in sync with customers and business strategy ... I particularly liked the simple language and benchmark examples."

*Paul Nelson, Vice-President Information Technology and CIO, **Rogers Cantel Inc.***

"Good checklist of things to do to implement a project."

*Tom Phelps, Vice-President, Investments, Strategies and Planning, **Noranda Inc.***

"Good examples of technology innovations."

*Sheilah Reid, CIO, **Xerox Canada***

"Interesting and thought provoking."

*Bruce Rosebrugh, Vice-President, Sales, **Diamed Lab Supplies***

"Be ahead of your competition. Do not wait for 1998 to declare the Year of the Tiger. Do it now. This book will give you that chance. Buy it. Read it. Share it. Ride it!"

*Fritz Scheuren, Ph.D., Professor of Statistics, **The George Washington University***

"I applaud you putting your wisdom in book form and like the tiger analogy a great deal ... A set of wisdoms that can bring 'wisdom' into our organization easily."

*Peter Shepard, Customer Services Manager, **Imperial Oil***

"A perfectly understandable set of guidelines for executives on how to manage computers. *Riding the Tiger* gives practical explanations as to why sound management must always come ahead of technology. The authors explain why the responsibility for information systems should not ever be abdicated to technical experts."

*Paul A. Strassmann, former Chief Information Executive, **Kraft, Xerox and U.S. Department of Defense***

"It reads well. It's accessible. It uses clear, concise prose. It is not prolix, a common problem with management books.... I also like the message — plan, think ahead, keep an eye on the bigger picture.... the Tiger is *unruly* and *can* be ridden."

*George Takach, Partner, **McCarthy Tétrault***

"Very easy and entertaining to read."

Heather Taylor, Senior Consultant, People Effectiveness,
AT&T Canada Long-Distance Services

"I love the TigerPearls ... a wonderful absence of technical jargon ... I think the text will be of particular appeal to 'generalists.'"

*Caroline Thornton, President, **NADUM Inc.***

"It is pitched at the right level for the [business manager] audience."

Al Venslovaitis, Vice-President, Information Technology,
The Globe and Mail

"Describes the nature of discomfort with the double-edged sword of information management well."

*Ken Wilson, President, Business Services Group, **Sprint Canada Inc.***

"An eye-opener to risks of CEOs not getting involved in information management."

*Don Woodley, CEO, **Oracle Canada***

"Recent studies continue to indicate that there is no correlation between the amount of IS/IT spending in an organization and the business benefit derived from that expenditure. An effective ROI can only come from a combination of understanding, commitment and vision on the part of senior executives. One of the best ways of accomplishing that is by reading this excellent new book, *Riding the Tiger*."

*Edward Yourdon, Author of **The Decline and Fall of the American Programmer***

"*Riding the Tiger* expounds the need for detailed planning, not just wishful thinking."

Ken Zurbrigg, Financial Services Marketing Consultant

RIDING THE
TIGER

How to outsmart the computer
that is after your job.

How not to bankrupt your organization
with information management.

How good clients get exceptional results.

ALISTAIR DAVIDSON
HARVEY GELLMAN
MARY CHUNG

HarperBusiness
HarperCollins*PublishersLtd*

http://www.harpercollins.com/canada

TigerPearl™ is a trademark of Alacrity Inc., Toronto, Ontario, Canada
Text illustrations by John Cadiz. Used by permission.
Questionnaires may be photocopied for restricted use
within companies and organizations.

First edition

Canadian Cataloguing in Publication Data

Davidson, Alistair F.F., 1953-
Riding the tiger

"A HarperBusiness book".
Includes bibliographical references and index.
ISBN 0-00-255763-0

1. Information technology - Management.   2. Information resources
management.   I. Gellman, H.S. (Harvey Saul), 1924-   .
II. Chung, Mary, 1952-   .   III. Title.

HD30.2.D38 1997   658.4'038   C96-931888-X

97 98 99 ❖ HC 10 9 8 7 6 5 4 3 2 1

Printed and bound in the United States

Authors' Dedications

This book is dedicated to all the people who made it possible and supported us through its writing: our clients, who have given us work, for without them none of this would have been possible; my co-authors, who have been a delight to work with; the entire Davidson family—Douglas, Evelyn, Neil and Lindsay—who through the years, over many dinner table discussions and arguments, fostered my interest in books and writing; Dr. Cho Man Chung, for his unstinting support and encouragement; our colleagues at Alacrity Inc., who continue to delight us with their wisdom, creativity and insights; and the late Ralph Fisher, who got me started and introduced me to Harvey.

Alistair Davidson

To my wife, whose love and support have always been there for me.

Harvey Gellman

To my father, whose confidence in the future is infectious. To Adrian, Daphne and Grace, the future is theirs. To the late William Li, who introduced me to the semiconductor chip.

Mary Chung

CONTENTS

Foreword xv
Acknowledgments xvii
Introduction: Tiger, Tiger, Burning Bright...1
      How To Read This Book..2
      What We Are *Not* Addressing in *Riding the Tiger*........................4

Chapter 1: How Information Technology Affects One Organization.............7
      The Bank of Glen Burnie

Chapter 2: Facing the Technology Tiger 15
      Like the automobile, the computer is not one thing. It has more
      than one effect. It is transforming your job, your business, your
      markets and all of society.

      A Whole New Set of Issues 17
      Too Big a Project Proposed, Too Little Achieved,
          Delivered Too Late, for Too Much Money 17
      A Ride on the Tiger Is, at Best, Rocky...23
      Costs of Information Management—Get the Big Picture............24
      Measuring the Investment Payback 26
      The Never-Ending Search for the Next Technology....................27
      We Have Seen the Light—It Is Digital and in Color....................28
      Surrounded by Tigers—Technology Is Changing
          the Way We Do Business..29
      The Challenge to the Tiger Rider 35
      Strategic Thinking, Not Computer Expertise, Is Key 38
      Summary 38

      The Bank of Glen Burnie Case Study: Contacting a Consultant.....39

Chapter 3: Leading the Tiger, Not Chasing Its Tail 43
        *Information technology should be guided by the business'
        strategic objectives.*

        Chasing the Tiger's Tail 44
        Business Strategy Is the Starting Point 47
        Useful Strategic Concepts and How They Affect
            Information Management 48
        Technology's Influence on Strategy 58
        Building a Sustainable Success Position (SSP) 59
        Leading the Tiger to Support a Sustainable Success Position 62
        Information Management Model for Achieving Sustainable
            Information Systems Capabilities 63
        Competitive Advantage through Information
            Technology—The Wal-Mart Story 68
        Summary 72

        The Bank of Glen Burnie Case Study: Developing the Strategy 73

Chapter 4: Running Away from the Tiger 79
        *The delinquent CEO fails to make sure that the information
        management of the organization is excellent.*

        Delegate and Avoid! 81
        Signals from the CEO 83
        The CEO Who Pays Attention 84
        Setting Strategies and Priorities 88
        Aligning Information Technology with Business Strategies 89
        How Organizations Develop an Information
            Technology Strategy 92
        Planning over Multiple Periods 95
        Setting Investment Priorities 96
        Working Smart 99
        Information Management Policies and Principles 100
        Sample Principles for an Organization 102
        Organizational Improvement Goals 107
        Assessing the Organization's Capabilities 109
        Improving Infrastructure and Technology 110
        Influencing Implementation 111
        Summary: The Role of Senior Management 112

        The Bank of Glen Burnie Case Study: The Delinquent CEO 114

Chapter 5: The Tiger's Backbone—Basic Anatomy 115
Policies and infrastructure for the corporate information highway.

Managing Where the Tiger Roams 115
The Highway for the Tiger...117
A Broader View of Infrastructure and Policies 119
Planning Policies and Infrastructure—Expect a
    Moving Target..121
Accountability...123
Technology Principles...126
Adequate Hardware 127
Excellent Software 128
Supporting Management Effectiveness.......................................131
Mobile and Temporary Computing 135
Managing Risks...137
Costing Infrastructure..140
Renting a Tiger—The Outsourcing Decision..............................141
Getting It Right the First Time..146
Motivating and Keeping Your Knowledge Workers 147
Customer Satisfaction..147
On Time and on Budget 148
Evaluating Technology...149
Buy versus Develop..151
Improving Infrastructure 151
Evolution Game Plan 152
Upgrading the Technical Capability of Your People..................153
Summary...154

The Bank of Glen Burnie Case Study: Infrastructure................155

Chapter 6: Harnessing the Power of the Tiger...161
*The people side of technology—the critical role of people in
information management.*

Informating People, Not Automating..163
Change, Change, Change 166
Stakeholders—Fellow Riders..168
Kraft Foods—In Control..170
The Philosophy of Decentralization..172
Good-bye, Boss. Hello, Team Leader. 174
The New Computer Literacy..180

Senior Management's Computer Literacy Can
    Affect the Success of the Organization.....................183
Connections between People Management and
    Information Management 184
Summary..185

The Bank of Glen Burnie Case Study: People..............186

Chapter 7: Adventures on Your Tiger 191
*Using information technology is like having a baby. You need
to keep feeding it. Just when you think you've finished raising it,
you have to send it to college and it costs you even more than
you thought possible.*

Projects—Where the Action Is......................................192
How to Spot a Project...192
Planning Projects 195
Should the Project Proceed?...195
Sizing the Project..200
Costing the Project..201
Choosing the Technology..202
Staffing the Project 203
Assessing and Managing Project Risk 205
Quality Project Process..211
Manage Expectations...213
The Importance of Cut-off Points..................................213
Deadlines 214
Project Team 215
Obtaining Buy-In and Involving the Management
    Team..216
Testing and Documentation 216
Installing New Information Technology Is a
    Process of Change...217
Why Projects Fail 217
Postaudits..218
Success that Lasts..219
Predicting Project Success...220

The Bank of Glen Burnie Case Study: Project Management.......223

Chapter 8: Riding Your Tiger with Finesse.......................229
Good clients get exceptional results.

Ignore Information Technology and Delegate to
  Experts at Your Own Risk 229
Everyone Is a Client...230
Good Clients Get Better Results 231
Information Technology Only Looks Like Magic 232
Know Your Own Reasons for Using
  Information Technology 232
Understand Your Competencies...233
People...233
Information Technology is a Catalyst
  for Change 234
Forward Thinking...234
Communicate Your Goals and Needs.......................................235
With Good Infrastructure, Quick and Dirty Projects
  Can Succeed...235
Software Is Always a Service 236
Open Systems Are Built, Not Bought.......................................236
Outsourcing—Riding Others' Learning Curves 236
The Future of Software Is in Layers and Modules....................237
Murphy's Law...238
Things Get Easier, but the Hurdle Is Always Being Raised 239
Commitment 239
Consensus...240
KISS—Keep It Simple, Stupid!..240
Good Clients in Partnership with Good Suppliers....................240
The Metropolitan Toronto Police Case 242
Three Times to Get It Right...244
What to Look for in a Project Plan 244
The Successful Project...247
Summary...248

Chapter 9: The Quick and the Dead 249
  The Conclusion to the Bank of Glen Burnie Case Study.

  Questions for the Reader 256
  Your Own Next Steps..256

Appendix I: Diagnostic Questionnaire..257
Appendix II: How One Large Organization Evaluates Its Projects............273
Glossary of Key Information and Technology Jargon................................279
Bibliography..293
Index 297

PERMISSIONS

FOREWORD

In *Riding the Tiger*, Alistair Davidson, Harvey Gellman and Mary Chung address a critical, outstanding need: in the increasingly competitive global arena in which we live and work, no business manager can afford to be without the skills necessary to deploy information technology effectively.

Notwithstanding all the packaged software that is available today, or all the project experience that has been accumulated over the past 40 years, projects involving information technology continue to fall short or fail with disturbing frequency. Davidson, Gellman and Chung have been through many such projects and share their experience, their expertise and their informed observations in this timely book. The lessons they outline will be of tremendous value to a great many business managers. Readers will come away with a better understanding of information technology, greater knowledge of how to apply it more effectively and an awareness of how to avoid common mistakes.

When the first desktop machines appeared in the late 1970s, I was very enthusiastic about the potential for applying personal computers to business problems. As these computers have progressed from limited stand-alone machines to networked powerhouses, that potential is being realized, and new uses and opportunities continue to be created. As we move into the future, the lessons appearing in this book become increasingly relevant to all business managers, in all types of business.

Over the past 25 years, in my work on the business applications of information technology, I have consistently noted the critical importance of effective communications. The cartoon showing sketches of the construction of a child's swing as perceived by differing project participants presents a compelling picture. The fact that "what the customer wanted" is so very different from the other views conveys a message with which many of us are all too familiar.

Davidson, Gellman and Chung present their broad range of comprehensive insights in the deceptively simple manner characteristic of high-quality communications. It is a particular pleasure that such valuable advice is now available from a Canadian source. *Riding the Tiger* is an invaluable reference tool from which many people will benefit.

Donald A. Stewart, F.I.A., F.C.I.A.
President and Chief Operating Officer
Sun Life of Canada

THE EVOLUTION

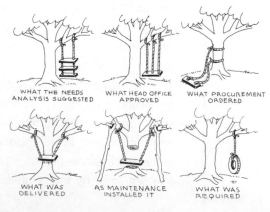

WHAT THE NEEDS
ANALYSIS SUGGESTED

WHAT HEAD OFFICE
APPROVED

WHAT PROCUREMENT
ORDERED

WHAT WAS
DELIVERED

AS MAINTENANCE
INSTALLED IT

WHAT WAS
REQUIRED

(Anon.)

ACKNOWLEDGMENTS

We would like to acknowledge the tremendous support of the many busy executives across Canada, the US and Europe who took the time out to read portions of our manuscript. Donald Stewart, in particular, deserves special mention for finding the time out of his hectic life as the new President of Sun Life Insurance to read *Riding the Tiger* and write the foreword. We are particularly pleased to have him write it as he is experienced in steering the tiger from his previous role as CIO. We are sure he will continue to pay attention in the future as well.

We would like to thank the staff at HarperCollins for their enthusiasm for *Riding the Tiger*, specifically Don Loney, our editor, who always remained optimistic, Jill Lambert for her initial interest in the book, Kathleen Richards for her valiant attempts to convert our rambling prose to English, Marie Campbell and Nicole

Langlois for their production editing, and Beverley Sotolov, our proofreader. Jane Stevenson played a special role as godmother to the book in introducing us to HarperCollins. A special note of thanks should also go to Rob Randall, a long-time expert in business publishing, writing and editing who made the book proposal possible. We also thank John Cadiz for his deft cartoons.

We sent out chapters of the book to many executives. Some were very knowledgeable about information management, others were more general management oriented. Some of them clearly have books in them based upon their insights. While we couldn't include every comment, there is always the next book. All the readers' comments and encouragement have aided us greatly even when exhorting us to do better. However, any mistakes in approach remain the authors'. In alphabetical order, the reviewers whose work reached us in time to be included:

Timothy Attia, Director, Consulting Services, The CGI Group
Paul Bassett, Senior Vice-President, Research, Netron Inc.
George Bedard, Partner, Bedard McGillivray & Associates
Gale Blank, Vice-President, Information Services Division, National Grocers Co. Ltd.
Catherine Aczel Boivie, Director of IS and CIO, BC Automobile Association
Graham Boundy, Director, Consulting, The CGI Group
Alan Brans, Director, Information Resources, Kraft Canada
Bruce Burgetz, Senior Vice-President, Information Technology, Shoppers Drug Mart
Robert Cavanagh, Director, Systems Support Branch, Ontario Ministry of Health
Tara Cramer, Director of Data Processing, Boeing Employees Credit Union
David Creighton, Budget Officer, City of Fairfield, California
Peter de Jager, President, de Jager & Co.
Michael Duffy, Manager Information Systems, GE Canada
Mark Dymond, Director, Consulting Services, The CGI Group
Douglas Enns, President and CEO, Pacific Coast Savings Credit Union
Ivor Faithfull, Director, ISO Automation, Philips Electronics Ltd.
Hugh Fletcher, Director, Consulting Services, The CGI Group
Jeff Gold, Director, Consulting Services, The CGI Group

B.B. "Ike" Goodfellow, President, Echo Bay Consulting
Tom Gove, Director, Corporate Affairs (Ret.), Procter & Gamble Canada
Karol Griffin, Senior Vice-President, Teachers Credit Union, South
    Bend, Indiana
Liz Grigg, Director, Information Systems, Cadbury Chocolate Canada
Andrew A. Grindlay, Professor, Richard Ivey School of Business (Ret.),
    University of Western Ontario
Ailsa Hamilton, Director, Integrated Justice Project, Ontario Ministry
    of Solicitor General and Correctional Services
Nader Hanna, Director, Consulting Services, The CGI Group
Jim Hayward, Vice-President, Consulting Services, The CGI Group
Brian Held, Senior Vice-President and CFO, Derlan Industries Ltd.
Elise Herzig, Director, Commercial Operations, McMaster University
    Nuclear Reactor
Loren Hicks, Vice-President, Consulting Services, The CGI Group
Alan Hutton, President, Star Data Systems
Donna Ingram, Acting Director, Information Systems Branch, Ontario
    Ministry of Community and Social Services
Paul Kennedy, President, IDC Canada Ltd.
Andrew Kinoshita, Senior Vice-President, Information Services, Ault
    Foods Ltd.
Gene Kotack, General Manager IS and CIO, Brewers Retail Inc.
Rocco Lallone, Communications Consultant, Bell Advanced Communications
Wilfred Loewrigkeit, Vice-President, Systems, National Life
Tony Loginow, Director, IS Development, Ontario Ministry of Finance
Don MacDonald, Vice-President, Technology and CIO, The T. Eaton
    Company
Duncan MacKay, Executive Vice-President, Nabnasset Corporation
Roger Mahabir, Director, Computing and Telecommunications,
    Metropolitan Toronto Police
Colin Maloney, Executive Director, Catholic Children's Aid Society
Al Martin, Senior Vice-President, Systems Research and Development,
    (Ret.) TD Bank
Joan McCalla, Information Infrastructure Branch, Director, Ontario
    Ministry of Economic Development, Trade and Tourism
John McLauchlan, Director, Consulting Services, The CGI Group

Bob Mingle, Manager of PC Options and PC Integration, IBM Canada

Hugh Moore, Chief Administrative Officer, Policing, Metropolitan Toronto Police

Lucille Nareen, Information Manager, Labatt Ontario Breweries

Paul Nelson, Vice-President, Information Technology and CIO, Rogers Cantel Inc.

Theodore Peridis, Professor, Schulich School of Business, York University

Tom Phelps, Vice-President, Investments, Strategies and Planning, Noranda Inc.

Cathryn Poulter, Director, Consulting Services, The CGI Group

Sheilah Reid, CIO, Xerox Canada

Bruce Rosebrugh, Vice-President, Sales, Diamed Lab Supplies

Janis Sears, ISVP, Technology and Services, Canada Life

Darrel Shaw, Director, Consulting Services, The CGI Group

Peter Shepard, Customer Services Manager, IS Department, Imperial Oil

Doug Smith, President, Filbitron Systems Group

Erik Lahn Sorensen, New Product Consultant, Dansk Teknologisk Institut, Copenhagen

Rejean St. Amour, Acting Vice-President, IS Technology, Ontario Lottery Corporation

Chris Stait-Gardner, President and CEO, Security Card Systems Inc.

Robert Steel, First Vice-President, Canadian Provinces, The CGI Group

Carolyn Swadron, Director, Relationship Support, Year 2000, CIBC

George Takach, Partner, McCarthy Tétrault

Ying Tam, Director, Consulting Services, The CGI Group

Heather Taylor, Sr. Consultant, People Effectivenesss, AT&T Canadian Long Distance Services

Caroline Thornton, President, NADUM Inc.

Al Venslovaitis, Vice-President, Information Technology, *The Globe and Mail*

Wayne Walker, Director, Information Management Facilities, Ontario Hydro

Mark Weber, Director of Finance, Teachers Credit Union, South Bend, Indiana

Ted White, President, Frederick T. White Associates

Doug Willougby, Vice-President, Finance, Pacific Coast Savings Credit
  Union
Ken Wilson, President, Business Services Group, Sprint Canada Inc.
Don Woodley, President, Compaq Canada Inc.
Ken Zurbrigg, Financial Services Marketing Consultant

And for those whose feedback came too late to be acknowledged here,
thank you too.

Alistair Davidson, Harvey Gellman, and Mary Chung,
at www.alacrity.com and www.tigerpearls.com

TIGER, TIGER, BURNING BRIGHT

Many organizations started using computers in the 1950s and 1960s. Yet many of today's systems are failures—in spite of all we have learned about using computers and developing software. Most information management systems are difficult to use. They fail to satisfy their users. They cost more than expected. They are delivered and installed late.

We wanted to write a book that would help nontechnical business managers understand more about how information technology is changing their organization. We wanted to help them play their role of shaping information technology in their business. We wanted to help them avoid many of the mistakes we see business managers making time and time again. If you don't read this book, you *will* learn these lessons, eventually, and probably at great cost to the business and possibly your career.

Our title is our metaphor for the problem many organizations are facing. *Managers are riding a technology tiger*. This makes for an uncomfortable place to sit. If you fall off, the tiger will eat you alive. If you master the tiger, you can outpace your competitors. But mastering and managing the tiger take some basic knowledge and skills.

In 1951, when Harvey Gellman was involved in the purchase of the first computer in Canada, computers were complex devices that only highly trained specialists could operate. In 1985, when Mary Chung and Alistair Davidson developed the first expert system for strategic planning in the world, most American executives still did not use computers. Now most managers in North America have computers on their desks.

Today, most of the projects that we work on are different from projects of a decade ago. Companies are spending more and more money on information management infrastructure and projects. These in turn support more and more tasks performed at the decision-making and managerial level. Both managers and front-line employees spend more time on software systems that change frequently. Integrating information from many sources is a common problem. Linking to customers and suppliers is a chal-. lenge that is shaking up many organizations.

Over the past two decades, computers have increased in power by more than 500 times. As a result, nearly every job in every organization needs to be reconsidered or redesigned. *Riding the Tiger* will help managers upgrade their knowledge so that they will not be blindsided by the inevitable computer-driven changes in their organization.

The computer is almost as commonplace as the telephone. But while managers may know how to bang out a memo, construct a spreadsheet or send e-mail, few know enough about what we call the New Computer Literacy. The New Computer Literacy is as much about how to change your organization as it is about computers. In fact, we prefer the term *information management* to terms like *computers* or *information technology*. We believe it gives more of the flavor of the challenges that managers are facing.

How to Read This Book

We have designed this book so that different readers can read it in different ways. The book is structured in layers (shown in the diagram on the inside cover of the book). It starts with the most general issue in chapter 2 of why computers are important and have changed the way orginizations work. Chapter 3 addresses the issue of linking your information technology strategy to your business strategy. Chapter 4 focuses on the role of a senior general manager such as the CEO. Chapter 5 focuses upon the policies and infrastructure that senior management should establish.

Chapter 6 deals with the critical role of people and capabilities in making technology work effectively. Chapter 7 is, in many ways, the heart of the book, because it addresses the practical issues of becoming involved in a project where information technology is a critical element. Chapter 8 deals with how to be on the receiving end of technical services from your own IS department or from a supplier.

While you can read this book in any order, we recommend that you read the introduction to our Plan-Do-Improve model at the end of chapter 3. This model provides a framework to which we refer throughout *Riding the Tiger*.

We pursue several themes. The first is the basis of the book and owes its origin to Harvey. Over 40 years of computer consulting, he has observed that a company only gets good information technology if its CEO demands good information technology.

Our second key point is that investing in information management actually reduces an organization's productivity unless there are specific improvement objectives that have already been established, are sought and measured. And with the types of computer systems being developed today, improvement requires that more nonspecialists, or "regular" managers, be involved in their acquisition than ever before.

Third, we believe that infrastructure in an organization is more about people than it is about hardware.

Fourth, all information management decisions must be based on one basic piece of logic. It is Plan–Do–Improve. At its simplest, this catechism reminds us that without plans, information technology is always implemented at considerable cost. Without pursuit and promotion of best practices, what is done is done badly. Without businesses seeking to improve the way they operate, they gain nothing from more use of computers.

Our fifth theme is that just because something can be automated it doesn't mean it should be. Automating a bad process just makes it more capital-intensive. An organization's overall strategy should drive its information technology investments. In many organizations, the limitations of its information technology determine the possible strategy. Good software not only solves short-term problems, it sets up the organization for future rapid improvement at modest, gradual cost.

Sixth, good project management is the key to success in implementing this technology. Good project management is particularly challenging, because it is really "change management."

Finally, we believe very strongly that information management is about effectiveness. It is always cheaper to postpone investments in information technology. But fundamentally, computers are inexpensive and people provide leverage. Investments in information technology should therefore be evaluated not on cost but on capturing opportunities.

What We Are *Not* Addressing in *Riding the Tiger*

You will notice that many topics you might expect to find in a book about information technology and management have been omitted. We do not recommend specific hardware or software or operating systems. We do not debate the merits of Macintosh or Windows. (We like them both for different reasons.) We spend little time on purchasing software packages, except as part of the acquisition process in managing a project.

We skim over the merits of mainframes or minis. There is a reason for this. Most organizations with mainframes and minis also have excellent specialists with extensive knowledge of this technology. End-users—most of us who use computers as part of our jobs but not our particular specialties—rarely get involved with such "hard core" systems. Our discussion in this book revolves around getting information off such systems.

The real growth in computer use lies with the "regular folks" who use computers. The kinds of systems regular users and managers are familiar with are in many ways more complicated and less stable than the systems specialists manage.

Paradoxically, the rapidly changing and evolving systems—the ones that can cripple or leverage a company—are the ones that won't work unless nonspecialist regular folks work with them. These people are the ones who will benefit from *Riding the Tiger*.

Information technology allows you to create terrible bureaucracies and awful information flows. There is no intrinsic advantage to any type of software unless you implement it wisely.

One of the authors recently talked with a general management consultant who was very interested in groupware, which is software used for sharing information among many locations. The consultant was enamored of the idea of lots of information flowing back and forth between people within an organization. He had lost sight of the objective of information management: to minimize work and useless activities. Making it easier to create bureaucratic paperwork and unnecessary communications had become his focus.

This kind of fascination with technology touches off many projects and investments that can wreck whole organizations. Avoid such boundless enthusiasm. Information management is important, but balance it with common sense.

We have written *Riding the Tiger* with two major concerns for our readers.

First, we would like the prescriptions and advice in it to be reasonably timeless. Most computer books date very quickly because they focus on a particular software package or, even worse, a version of the software package. The advice in *Riding the Tiger* should transcend the period in which it was written. We have spent little time on the merits of this technology or that software program. Instead, we have focused on the larger management, policy and project issues.

Also, we have written the book assuming that the readers are business managers. We do assume they are computer users, but *not* programmers, *not* information technology professionals. Information technology professionals will find the book useful in its discussion of the business side of their role. They may also find it useful for educating their business manager clients about the problems they face in developing information management projects.

Throughout *Riding the Tiger*, we provide aphorisms, or TigerPearls, that help the reader by providing a summary of key points. One of the early reviewers of our manuscript, Paul Basset, has suggested that Pearl stands for Plan–Execute–Analyze and adjust, Repeat the Loop—perhaps another way of talking about Plan–Do–Improve. Another reviewer suggested that

TigerPearls should have been called TigerPaws—thoughts that give pause for thought.

For all of you riding the technology tiger, welcome to the driver's manual for your tiger.

Riding the Tiger
is written to
address the
many ways
in which
information
management
affects you in
your organization.

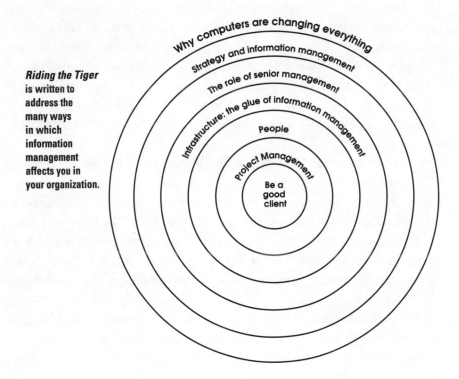

chapter 1

HOW INFORMATION TECHNOLOGY AFFECTS ONE ORGANIZATION

THE BANK OF GLEN BURNIE

All managers eventually reach a difficult point in their careers—one where they must make decisions about things they really don't understand very well.

How they deal with this situation can make or break their careers. We are going to begin this book with the types of questions about *information technology* and *information management* that may worry you. In later chapters, we will address the issues of strategy and information technology, the role of CEOs and senior managers, infrastructure, people issues, project management and what being a good customer means.

We begin with our fictional bank, the Bank of Glen Burnie. After each chapter, we will return briefly to it as a way of illustrating the themes of *Riding the Tiger* developed in chapters 2 through 8. We will show how the themes of each chapter are experienced by the bank's management as they develop their own business and information management strategy.

You have been appointed the president and chief operating officer (COO) of a relatively small US financial institution of $3 billion. You are now wondering what you should do to help the business grow or perhaps just survive. Americans take for granted that there are many financial institutions in their country. In most other countries, the number of financial institutions is much smaller. In Canada, France, the UK and Germany there are a small number of surviving large institutions.

Our hero's name is Steve Arbeit. Times are tough and the forecast calls for stormy weather. Debit cards, the Internet, home computer banking, shrinking margins, obsolete computer systems, increased rate of change— all add up to change, and banks have never been good at change.

He is particularly worried about the Internet. How does it change the economics of his business? One friend said to him recently, "Don't worry about the Internet. It's just slow television."

THE RULES OF THE GAME ARE CHANGING

The Cast of Characters at the Bank of Glen Burnie

Aldo Moretti, Chairperson and Chief Executive Officer
Steve Arbeit, President and Chief Operating Officer
Peter Schultz, Vice-President, Information Systems, and
    Chief Information Officer
Gail Bartok, Vice-President, Human Resources
Martha Rodrigues, Vice-President, Operations
Kathy Smith, Branch Manager
Jeremy Havelock, Vice-President, Finance, and Chief
    Financial Officer
Ron Silver, Vice-President, Marketing
Bill Underwood, Facilitator
John Ho, Director and Dean of local business school

Like most managers, Steve does use a computer. He knows how to check his e-mail. He types passably well, but slowly. He regrets not having taken typing in high school when he was a kid, but in those days, real men didn't type. He's pretty good with a spreadsheet. He uses the World Wide Web occasionally. His kids use CD-ROMs for their homework. In the past year at the bank, there has been a mad rush to pursue information technology for his organization.

There are too many connections, he thinks. There are lots of choices and he is not sure he really understands them. He decides to send an e-mail to his old friend and teacher, Professor Bill Underwood. As Bill always used to joke, when it comes to information technology, he's pretty much "been there and done that."

In his new role, Steve would like to launch more new products than has been possible in the past. The problem is, as he knows from experience, that every time you turn around, the IS (information systems) department says, "No, we can't do it that quickly." His IS department determines what can and cannot be done, rather than the marketing department. This is extremely frustrating. He wonders if client-server computing isn't the answer. It seems too simple that one technology could solve all these problems.

The chief financial officer, Jeremy Havelock, likes computers. That's part of the problem. Every time a new supplier calls, he is as easily seduced as an ice cream fanatic in a Baskin-Robbins store. The technology keeps changing so quickly. Just when you think you have a fix on it, it changes again.

It's pretty hard getting hold of the IS director, Peter Schultz. He is always running around to conferences, and when you can reach him the answer is always no. He is a good person, but his department does not seem to be doing much more than sticking fingers in the dike of computer issues and problems threatening to burst.

There is ongoing debate in the organization about the number of employees its operation really needs. Many of its competitors are laying off 30 to 40 percent of their people. The board is pressing the bank to do the same. Steve is worried that if Glen Burnie offers a downsizing program the good employees will be the ones who leave.

He has heard a rumor that IBM had this problem at the Olympic Games in Atlanta. Their downsizing meant they lost the people who had worked for them before on the Games. That's why things didn't run as smoothly as in the past.

The Bank of Glen Burnie has a legacy. Actually, it's a "legacy system." It's an old clunker of a minicomputer. It does not do its job very well, but replacing it would require a huge amount of work and money. Steve wonders what he should do. Replace it? Try to extend its life? How would they implement a new system? One supplier has suggested a three-layer architecture. Steve's not sure what that means. It sounds expensive.

There seem to be lots of personal computers in the organization. They do not seem to be doing much for the bank except increase costs.

What is really going on here? Maybe they should just stick with terminals and hope the problem will go away.

In several months, the bank will kick off its strategic and business planning. Steve faces all the conflicting demands for more computers, more software, faster networks, more departmental servers and a new telephone system. As chief operating officer, he senses that his business strategy, his people and his computers are marching off in completely different directions.

Just as Steve is getting ready to leave his office, Peter Schultz calls him on the phone. The main computer has broken down and the transaction records have been corrupted. The backup tapes failed to restore the data properly. Steve authorizes the people who need to come in on the weekend to reconstruct the transaction records. At least the computer is paid for. He feels his blood pressure rising.

Riding the Tiger can help reduce your risk of being thrown or eaten alive by the tiger. It will lay out for you the key information that you need to know to survive in the topsy-turvy organization you will inevitably work in.

We have structured the book to help the nontechnical business manager or computer user deal with information management by looking at the issue from different points of view. Information management runs throughout an organization and cannot be dealt with easily, as one entity, so we have structured the material as follows:

- **Process Issues.** The Bank of Glen Burnie case illustrates how a "real" group of managers trying to improve the organization of a small financial institution might address information management issues. Beginning in Chapter 1, the case will develop progressively through each chapter.
- **Problems.** Chapter 2 focuses on the types of problems that people run into all the time when they try to change their organizations and their information management.
- **Strategy and Information Management.** Chapter 3 offers a framework for thinking about how information management can support your organization's strategy and how you can seek competitive advantage, build and maintain it.
- **Leadership Issues.** These issues are covered in chapter 4. In the past, some senior managers have paid little attention to the information management of their organizations.
- **Infrastructure.** In chapter 5, we distinguish between business initiatives that require information management projects and "infrastructure," the glue that holds an organization together.
- **People Issues.** Chapter 6 looks at people and computers. There are so many ways they can support and fail each other.
- **Project Management.** Chapter 7 presents some general conclusions about becoming involved in information technology projects. We offer rules of thumb and tricks of project management to help ensure success.

- **The Good Client.** Chapter 8 tells what it takes to be a good client. Good clients do get better results than bad ones do!
- **Resolution of the Case.** We return to the case of the Bank of Glen Burnie in chapter 9 to see how they have managed their own transition to mastering their own technology tiger.
- **Diagnostic Questionnaire.** Once you have finished the book, take a look at your own firm and see how it stacks up. The questionnaire helps you identify the information management activities in your own organization.
- **Keeping Up-to-Date.** Readers who want to keep up with important management developments but don't want to flounder through reams of technical information in computer magazines provide can subscribe to the *Riding the Tiger* newsletter. It is designed for the person who wants to keep up, but is not a "techie."

Waiting for Bill Underwood

Steve leaves the Bank of Glen Burnie late that night. He wonders what Bill is going to suggest as he drives home. He feels his brain is going in circles and is grateful for recent research that suggests up to two drinks a day is good for the health of your heart.

Let's take a look at why information technology is important and why Steve ought to be worried. He has just climbed onto the back of the technology tiger. He needs some driving lessons and probably a road map.

BEFORE YOU GO ON . . .

Spend a few minutes considering Steve Arbeit's position before you read any further. At the end of the book, you can review how well you anticipated the evolution of his bank and his success as COO.

Can the Bank of Glen Burnie survive with all its problems?

Should Steve be looking for a new job because he doesn't know enough about information technology?

Is downsizing the answer for this bank?

What are the major forces affecting the Bank of Glen Burnie?

What kinds of processes should the bank follow if it changes its strategy?

What technologies are likely to be most important to the bank?

Who needs to be involved in changing the organization?

What are the smaller and larger competitors of the bank likely to do?

How should the organization measure and control itself?

What should the role of consultants be for this organization? Should this organization be seeking answers from its consultants for a better way to address the issues with which it is faced?

chapter **2**

FACING THE
TECHNOLOGY TIGER

 TigerPearl Like the automobile, the computer is not one thing. It has more than one effect. It is transforming your job, your business, your markets and all of society.

We, the authors, are often reluctant computer users.

We use computers because there is no other way to do the tasks we need to do. And, maybe unfortunately, because we use computers a lot we constantly try to do new things with them. So our machines freeze or crash or stop working and we waste time. Through perseverance, we learn how to do things better. The process costs us dearly; each new benefit is bought with great frustration.

That is the essence of riding the tiger of technology. When it comes to computers, you're often damned if you do *and* damned if you don't.

Succeeding in any organization is always an unpredictable process. But like the process of

Darwinian selection, where organisms are selected for their ability to survive and reproduce, you are hired for your skills and your ability to create value that can translate into success for the organization. The more you know about computers, information management and their consequences, the more valuable you will be to your organization.

Today, your effectiveness is based not just upon your skills and knowledge, but also upon the information management of the organization. If you cannot assess your organization and its capabilities, you may run the risk of losing your job in a sudden downsizing. If your role is ineffective due to poor information management, then you must attempt to influence your organization. Your objective will be to make it more effective. Only organizations with effective information management can provide you with long-term employment.

JUMP ON OR BE DEVOURED

A Whole New Set of Issues

For most managers, the experience of using personal computers and thinking about information issues is a relatively new phenomenon. Typical Baby Boom managers might be in their forties today. When they began their careers in the 1970s, computers were used exclusively by information systems professionals.

Most managerial computer users did not start using computers until the mid 1980s. Even then, that use was restricted primarily to spreadsheets.

In the late 1980s, managers first used computers in a big way, so the widespread use of computers is for most of them new knowledge and a recent skill, and an area in which they have received little formal training.

The curve is now accelerating dramatically, so that people are increasingly drawn to both computer use and redesigning and improving their organization in response to the technology. Redesign is tough to do well, a fact that Machiavelli, perhaps the first writer on reengineering, pointed out in *The Prince*:

> *There is nothing more difficult to plan, more doubtful of success, nor more dangerous to manage, than the creation of a new system. For the initiator has the enmity of all those who would profit by the preservation of the old system, and merely lukewarm defenders of those who would gain by a new one.*

Too Big a Project Proposed, Too Little Achieved, Delivered Too Late, for Too Much Money

Many of the computer projects that draw managers into new roles happen by accident. Someone in the organization sees an opportunity to save money or generate new business. He or she assigns the company's own information systems (IS) department to build the computer system or, more frequently these days, seeks outside help. Whether internal or external, the ideal developer puts down on paper the project specifications and has the client approve them. Months or years later, the software is delivered to the customer. If things have gone well, the customer is reasonably happy with the system and the project is considered completed.

Except, that's not what usually happens.

In reality, managers in the busy 1990s don't have the time to specify their organization's requirements properly, so when the software is delivered it isn't really what they needed. Either they didn't think through the problem enough, or they gave specifications that were too vague, or the business changed during the project. Requirements have to be revised and the costs start to climb. Two years later, a new manager comes in to solve the problems with the software that everyone now knows, with perfect hindsight, should have been utterly different.

In some organizations, it takes so long to develop software that by the time it's ready, the business or market has changed and the software is obsolete before it's ever launched. In the 1970s, one could assume a software project would take two years to develop and then could be used for five years. In the 1990s, many projects must be done within six months because the products have much shorter life cycles. In two years, the product may have been replaced.

Assuming that the software did work well and the managers were pleased with it, another wrinkle appears. Generally, the person authorizing the software is not the one who uses it. When the software is delivered to the actual users, they resist it. It means learning something new or, worse, the person who laid out the specs did not really understand what the users needed. The costs climb further.

Given all this, it seems incredible that anyone would bother with computers at all. That they do seems even stranger when you consider each group's role in the project and how they experience it.

Customer: *"I can't get no satisfaction."*

Typically, managers who have invested in the system are frustrated. They have exceeded their budgets and usually they look bad to their bosses. The system isn't working yet, so they feel their careers are on the line. And when the system is eventually delivered, it can be underwhelming in performance.

The obvious people to blame are the folks who developed the project. If external consultants did the work, then clearly they lied to get the business. If the project was developed internally, then it is clear that personal incompetence is to blame. The general manager always feels firing managers in the information systems department is so therapeutic. Being chief information officer, or CIO, can be one of the most dangerous positions in an organization.

Consultant: *"Customers are often shortsighted."*
Whether an internal or external developer, the developer is typically frustrated because the client didn't properly specify what the organization needed up front. Clients often say, "Our budget wasn't big enough to do the project right." They don't appreciate that it takes time to build systems right. At the beginning of the project, they signed off on the requirements. Then they kept changing them. Even worse, they have selective memories—they don't recall how their understanding of the problem kept on changing.

Users: *"Why didn't they talk to us first?"*
Users often dislike software they had no part in developing. They tend to have a better understanding of the tasks they have to perform than the specifier. The users and what they really need have been ignored.

Hardware vendor: *"I gotta meet the client's budget to get the business."*
The vendors supplying the hardware face their own pressures. They have to meet the budget requirements. The vendor sells hardware to meet the client's price requirements rather than their performance requirements. The selected systems application turns out to be too slow. (Rarely does someone complain that the application is too fast.) The hardware vendor's goal is to sell the hardware that will lock in the account by keeping the client dependent on it. There's always an opportunity to make money off ongoing service and a later upgrade sale. "Yes, we can always sell them more memory and a faster processor later."

Information systems department: *"You can't always get what you want. But if you try, sometimes you'll get what you need."*
"We could have done it better than the consultant. We just don't have the internal resources. We understand the business a lot better than an outsider does. Unfortunately, we've got to fix the on-line order entry system right now and can't get to your problem for another two years."

With all this, it's a miracle we continue to believe in computing technology.

Frustration is a normal part of using new technologies. Setting up methods for reducing frustration and capturing learning is *the* information management task.

If you work in any organization today, the chances are close to 100 percent that you'll face the problem of using, buying, upgrading or getting rid of computers. Your job will be affected by your company's policy decisions and the skill with which the organization makes *you* effective.

You'll also be involved in what we like to refer to as information management projects—projects where you as an end-user, or a manager, will be called upon to figure out how to improve the information management in your organization. Computers are now so deeply embedded in organizations that only the users and the business managers can establish what the organization really needs. Gone are the days when the technical specialists knew all the answers.

If your organization is a bad one and you do not feel yourself becoming constantly more effective, then *both your organization and your job* are in danger.

If your organization is a good one and you feel you are learning and becoming more and more productive all the time, then *your career is likely bright.*

But if you can make yourself the kind of person who is instrumental in improving your organization and making others more effective, then you can almost be guaranteed a path to success. You will remain one step ahead of the next technology tiger that's after your job.

Now, improving an organization is a dangerous task. It means taking risks. It means developing new expertise. It means challenging the status quo. Perhaps these are all things you want to avoid. But we suspect that, with the accelerating use of computers, *making a decision to do nothing is actually riskier than attempting to keep up with the changes.*

This year's computer fashion is the old-fashioned one with a new set of unsolved problems.

Like any area of business, computers experience waves of fads and fashions. The cynics would say that each fashion has its true believers, so that reasonable debate over the merits of each fashion is almost impossible. Over the past 30 years, we have seen five major waves of this technology:

- Mainframes
- Minis
- Personal computers and engineering workstations
- Local area networks
- Wide area networks and the Internet

Some joke that no sooner had people figured out how to make mainframes work reliably then along came minis and a new generation of experts. Everyone had to independently reinvent all the mistakes that the mainframe experts had solved. Then came personal computers, with mistakes spontaneously reinvented by a whole new group of users and programmers. And today, similar mistakes are being reinvented in networking. And so it goes.

What makes today different is that, in the past, *very few people actually used mainframes or minis.* The massive explosion in personal computer use and networking means that millions of people, nonspecialists, are doing an extraordinary variety of things on computers that were not possible, affordable or even dreamed about on more expensive machines. Ask yourself these questions:

- Who could have conceived of doing desktop publishing on a multimillion-dollar mainframe or a multihundred-thousand-dollar mini?
- Who could have thought about devoting an entire mainframe or mini to accepting voice dictation from a manager? A secretary would have been cheaper.
- What small business could have afforded to use a computer for direct-mail marketing when the cost of the computer alone was more than the business' annual revenues?
- Who would have thought of letting children have a computer to look up information in an encyclopedia when the costs were so high that only specialist librarians in high-priced consulting and law firms could afford access to on-line databases?

As the costs have dropped, so accessibility has risen. And so has the number of users. It is not farfetched to imagine that most organizations will one day have more computers than people. Some organizations, like our own, have already reached that point.

If you are trying to look at the impact of a new technology, look at its payback figures. When the payback is irresistible, so is the technology.

When a particular form of technology drops in costs, it reaches a point where it becomes downright irresistible. This is the point we've reached with personal computers. Since Intel's first generation of microprocessors, the power of a personal computer has expanded roughly 500 times.

We believe that this increase in capability means that just about every job in every organization either needs drastic rethinking or is already extinct.

E-mail is important. It changes the economics of many business activities.

Your job is not safe unless you understand how you can improve it and make yourself more effective—more indispensable. Even if your job is safe, your career is not safe. Engineers have for many years grappled with the rapid obsolescence of their knowledge. Now all managers are pressed to upgrade their knowledge of information management—what we call the New Computer Literacy. If you lead a department or an organization, you must know enough to make sure that you improve your operation as your competitors become more aggressive and your customers demand more.

Not all uses of computers make sense. Not all ways of building software are successful. Not all projects are consistent with the culture and objectives of your organization.

Even worse, there is a built-in bias in most organizations toward investing in the wrong projects—the ones with low payback.

Computers are now everywhere. Their newest users are now the most powerful because they are running our businesses. Most organizations are changing so fast that their information management requirements are changing even faster. As a result, most organizations use their computers poorly. Even worse, some organizations have built-in idiosyncrasies that make them use computers ineffectively.

Having access to lots of information is a pain. You want access to high-quality information. Develop your reputation for good information management and people will flock to you. You will be an employer people want to work for.

A Ride on the Tiger Is, at Best, Rocky

For every success story in harnessing the technology tiger, there are probably 10 tales of failure and discontent. You see the symptoms everywhere:

- Unhappy users
- Large information systems budgets committed to maintaining antiquated systems
- Technology that does not support an organization's new directions
- Projects delivered too late for too much money and with little to show for it
- Users who refuse to adopt new software
- Not enough resources to support all the proposed information technology projects

The list goes on. It is not easy to use information technology to its fullest potential. For every decision you make, you must consider many choices in technologies and implementation methods. For instance, you need to

- choose infrastructure, network, hardware, software and vendors,
- decide what resources and people you'll need,
- decide which projects to implement and how to implement them,
- weigh benefits today against benefits in the longer term.

Worse still, the decisions you make today may no longer make sense tomorrow as the technology and business requirements change. How much risk should you take? Should you try to play it safe and follow someone else's lead? Will excessive conservatism cost your company's business its competitive advantage?

Organizations find they don't have all the answers for the technology and business issues that can overwhelm them.

New questions then arise: Can and should you transfer your problems to experts by outsourcing all your information systems tasks? Should you purchase packaged programs? There are no simple answers.

You'll find the technology tiger, while promising you *power* and *leverage,* a tough animal to ride. There are many questions to be answered and decisions to be made. If you are not careful, you may rush toward the wrong destination or fall off and seriously injure yourself and your organization.

Computing technology represents a significant investment for many businesses. Organizations have to manage their investment, development, maintenance of and withdrawal from information systems with skill. Do it right and your company grows. Do it wrong and your company dies.

Costs of Information Management—Get the Big Picture

Most managers have the wrong ideas about the costs of information management. Like the blind man and the elephant, most see only one part of the whole. This creates problems when they try to manage technology expenditures.

Recognize at the outset that nobody gets it right the first time. The chances are good that any system will not be reasonably stable until your organization embarks on its third version of the system. As a result,

- managers don't budget enough money to develop a system, and
- they are upset when they learn they have to invest more money in it when setting it up.

Paul Strassmann is the former CIO of Xerox and the Pentagon and an influential writer on information management. In his 1985 book *Information Payoff,* he observes that "The history of information technology can be characterized as the overestimation of what can be accomplished immediately and the underestimation of long-term consequences."

We would amplify his observation. The most fundamental managerial misconception about computers is that the *up-front cost of ownership,* the most visible part of the acquisition process, is the most important. In reality, with as much as 80 percent of budgets being spent on maintenance (fixing and improving information technology), it makes sense to select solutions and strategies that have low maintenance costs and can be managed, improved and upgraded easily.

Second, organizations that do all things for themselves don't have a hope of succeeding. They can never gain enough expertise to make the information technology project a success. *Using a knowledgeable supplier* can be much less expensive and risky than paying the supplier a profit.

Use of outside suppliers may not sound like an important issue, but information technology costs are very influenced by expertise. Good programmers and a good project manager can bring in projects at a much lower cost than those project teams descending a steep learning curve.

The flip side of using suppliers is that if a firm contracts out the development of the system, it cannot acquire the expertise necessary to maintain the system. The right balance of purchasing and outsourcing versus internal development is a major strategic issue. It strikes at the organization's core competencies. These in turn influence the organization's competitive advantage down the road. Figuring out the costs and benefits of outsourcing is a complex issue. We'll return to the topic later in the book.

The third issue is that of the *cost of the perfect decision*. Since computing technology is constantly changing and demand is always growing, organizations must continually assess new technologies and ways to implement them. The evaluation is part of the cost of the transaction.

For many organizations, more time is spent evaluating the choices than the decision justifies. The classic example is choosing PCs. While it might have made sense to worry about hardware when it was expensive, a convoluted decision-making process to purchase IBM versus Compaq PCs is no longer required. It may even be cheaper to buy some of both brands and compare their performance.

Last, incremental costs are a large issue in information management. Systems and architectures—that is, the system's framework—that can be expanded easily and allow for modular replacement and upgrade can offer attractive incremental costs.

Many managers make the mistake of believing that one large technology purchase will be "the big one" that will last for many years. They think that when the system becomes obsolete, they can just replace the whole thing. What happens is that the system reaches this point sooner than expected, and the budget is never enough to replace everything at once. The fundamental fact about computing technology spending is that you have to be prepared to make regular, useful smaller investments toward achieving your final goal.

Measuring the Investment Payback

Businesses have to deal with new products, new organizational structures, reengineered processes and new business issues all the time. As a result, your software needs to change quickly, too, to adapt to new business conditions. Chances are good that once you own a piece of software, maintaining and feeding it will cost you more time and more money than you ever anticipated.

With so much money being spent by organizations on shoring up, jury-rigging and maintaining older computer systems, practically nothing is left over in the budget for developing the new systems that help an organization improve its competitive position. A legacy of investment in different information technologies becomes a financial sinkhole. Computer systems are simultaneously too expensive to replace and too expensive to maintain.

Most of this technology no longer affects isolated functions but a range of an organization's areas and processes. It is now nearly impossible to isolate the impact of a computing investment.

We argue that the cost of information technology is and should be often totally irrelevant in your budgeting. What counts is the economics of a "business initiative." By this we mean the business processes and strategies the information technology supports.

In other words, if your information technology enables you to raise your profit level, it's a good investment, regardless of what it is costing you. The cost of the initiative can include new investment outright plus a lot of reengineering and allocated costs. There is no magic about a cost–benefit ratio. It can only be considered relative to the business initiative it supports.

In *Riding the Tiger* we distinguish between projects that are increasingly "owned" by the business units and departments, and the infrastructure that (1) provides the glue for exchanging information in the organization and (2) that builds capabilities to allow the organization to reap economies of scale.

The Never-Ending Search for the Next Technology

As most people know, computers were originally invented to perform mathematical calculations for the military in the late 1940s. These first ones were big and expensive and hard to use. They were also slow and tended to be used in highly centralized organizations.

Only highly trained specialists with PhDs, like Harvey Gellman, could operate them. This remained the case until the advent of the Macintosh in the early 1980s. The Xerox Star and the LISA, predecessors to the Macintosh, and the Mac itself sparked a revolution that made it possible for less technical individuals to use computers.

As computers have become more powerful and easier to use, they have found their way into more jobs and tasks. They appear at home and in the office as personal computers. They are embedded in all the machinery we use or that affects us, from automobiles, appliances, production machines, control mechanisms and medical devices to communication devices.

Every day we hear about the next marvelous use of computers. But not all of these uses are divinely ordained. The development of computing has not been a smooth and logical path.

There is an entire industry devoted to the forecast of technological trends. Its workers carry out a job somewhat akin to that of stock market analysts. Chance and market forces have major influence on the computing market. The best technology is not automatically successful. Standards will not be set by the time you need them. Rapid improvements mean short product life cycles and a high rate of obsolescence. The obvious user requirements seem to take forever to fulfill. Your tiger has to dodge many traps and avoid taking many side paths that lead to dead-ends.

The history of computing technology is the story of product life cycles, clashing like icebergs, often crushing users between them.

Technological development will continue to be quirky and unpredictable because the nature of product and market development is inherently risky. We know that there are good ways and bad ways to approach computing. Good ways cost 10 or 100 times less than the bad ones. Good ways mean planning well, doing it right and improving the business. They mean good design, competent people, a willingness to accept mistakes and a commitment to consistent improvement.

While it is healthy to be skeptical and take a wait-and-see attitude, some business people demonstrate a healthier appetite for risks and its promises of opportunity and competitive advantage. There is no single answer for latching onto the next winning technology, but there are ways you can make your bet more successful.

We Have Seen the Light—It Is Digital and in Color

When the 70-year-olds around us start taking computer lessons and surfing the Net with ease, we know that the world has changed. Nerd is cool. Hollywood glamorizes the computer by projecting it into our consciousness in nearly every film. Unfortunately, the view of information technology that vendors promote and Hollywood romanticizes does not address the nuts and bolts of how these apparently magic uses of computers come into being.

The computer is glibly presented as the bridge to the twenty-first century. It is no longer just a gadget for a distant future portrayed in science fiction films. It is a door to new wonders. It promises you'll be set for the future if you step through that portal.

To be fair, in every organization, managers *are* using computers for more and more tasks. Many of us regularly use our computers for word processing, spreadsheets, databases, presentation graphics, brochure design, statistics, faxing, e-mail, contact management, accessing the Internet and so on. In the future we certainly can expect to use our computers for telephony, voice recognition, video conferencing, home banking, booking theater and airplane tickets, and who knows what else?

Twenty years ago, it was hard to believe that computers could ever be portable. It was almost unimaginable that one person might pack five computers in a suitcase, fly somewhere, set up a temporary network there and run a simulation program to train managers. Yet this is what one of this book's authors does regularly.

Even experts are amazed at how rapidly computer technology changes and grows. For those new to the technology, computing is both exciting and intimidating.

Even if we accept the optimistic vision of the future, we need to ask ourselves: Where will it take our business? What will be our individual roles in this process? Will we be able to keep up or will we be left hopelessly behind?

To address these questions, we think a historical parallel is useful.

Surrounded by Tigers—Technology Is Changing the Way We Do Business

In the nineteenth century, the servants in a middle-class Victorian household performed the domestic chores of preparing food, washing laundry and cleaning. Today, we have fast-food outlets, frozen food, dishwashers, self-service laundries, washers and dryers, microwaves, answering machines and so on. The market system has gradually sought out tasks in the home and systematized and automated them. The middle class is correspondingly larger. All of us who might have been servants of a smaller Victorian middle class are now ourselves middle class because we can afford the same services, delivered in a totally different way.

The same phenomenon occurs in business. Tasks that we previously did in-house, often inefficiently, are now automated. We buy these services from suppliers who can offer them to us at attractive prices through their own greater economies of scale. For instance, the labor-intensive and repetitive writing, typing and correcting that secretaries used to do, a manager now does on a word processor. We now "desktop-publish" (a new verb in the English language) and print most documents ourselves using software products and laser printers rather than send documents out to be typeset and printed.

The revolution continues within organizations and home offices. Computing technology is incorporated more and more into all aspects of business. Processes are reviewed and redefined to take advantage of the technology, to squeeze out redundancy and inefficiencies and create new capabilities. The technology tiger is prowling throughout our organizations.

TIGERPEARL

The cost of wasted effort is the reward you would have received from doing things right.

In this section, we'll demonstrate how five key areas of business are being improved by information technology.

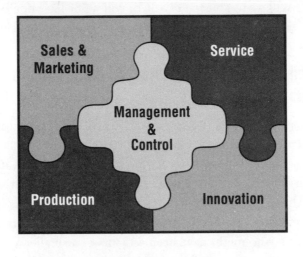

Sales

Sales can often be improved with IT. Sales representatives in the field are an excellent source of information about customers. They deal with customers face-to-face. They know what their customers want, and they hear about what their competitors are doing. Few companies do as good a job of tracking and exploiting sales information as they should.

To use this information in the heads of the sales reps effectively, we try to make it easy for the sales reps to share this information with other departments such as marketing and finance.

Today, many companies equip their field reps with portable laptop computers, as well as powerful sales tracking and proposal-writing software. By connecting to the company's computer network, they can place, verify and query customer orders and billing issues, and even check inventory levels or production lag times.

Examples of sales automation appear in every industry:

1. A baking company produces goods that are worthless 72 hours after they create them. It is therefore important to know exactly when and where customers will buy. Sales automation tools helped the following baking company improve its estimates of customer demand.

One company has issued its field reps hand-held computers and portable printers. Every evening, company computers send all the latest product data, price changes and new-customer data into each sales rep's hand-held computer, which rests in its docking station at a distribution center at night. Just after dawn, the sales reps pick up their palmtops and check that the type and number of bakery products they ordered have been loaded correctly onto their trucks.

The sales representative then drives the route. At each store he or she takes all stale products off the shelves, enters the data into the palmtop and then fills up the shelves with the fresh goods. The palmtop computer automatically generates an invoice that takes into account how many stale products from the previous day were not sold and how much fresh product was delivered. The sales rep then enters his or her estimate of the next day's order. This means that drivers can track demand on a daily basis, by account.

The time the drivers save on their end-of-the-day paperwork—two hours a day and more on average—they spend in the stores, straightening the shelves and making sure the product displays remain appealing. After running the automated system, the company learned its business was not spread out evenly during the week. It turned out that on Mondays through Wednesdays, the company made 35 percent of its sales, and on Thursdays through Sundays, 65 percent. In the past, the company had delivered too much product early in the week, which meant a lot of stale returns. It also meant that the compnay ran out on the weekends. The company has adjusted its baking schedule accordingly.

2. One company that sells laboratory equipment has also given its sales reps laptop computers. The reps now send weekly reports automatically from their laptops over standard telephone lines to the sales manager's computer. These reports categorize all potential customers according to the "maturity" of the rep's sales pitch. The sales manager can check the status of all new, pending and fulfilled business. He can "drill down" to get the details of any one sales call or lead.

The reps' laptops can provide full-color sales presentations. The company has created a database of hundreds of colorful presentations. When reps want to demonstrate a piece of equipment they merely dial into the server at headquarters, download the presentation they need, modify it for their own use and display it for specific customers. They can store it on a floppy disk until the next time they might need it or delete it. If they have a good idea, they can add it to the marketing database server for their colleagues to try.

Sales reps in different territories can rarely get together face-to-face, so they communicate and share ideas through computers. The reps can log on to a Lotus Notes "discussion" database to chat with one another.

The main benefit of sales automation to this company is the "leveraging" of knowledge across the organization. Though originally intended only for the field sales force, the setup is now being used widely across the company. The marketing people have become interested in what the salespeople could tell them about what was happening in the field, and departments that were separated from one another are collaborating more and more.

Marketing

By improving their understanding of their customers' requirements, many organizations can adapt their positioning, pricing and product lines. This helps companies introduce new products and services efficiently. Information technology has made the analysis of large volumes of customer information possible.

For example, L.L. Bean discovered through their customer database that they were serving primarily upscale customers who like the *idea* of hunting, but are not *actual* hunters. They adjusted their market position as a result. Similarly, "frequent flyer" account databases allow airlines to schedule, price and serve their customers based on the customers' patterns of use of their services.

By combining different technologies, businesses can customize their services and/or goods very precisely with prices and delivery times that compete with mass merchandised goods. They offer a unique bundle of features that may be difficult for competitors to match. Dell Computer and Gateway sell computers assembled for individual customers' orders. Levi Strauss can manufacture its clothing according to a customer's actual measurements.

Customer Service

Customers expect to know the status of a company's dealings with them— shipping, account and service status. For example, they expect to be able to access information about their accounts on a 7 x 24 basis (seven days a week and 24 hours a day). Customer service centers, as a result, are growing like wildfire. They are demanding more powerful computing technology to support their work. Dow Jones is using new technology that seamlessly combines information about a customer with a telephone call. As a result, a telephone service call coming in can be passed to different support personnel with a data screen. The computer screen and information on the customer can be passed on to an employee with the right expertise to answer the customer's question or solve a problem.

In hospitals, the patient's data from different departments and physicians can be collected and shared on-line, saving time and allowing physicians to make better decisions with more complete information.

Customers can now access information about themselves directly. American Airlines frequent flyers and American Express card users can download their account statements over the Internet.

Production

The use of computer controls, manufacturing requirements and planning (MRP) systems and robotics in manufacturing have advanced production efficiency and effectiveness. The use of electronic data interchange, or EDI, shortens the ordering and manufacturing cycle and therefore reduces inventory. Combining electronic and physical networks greatly increase consumer convenience. In home shopping, for instance, a person watches the television network and orders a product by telephone. The EDI network transfers the order to the point of production. Finally, the physical distribution network delivers the goods.

> *Boeing was able to integrate its Computer Aided Design (CAD) with its production. More significantly, it was able to simulate the assembly process before creating the machine tools and was able to identify problems that cannot be foreseen otherwise. "Simulate Before You Build" is already happening, to a degree. Northrop built the B-2 stealth bomber without paper. It was simulated in a computer instead. Some industrial experts call the B-2 "the most complex system ever to be simulated." The entire*

project was designed as a simulation so intricate and precise that Northrop didn't bother fabricating a mechanical mock-up before actually building the billion-dollar plane. Normally a system consisting of 30,000 parts entails redesigning 50% of the parts during the course of actual construction. Northrop's "simulate first" approach reduced that number of refitted parts to 3%.

Kevin Kelly, *Out of Control*, 1994

Many of today's services cannot function at their scale level without using computing technology. The international financial network allows banks and other financial institutions to deliver across international borders within seconds. Credit cards can be validated almost anywhere in the world in seconds. Retrieval in foreign funds is made possible through the international network of automated teller machines (ATMs).

The airline reservation system has progressed from the agent's network to the Internet. Telephone companies' operator services are possible because a large database of information has been married with a digitized voice recognition system.

Management and Control

As executives started to use computers, three things happened. First, they wanted information that was not tracked before. Second, they wanted to be able to get at the information easily, wherever they were. Third, as a new category of users, they demanded completely different types of models and tools to suit their management needs. As soon as information from financial and marketing decision support systems became more accessible to managers, many became interested in linking this information to other data in the business.

As a result, we have seen the rise in *data warehouses*, which allow managers to

- seek out meaningful relationships in their business,
- drill down into details, and
- find conclusive summary information.

* * *

Data warehouses can be developed for multiple purposes, for management control of the business as well as for a more detailed understanding of customers.

For example, the Canadian national mail service, Canada Post, believes that its operations are one of its most important assets. As a result, it has a war room that allows senior management to track the state of its operations in detail.

Alacrity Inc. provides a planning and control system that supports decentralized decision making. It also helps make sure that the overall corporate objectives are supported by business units. (Managers can track the activities and budgets planned for supporting their companies' strategic goals.) The planning system works with a decision support system that allows information to be shared.

Information about competitors and the marketplace can be routed to the marketing department and senior managers to help them in their planning process. For instance, through a sophisticated sales information system, scanner data allow grocery chains such as Safeway in the US, Loblaws in Canada, Sainsbury's in the UK and the Coop in Switzerland to learn about the performance of specific brands. This in turn enables them to develop house brands to compete with the name brands.

Innovation and New Products

Innovation in the investment industries has been greatly enhanced. Sophisticated financial models allow for quick creation and customization of new financial products with complex features.

Ford can bring together a global design team to work on a car development project, for example, through a combination of video conferencing, a high-speed network and Computer Aided Design (CAD) machines.

The Challenge to the Tiger Rider

All these examples of innovation should demonstrate that it is no longer possible to ignore information technology. *Your* challenge now is to convert your colleagues who may say:

- It's too complicated.
- It changes too fast.
- It's too specialized.
- It's too risky.
- Let's leave it to the information technology managers.
- Let the experts ride the tigers.

Your colleagues need to be convinced that your business is on the line and their jobs are on the line under this onslaught of tigers. If they are still not interested, there are 10 good reasons they should be:

1. About 90 percent of all managers now use computers. As an input into business, computing has also come down in cost by a factor of three in the past three years. Any economic input with such a dramatic effect and cost curve cannot be ignored.

2. If you work for an organization considering reengineering, computers are an essential part of any such project. But understanding the important role of information management in improving an organization's processes is just the beginning. You must be persistent. New information systems are rarely right the first time. Good information management arises gradually from many small decisions and improvements.

3. Companies that do not use computers can lose out to competitors in cost and response time. You may not be able to create competitive advantage by using computers, but you will definitely create a competitive disadvantage if you don't.

4. Serving customers well was easier when you knew them personally. In large organizations, few of us can get to know our customers anymore. Customer knowledge gained through computer information can help us provide personalized service.

5. Computers can often help managers gain information and knowledge that help them spot opportunities faster than those managers without computers.

6. Only a computer can eliminate the redundant entry, assembly and retrieval of data.

7. Competitive scale efficiencies today can only be achieved through computing technology.
8. You cannot perform many tasks in organizations today without computers. Think of Computer Aided Design and engineering, consolidating hundreds of spreadsheets or retrieving of millions of pieces of data about a particular market.
9. Computers can be used to increase corporate knowledge and increase the speed of learning in the organization.
10. If you are fortunate enough to be able to influence what your organization does, then what you believe about what is important in using IT can make or break your organization.

You can no longer enjoy the choice of ignoring information technology. Both public and private sector organizations are run today with people and procedures, and silicon and software. Business managers may not need to program, but they do need to understand the technology, its power and pitfalls.

You don't need to know how to build a car to know enough to drive one. You do need to know *when* to maintain it. Leaving knowledge about your car to specialists would mean that only chauffeurs could drive!

In the early days when cars were introduced, Mercedes-Benz predicted that its market would never be larger than one million vehicles. The company reasoned that there could only be a maximum of one million chauffeurs available to drive them. Enough said.

Computing technology is now too important to remain the exclusive playground of specialists. These experts need to work with and learn from business managers to carry out their jobs properly. They already recognize that computing technology must be aligned with business needs. Computing professionals cry out for greater understanding, involvement, commitment and leadership from the others in their organizations.

> ## Strategic Thinking, Not Computer Expertise, Is Key
> - Strategy is about figuring out the most effective use of your resources.
> - Planning is about anticipating the multiple consequences of your investments on the different areas of your business, on your customers, on your competitors, over various time periods.
> - Policies are about making life simple in your organization.
> - Reducing the bureaucracy and the number of policies in your organization is the way you empower people.
> - Training is how you upgrade your people.
>
> These are the tools of the business manager.

SUMMARY

The real issue for you as a business manager is *strategy*. What knowledge should you master so you can harness the information technology available in a way that will support the objectives of your business? What can you do to increase the probability of success of information technology projects in your organization? What kind of framework would you find most useful for working with this exciting, complex and changing technology? These are the issues that we will address in the next chapter.

How can you ride the technology tiger, steer it and not be eaten alive by it?

The Bank of Glen Burnie Case Study:

Steve Arbeit's office, Bank of Glen Burnie, Thursday evening.

CONTACTING A CONSULTANT

Bill Underwood, Facilitator: Hello, Steve, it's Bill.

Steve Arbeit, President and COO: Boy, am I glad to hear from you!

Bill: Got your voice mail. What seems to be the problem?

Steve: Well, I've just been appointed President and COO for the Bank of Glen Burnie. I'm embarrassed to admit that I'm feeling a bit out of my depth over what I should be doing with the computers here. We seem to be spending a fortune on them and not getting results. My Board of Directors and the CEO have put pressure on me to turn the place around. I don't have much time before they are going to start expecting results. And I'll probably have to do some downsizing, which I don't want to do.

Bill: Steve, you're not alone. There're a lot of executives in your shoes. They're shocked at how fast things are changing. If it's any consolation, even specialists have a hard time keeping up.

Steve: Oh great!

Bill: Now, don't worry. If you need some help, I'm sure I can supply it. It is difficult, but it's not impossible.

Steve: So what do you suggest?

Bill: Have you got some time now to talk about the bank?

Steve: Sure, now's good. Let's talk.

Bill: Okay, why don't we start off by figuring out what's going on in your industry?

Steve: Shouldn't we focus on our computer problems first?

Bill: Can't help you if I don't know what you think is happening in your market.

Steve: Okay. Well, the big problem is that banking is not as profitable as it used to be. With all the changes in regulations, it's become a lot easier for the big banks to get bigger. They're making it really tough for a small player to compete. You know, we've only got three billion in assets, but our competitors seems to get bigger and bigger. The number of banks is shrinking. We're down to 10,000 banks from 14,000 when I started in this business, and the pace is accelerating. I can see 50 percent of the banks disappearing in the next five years. I don't know the numbers on savings and loans, but I think they're down to 2,000 to 3,000 institutions. Credit unions are going the same way.

Bill: Go on.

Steve: We used to worry about only two or three local competitors, but now every time I turn around there's another national or super-regional competitor going after my customers. And they're not just banks. They're car leasing companies like GMAC and Ford Credit. Even AT&T is in on the game. AT&T is actually the second largest issue of credit cards in the US. They came out of nowhere. They and Sears are big competition for us in credit cards now. Then there are the national banks such as Citibank and the super-regionals such as FirstUnion and NationsBank. I tell you, it's tough. You know, even the credit unions are more aggressive.

Bill: Sounds bad, all right.

Steve: And if that wasn't bad enough, we're worrying about whether the debit card is going to replace checking accounts and make our automated teller machines obsolete.

Bill: Perhaps you could explain that one to me, Steve.

Steve: Well, if you can go to your store and pay for your purchase with your debit card, you can also withdraw cash with your debit card. Who needs an ATM then, except maybe for account balances? Then, of course, there's home banking and the Internet delivery of financial services.

Bill: You mean computer banking? Doing things from home with your computer?

Steve: That's right. I just learned that almost half our households now have computers, so it isn't going to be long before we'll be under real pressure to have banking via the Internet. It's going to change the way we do business.

Bill: So, Steve, what I'm hearing is that you've got lots of competition.

Steve: And it's going to get worse once everyone does banking over the Internet. They'll compare our deposit rates with everybody's in the known universe. It's going to be brutal.

Bill: And loans, too, I suppose.

Steve: That's right.

Bill: So you're worried you may not survive. Or that people won't have a reason to do business with you, because the bigger financial institutions will be more competitive.

Steve: If that was all, that would be one thing. But at the same time I've got all these problems. Profits aren't high enough and everybody in the organization seems to want to buy 10 computers. The capital budget requests last year were up 400 percent from the previous year. My board of directors is *never* going to approve all the stuff that's going to show up in this year's budget.

Bill: I see. So what I'm hearing is that you need to figure out your strategy. What is your mission? Why should customers want to do business with you? What do you stand for? Then you'll be able to figure out how you should be using your computers best. Does that make sense to you? It sounds like you need to figure out how to make more money, too.

Steve: It does. That's the what. What about the how? Any recommendations?

Bill: Well, if I were in your shoes, I might want to consider a planning retreat. That would get your colleagues involved. You might want to think about getting a consultant in to help you, too, a facilitator.

Steve: I'd rather use someone I know. And someone who can handle strategy *and* computers. That's a hard combination to find. Are you available, Bill?

Bill: If we did it over a weekend, I could be.

Steve: Okay, that's fixed. I'll get back to you with a date. I'll speak with my colleagues and browbeat them into giving up a weekend.

Bill: Guilt works!

Steve: So does the fear of losing their jobs.

chapter 3

LEADING THE TIGER, NOT CHASING ITS TAIL

INFORMATION TECHNOLOGY SHOULD BE GUIDED BY THE BUSINESS' STRATEGIC OBJECTIVES

There are three different dimensions to the economic task: (1) The present business must be made effective; (2) its potential must be identified and realized; (3) it must be made into a different business for a different future. Each task requires a distinct approach. Each asks different questions. Each comes out with different conclusions. Yet they are inseparable. All three have to be done at the same time: today.

Peter F. Drucker,
Managing for Results, 1964

Chasing the Tiger's Tail

Forty-five years ago, you had to be in the military, big government or a large and advanced organization to justify owning a computer. By the 1960s, computers were being used by most medium-sized and large businesses for their record keeping and accounting systems. In the 1980s, computers became affordable for individuals. Computers are now everywhere in organizations and in the telecom links that tie together different locations and organizations. Every time you turn around, computers are being used for something new.

The release of computing power to end-users is the basis of the enormous growth of the computing industry in the past 20 years. Who today has not heard of Bill Gates or Steven Jobs?

The rapid growth in smaller computers has happened in a relatively unplanned manner. When computers cost little more than an electronic typewriter used to, managers will buy them when they can personally or departmentally justify the cost. When a computer is an expense account item, a manager will not pay a lot of attention to organizational policies when buying it. As long as the computer is a personal tool and the person buying it does not need to exchange data with the rest of the organization through it, he or she won't consider broader standards and policies important.

BUSINESS STRATEGY SHOULD DRIVE INFORMATION MANAGEMENT

Disconnects in Information Systems

However, the cycle of computerization has changed. The central information systems department still exists and manages the basic infrastructure of transaction processing and networks. But now, business units and departments want to link their often randomly acquired and developed systems to the central systems. For many areas within organizations, this is the cycle of computerization:

- Buy PCs and software packages.
- Set up a local area network to share files and printers.
- Set up a client-server database for departmental use.
- Build an application.
- Recognize the need to communicate with traditional mainframes and minicomputers, suppliers or customers.
- Discover a need to invest in departmental staff or acquire access to support for the applications purchased or built.

The company ends up with an expensive high-maintenance system, particularly if the system at that point cannot be linked easily with the traditional systems or other independently developed systems in other departments. You have created islands of information. But whether the capabilities developed are expensive to maintain or not, the question is: Has the investment advanced the capabilities of the organization and supported its key strategic business initiatives?

Increase in Capital Expenses

Arming employees with computers is not enough. Some would argue that merely giving a computer to an employee makes that employee more expensive. The capital cost per employee increases with no corresponding increase in his or her productivity. Computerizing without changing the nature of the work your organization does will not automatically benefit your business.

Adding computers always reduces productivity. Computers only increase productivity if you change the way you run your business.

Consider General Motors. It has invested a huge amount in information technology capability through acquiring the technology-oriented EDS and Hughes. The important question for its core automotive business has been: Has acquiring this capability made GM more responsive to the marketplace? Has the quality of GM products improved faster than that of its competition? Has GM been able to increase its productivity in order to gain a cost advantage? To date the answer to these questions is probably no.

For GM, the decision to invest in technology subsidiaries has been financially profitable but should have been secondary to the issues of cultural change. On a smaller scale, GM has had successes with its Saturn division, which has developed a superb reputation for its management–union relationships and the quality of its products.

Which Technology and When

The wide variety of available technology can be frustrating, particularly when it represents large risks and rewards and so much is still in development. Should a financial institution invest in telephone banking, computer-based home banking or both? How quickly will customers buy the new services? When is the best time to make these investments?

As soon as you purchase a powerful computer notebook, for a fraction of last year's price, and you are celebrating your purchase, you will find a more powerful machine with an even more attractive price.

New Business Opportunities

In spite of these uncertainties, the decrease in the cost of technology has enabled us to increase our ability to do many things. For example, customer service centers now handle customers 24 hours a day, seven days a week. Technology has changed our entire expectation of service from most businesses.

The Internet is another such enabling technology. Specialty magazine publishers can now broaden their geographic reach to all of North America and increase their revenues by creating successful web sites. They can broaden their markets with computing technology rather than traditional distribution through stores and the mail.

Leading the Tiger

It's easy to be overwhelmed by all the technological choices. But there is a way out. Information technology (IT), like many other business decisions, needs to be guided by the business' blueprint—its strategic plan. If you don't know where you are going, any road will take you there, as the saying goes. So you'd better figure out where you are going.

Committing your business to a strategic direction is the only way to avoid chasing your own tiger's tail. It is also the only way users can help make technology work for their businesses without fragmenting them, creating islands of information and perhaps even bankrupting their organizations.

We need to see beyond the technology choices and address the bigger issues. With limited resources, management needs to separate the tactical problems it faces from the more important and bigger strategic issues. A pattern of good decisions can make the difference between a healthy growing business and one struggling to survive.

Business Strategy Is the Starting Point

As we will keep emphasizing, an organization must have clear strategies before it can expect its information technology to achieve its full potential. What makes strategy a difficult concept to write and talk about is that the word is much abused in the 1990s.

Every manager, every consultant and policy maker talks constantly about his or her strategy. In our experience there is little overlap between the meaning of the word and the ways most groups of managers use it. When we work with a group of managers in a planning retreat, one of our first tasks is to establish a common vocabulary. Otherwise, our words sail past each other like ships in the night.

TigerPearl

Good strategies are about what you are not going to do.

In our view, establishing a strategy is about identifying objectives and the means for reaching them. For companies, there are generally different types of objectives and different ways to reach them.

Practicing the art of leadership here demands investing time and resources to solve short-term problems and building toward longer-term improved benefits, solutions and competencies. Also—and this is crucial— it is about involving the members of your organization in developing and implementing those strategies.

This book does not discuss how you should develop your own business strategies. We are more interested in exploring with you how some of the most important strategic concepts should affect your approach to information management.

Useful Strategic Concepts and How They Affect Information Management

Mission

While the concept of a corporate mission goes in and out of fashion, we believe companies ought to "stand for something." Most small and medium-sized companies have values that are important to them. A mission statement should express these values.

We are evolving toward a knowledge-oriented society. A mission provides a framework that can empower employees to make difficult decisions. It galvanizes employees to work toward a central goal with a set of common values and understanding.

In a downsized corporation, eliminating bureaucracy means giving employees more power to affect the experience of customers using your product or service. A mission should authorize employees to make decisions they know the company would want them to make, even though there is often no precedent and no superior to ask for permission to do so. When a company implicitly delegates authority to its front line, information management becomes critical. It can help give the employees solid information on which to base their decisions.

Missions also do something else. They limit what the corporation is prepared to do by outlining the boundaries beyond which the company has chosen not to move. This limit is particularly important because strategy is as much about what a company will not do as it is about what it will do.

When applied to information technology, missions provide an evaluative framework against which the value of a proposed IT project can be evaluated.

We recently worked with a financial institution to help it refine its mission. It had previously concentrated on selling financial services. We worked with its people to change their mission to creating and purchasing services *on behalf of its customers*. With this purpose established, the management team quickly realized it needed to develop more information technology and information management capability. This new capability will help the company track the spending patterns of its own users and its customers' use of financial services. This way it can fulfill its commitment to serving its customers. Better, more detailed knowledge about its customers was the only way the company could carry out its mission.

While the management team had known it was going to need to spend money on upgrading its information systems, the mission gave them new fervor and enthusiasm. It excited them to work out new ways that their business could serve its customers. The pay-offs from knowing a great deal about its customers were so critical to the company's success that there was no debate over the development. These information systems for tracking customers were clearly strategic information systems for the organization, critical to its survival and growth.

In other words, a mission provides the framework from which the basic policies and information infrastructure of the organization can be determined and prioritized.

Customer Segmentation

When customer needs vary widely and form large enough pockets to be reached and served economically as individual markets, you have *segmentation*. Since the late 1970s, segmentation has become increasingly important. Today, markets segment in many different ways—according to demographics, use, geography, life-style or psychographics (the psychological profile of customer groups). Each segment may have different needs, different perceptions of value and different pricing requirements. These differences affect the activities an organization can afford to pursue to satisfy these needs.

Businesses have capitalized on the opportunity to package products and services targeted at different segments. In the long-distance telephone business, where telephone companies analyze patterns of calling, you can choose the carrier that gives you the best discount, according to your long-distance phoning habits.

To market to a narrow segment, a business needs detailed customer information. This often requires new information management strategies. Powerful technology now enables "database marketing." Businesses improve their ability to identify small customer segments and their purchasing habits based on their gathering and analyzing of market and customer data. For example, Citibank tracks the consumption behavior of its customers to predict what financial services they require. Information technology now permits some industries to move away from marketing to a segment to marketing to individuals—each a segment of one. One of our clients, a financial services company, aims to provide completely customized financial services within which the pricing of one product can be offset by the pricing of another product.

Any business that needs detailed segmentation information such as customers' demographics, psychographics and purchase habits needs a superb customer database. Investment in data warehousing and data mining should be high on its information technology agenda.

The Cost Drivers

For each activity in a business organization, there are likely to be a limited number of choices that will affect the economics of that activity. These include

1. changing the scale of the activity,
2. changing the activity to support more products (economies of scope),
3. changing the level of capacity utilization,
4. obtaining a lower per-unit cost from experience (learning curves),
5. reducing the total length of time it takes to produce the product or service.

Information technology often changes the economics of a particular activity.

Activities with Different Cost Structures and Drivers

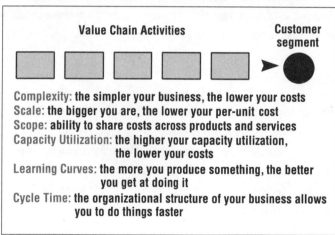

Value Chain Activities   **Customer segment**

Complexity: the simpler your business, the lower your costs
Scale: the bigger you are, the lower your per-unit cost
Scope: ability to share costs across products and services
Capacity Utilization: the higher your capacity utilization, the lower your costs
Learning Curves: the more you produce something, the better you get at doing it
Cycle Time: the organizational structure of your business allows you to do things faster

Scale

In many cases, the cost of an activity relates directly to the size of the overall operation. Unfortunately, a company with many locations has had to split up its operation. It may, as a result, not gain the advantage of *scale.* Networking may be the key to restoring such an advantage so that resources can be shared across locations, buying power taken advantage of or learning shared.

Scope

For a company such as Nabisco that started off distributing biscuits, it is no great leap for it to add crackers to its product line. This represents an economy of *scope*. The opposite of scope is *complexity*. At a certain level of complexity, say in a multiproduct factory, the additional costs of managing the complexity lead to decreasing economies of scope.

Capacity Utilization

Capacity utilization is a well-recognized cost characteristic. In general, the higher the level of use, the larger the number of units over which the fixed costs of the activity are spread. Telephone companies would like to encourage a greater volume of calls in the evenings and on weekends, when they have capacity available. So they discount their long-distance services to shift volume to these periods and to target different segments of the market such as the home user, who is typically more sensitive to telephone prices.

Learning Curves

Learning, or experience, curves are one of the oldest ideas in modern strategic theory. The concept is that the more you produce of something, the better you become at it. So if you have produced more than your competitors, your cost per unit will be lower than your competitors' costs, which will enable you to drop your price and sell more. Of course that would reduce your costs even further. The entire computer business exemplifies the experience curve.

The less obvious strategy is pricing your product in a growth market based upon where your costs are going to be. By offering low prices, your volume goes up. At the same time your costs go down, which justifies your initial decision to set prices according to your anticipated future cost structure.

Cycle Time

In the 1980s, many businesses tried to reduce the total time it took their companies to operate through the business systems. Japanese car companies originally moved to manage their inventories better by minimizing them because land is scarce and therefore expensive in Japan. The issue of minimizing time has now extended from manufacturing to new product development. In short, less time spent producing a product normally means less money expended and a cleaner process.

Managing for Quality

While *quality*, strictly speaking, does not drive costs, most companies find that managing for quality benefits their businesses. First, it is generally cheaper to build a consistent level of quality than to have to build in rework loops to allow for fixing and repairing problems. Second, if you can build a consistent level of quality, you will probably have a better manufacturing process and find you can build a superior product that will command a premium price.

Improving Your Competitive Position—HPV/LDC

To compete, a business must offer a point of differentiation. The basic two choices are

1. provide a product or service of High Perceived Value (HPV), or
2. deliver the product or service at the lowest total cost to the customer possible (Low Delivered Cost, or LDC).

The perceived value and low cost are relative. They depend on the definition of the market you serve. As long as the customers in your segment find your product offers the highest perceived value, you will have a competitive advantage in that segment. For example, in the computer business, "value" for a home user is something different from "value" for a chief information officer. The home user probably does not care about networking and the total life cycle cost of ownership and support. The IS director cares most about maintenance costs and compatibility issues.

Moving along the curve from A to B is a marketing decision. Moving diagonally means a change in strategic position.

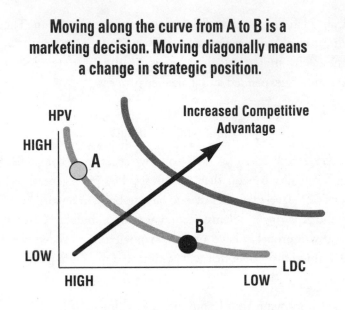

HPV = High Perceived Value by customer.
LDC = Low Delivered Cost to customer,
taking into account all costs.

Your competitive position is not permanent. Not only do competitors shift in their relative positions, their innovations can change the rules of the game. Computer advances can improve the benefits technologies offer or reduce costs. They can alter your marketing position along the curve or push you out to the next level of competition. This is where technology can affect your competitive strategy.

The competitive position of your business also affects information technology. Competitive strategy suggests what infrastructure investments take priority—those that increase perceived value or those that reduce costs.

In the furniture business, traditional department stores offered a downtown location, their own credit card for financing the purchase, delivery and assembly but a relatively narrow selection of furniture. Their furniture was typically high quality, probably even made out of real wood, but expensive. Their market point was probably in the 1950s, when two-career couples were less common and furniture shopping was stereotyped as woman's work.

Today, the aggressive international competitor IKEA has created a destination retail category killer. With typically only one store in any city, buyers must drive long distances to get to its warehouse outlet stores. The chain's typical buyers are the apartment-living, two-career couples who want low prices and high style. Because IKEA stays open late, a couple can drive to the store in the evening. They have to put the furniture in the car (or on the roof) themselves, but this highly taxed two-career couple can own stylish (but not long lasting) furniture by not paying for a downtown location, by not paying for delivery, and assembling the furniture themselves.

The strategic advantage of IKEA is reinforced by its global strategy of pursuing economies of scale. It ships knock down furniture around the globe and contracts with suppliers for such huge volumes that it has economies-of-scale advantages in addition to the low operating costs of its single-city warehouse outlets.

Core Competency

More managers recognize that competence, capabilities and knowledge are not only business inputs but also differentiation factors. The concept of core competence helps managers identify the capabilities, processes and knowledge with which they can differentiate their firms and others and help their companies weather changes.

Information technology can be designed to support and enhance these identified areas of competence and even make them possible. It is now common to refer to computing as an *enabling* technology. We believe that not only should business strategy drive information technology and create differences in business performance, but it should also be designed to affect the *capabilities* of the organization. The goals of better performance and greater capabilities should be clearly stated and sought in your planning process.

Business or Activity Systems

Economists have also often failed to relate administrative coordination to the theory of the firm. For example, far more economies result from the careful coordination of flow through the processes of

*production and distribution than from increasing the size of pro-
ducing or distributing units in terms of capital facilities or workers.*

Alfred Chandler, *The Visible Hand: The Managerial
Revolution in American Business*, 1977

One of the latest techniques for developing strategy is called *business systems analysis.* The name is somewhat misleading, in that "systems" does not
refer to computer systems, but to the notion of a business as a system of
connected activities. To succeed in business you must have a clear idea about
the basis on which you are competing and align your activities so that you
can achieve your goal. It implies having the confidence and courage to focus
on a chosen strategy and not allocate resources to lesser opportunities.

Your organization's activities represent its "business system." Each activity
can be done efficiently or inefficiently. Improving your competitive position
means two things: first, you leverage what you do well so that your cost structure for key activities is lower than your competitors' for the segment you are
targeting. Or second, you can manage the way you create the perception of high
value for your product or service.

Information technology can give a business system the means to support a
differentiating strategy. Your company must align itself with its desired goals
through its information technology because that technology affects structure,
processes and people—all the important ingredients of your business.

Selective extravagance

Tom Bonoma, a former head of the Harvard Business School MBA program, has suggested that excellent companies tend to identify one aspect of
their business and are selectively "extravagant" in investing in that portion
of the business. By this he means that the organization invests more in that
activity or capability than some might think necessary.

IBM's historical emphasis on customer service is one example of this.
IBM has always stressed its ability to solve customer problems. When a
problem is not solved, it escalates, within a certain time, to the next level of
management. Eventually, if the problem is not solved, it reaches the attention of the CEO. This strong and almost extravagant focus on resolving

customer problems has proven invaluable to the corporation over the years, particularly with significant customers who are heavily dependent on their system. Unfortunately, in a world of commodity hardware and software, IBM is learning now that reliability without labor intensive support presents a new and different factor critical in its mass market business. IBM, today, requires a different business system and different alignment of its strategy, processes and people to meet the new challenges.

Critical Success Factors

Strategies often require certain events or performances to take place so they can succeed. For example, a strategy may require the consistent and error-free delivery of a service or the completion of a product, with a certain level of performance to be achieved.

Defining *critical success factors* helps in the implementation of information technology. These factors identify what is needed to build the final performance goals. The organization's information technology should contribute to the achievement of critical success factors. This can include decisions on infrastructure, technology choices, project design and even sourcing.

The concept also applies to planning for IT. By identifying these factors, project managers can more easily determine what they need to make the project succeed. A similar approach focuses on managing risks through looking at *critical risk factors.* Rapidly changing technology or complex projects are full of risks. By identifying the biggest risks up front and dealing with them, managers will ensure those projects a much greater chance of success.

Critical success factors, or CSFs, help managers determine policies and performance goals for their organizations. They can also help the company select the projects it will pursue.

Portfolio Analysis

Portfolio analysis helps you allocate resources among different opportunities. The traditional approach to portfolio analysis takes different business units and compares their competitiveness in the marketplace as well as the attractiveness of the markets in which they compete. Generally, the cash flow from each business is considered. This gives us a way to allocate limited resources to the areas of opportunity. Other portfolio models take into account which businesses are emerging, growing, maturing or declining at any one time.

The decisions you make usually involve maintaining a reliable cash source from the mature businesses to fund the hopefuls, get rid of the non-performing ones and identify strategies for the uncertain ones.

Portfolio decisions affect IT investments particularly when the business units share technology infrastructures. The acquisition of other businesses may seem to have little to do with information technology. But service delivery systems and decision support systems are now vital parts of any business. Incompatible systems from the acquisition can be a real headache for a management team.

The concept of portfolio analysis can also be applied to information technology itself. (See chapter 7 for a discussion of its application.)

How should we select strategies?

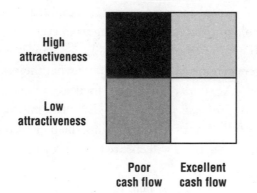

An example of a portfolio grid for classifying business products.

Technology's Influence on Strategy

While business strategy drives which technology should be adopted, technology is itself a strong factor in enabling a business strategy. Information technology can:

1. change the cost curve of an input factor,
2. provide new ways of delivering and selling,
3. help add value to your business service.

In other words, it can change how businesses segment, deliver, sell, market and produce. In the financial services industry, for example, the availability and the adoption rate of the technology by customers drive how fast strategy can be changed.

Technology causes as much excitement as it does confusion. Because there are so many possibilities and because different technologies are at different stages of maturity, many managers are concerned about which technology they should "bet on."

As a manager you must increase your understanding of the models of technology adoption and evolution. The history of technology is the history of product and market life cycles. It is foolish to "bet on" a technology without understanding the forces of the market.

Technology-push and technology-pull should not be confused. Both are happening in organizations at the same time. As a result, managers also need to master basic strategic concepts of business and evaluate how the technology in question relates to the strategic issues of their businesses. Managers who want to ride their tigers well will develop their own strategies for managing technology, based on their understanding of both technology and business.

Building a Sustainable Success Position (SSP)

As any manager already knows, to survive and excel, a company has to be competitive. Since the business environment changes rapidly and competition is fierce, business leaders have to attain winning positions and also find ways to maintain them.

A successful strategic position can be based on either High Perceived Value (HPV) or on Lowest Delivered Cost (LDC). To stay in its chosen competitive position, your company needs an activity system that supports and improves that position. Otherwise, it is only a matter of time before a competitor copies you and wins that position itself. Such an activity system may combine processes of the value chain (the series of activities) ranging from customer service, product order and delivery, to sale processes.

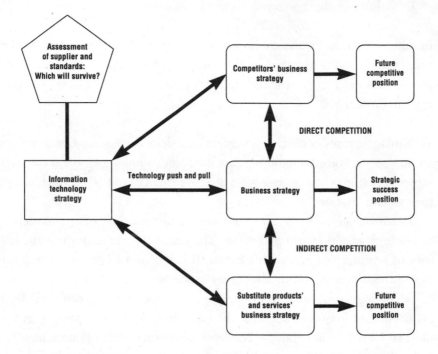

A good strategy solves several problems at the same time. Good software also solves several problems at the same time. Great software fixes a group of short-term problems and provides a framework for making it easier to solve longer-term problems later on.

Alignment

Visionary companies don't put in place any random set of mecha-nisms or processes. They put in place pieces that reinforce each other, clustered together to deliver a powerful combined punch. Notice the clustering at Ford: statistical quality control methods reinforced by employee involvement training reinforced by participative management training programs reinforced by promotion criteria based upon participative management skills. . . . Attaining alignment is not just a process of adding new things; it is also a never-ending process of identifying and doggedly correcting misaligments that push a company away from its core ideology or impede progress.

James C. Collins and Jerry I. Porras,
Built to Last, 1994

A common challenge is to make sure everybody understands the shared objectives of the organization. A slightly less obvious concern is ensuring that the supporting systems, activities, incentive plans and culture also support the firm's strategy. Tying together the strategic objectives and the investment decisions of the organization and the people issues is often called *alignment*.

For entrepreneurs, alignment is common sense. Their businesses are small enough that the managers can see clearly the performance of individuals. In a larger firm, the connections between the many complex components of the business are less obvious.

To make a strategy successful and deep enough that it's difficult for competitors to imitate, the managers must align their organization's technology and people with its strategy. The business needs structure and processes that allow people to do their work effectively, and information management that supports these strategies.

An insurance company that positions its sales representatives as knowledgeable financial planners would be a good example. The range of products available would then increase and customer interaction would have to become more consultative and less sales-oriented. The information technology supporting this might include financial planning software that helps sales representatives provide financial planning advice to their clients. Management would also have to tie the incentives for the sales representatives to customer satisfaction rather than sales volume.

Just as water drains to the lowest level, so management practices tend to follow the easiest course, not necessarily what the strategy demands. The right IT and management practices can make visible the key measures of performance and the key information that makes a strategy work.

Leading the Tiger to Support a Sustainable Success Position

In essence, *Riding the Tiger* considers how you can harness the power of the tiger to support a sustainable competitive position in *your* business. Many books on technology have laid out models for specialists in information technology management. We are interested, however, in outlining a more strategic framework that presents technology problems through a broader business perspective.

A useful model is one that can guide both the organization's decision making and the individual's with regard to riding the technology tiger.

The first question is, What is the scope of information management? We think it includes people, policies, infrastructure, technology and project management. We group these into three areas: leadership, policies and projects. This is the framework under which we shall examine information management issues.

To manage information and information technology, managers must plan. The question they must ask themselves is, Planning to what purpose? In our view, the purpose of information technology is to improve both business performance and the capabilities of the organization. Like other investments, the technology must lead to improved sales, margins or profits in the short or long term. Moreover, it should improve the organization's capabilities. We have therefore made improvement the third aspect of information management activities.

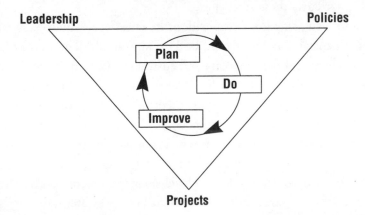

The cycle of Plan–Do–Improve is a continuous process. It never stops. In our illustration, these three activities form a circle with each stage feeding into the next. And this circle of activities works within the larger context of the leadership, policies and projects of information management. The issues a leader focuses on, the policies senior managers establish and emphasize and the projects managers select frame the environment within which information management and improvement take place.

Another way of thinking through the relationships between strategy and IT is to see this model as a nine-box matrix, which we will review in the next section. With the aid of this diagram, you can focus on the information management issues of leadership, policies and projects—in other words, by row.

Or you can review them through the cycle of Plan–Do–Improve—by column. The rest of this chapter outlines the Information Management Model. Throughout the book we will refer back to different parts of this model in greater detail.

Information Management Model
for Achieving Sustainable Information Systems Capabilities

	Plan	Do	Improve
Leadership	• IT strategy supports business strategy • Investment strategy	• Redesign process • Motivating for excellence	• Business performance • Organizational capabilities
Policies	• Accountability • Infrastucture plan	• Technology choices support principles and infrastructure • Sourcing decisions	• Evolution and replacement of infrastructure • Technology capability
Projects	• Project portfolio • Project planning	• Developing quality processes and reaching that goal • Involving users and training	• Measures of performance • Developing and attaining quality and competence

Brave reader, you are mounting the back of the technology tiger. This framework, like your saddle, can help you find your seat and hold on to it.

Leadership

Leadership features strongly in all phases of information management. Business needs leadership to guide its use of information technology. Organizational goals affect the choice of projects, and leadership in quality processes affects how successful implementation will be.

The first basic rule is that the organization's strategy is the critical driver of any information management project. Clearly, there is no point in developing capabilities for areas that are not important. Just because a project is "do-able" doesn't mean it *should* be done.

For example, one of the finest restaurants in the world operates through an interesting approach to information technology. Located in Switzerland, it boasts the maximum of three Michelin stars. In spite of having fewer than 20 tables, the establishment uses a database to track the experience of every customer who dines there. It tracks who the waiter was, what the individual customers ate, what wines they drank. The owner does not want to offer them the same menu or experience the next time they visit. For this restaurant, excellence and the unique experience of dining are a work of art that sets it apart from all other such establishments.

Its use of IT differs from that of a fast-food outlet such as McDonald's. McDonald's would not be interested in, nor could it afford, a record of the dining experience of an individual customer. More likely, it is interested in tracking the volume of its product items, the consistency and efficiency of its delivery and the impact of its advertising. The information technology plans for the two restaurants are vastly different because of their divergent competitive positioning. The three-star restaurant holds a High Perceived Value position, while, relative to the Swiss restaurant, McDonald's favors a Low Delivered Cost position.

If strategy is about leverage—doing the right thing and doing things right—then figuring out what to automate, what to buy, who to staff your business with, how to involve and support your users, how to manage transitions and how to manage technical risk set a complex task for a manager, even one who has mastered and knows information management better than his or her counterparts.

You can't solve your problem if you forget your purpose.

Good information management starts at the top. The highest level of management determines the role it wants information technology to play. Senior management should address the investment strategy of technology specifically because of the degree to which technology can affect the success of the business strategy.

This level of management, whether at the top of the organization or in a line activity, must also identify the overall business performance and capabilities improvement goals for the business and its use of technology.

Senior management can and should influence how information technology is implemented. The managers should encourage the organization to redesign and improve their processes as required. The implementation stage is complex and frequently frustrating, and senior management can motivate the organization to pursue excellence in implementing both business strategies and IT strategies.

Values and corporate culture *do* count, and management typically sets the standard. Building good information systems always requires perseverance, so protecting senior management and having their commitment are critical.

Policies

Traditionally, as we have noted, the information systems function has been centralized. With the personal computer revolution, information technology has been distributed to more and more users. Many hardware and software decisions have been assumed by departments or line business units. These business units have typically decided that their business needs for information technology were so great that they could not wait on the central information systems department to help steer them.

The challenge today is to develop a model of coordination and accountability for IT decision making that meets both corporate as well as individual user needs.

The larger the organization, the more opportunity it has to benefit from standards and policies and a centralized investment in infrastructure. The challenge is always to put in place the *fewest policies* that will promote entrepreneurial behavior in the business unit manager.

The other significant corporate decision centers on the infrastructure plan. If your business lacks a basic infrastructure, it will accomplish little. Similarly, if a person has poor arithmetic, reading, writing and problem-solving skills, then subsequent personal development is likely to be difficult. We see a business' infrastructure as equivalent to an individual's sound basic education.

Without basic infrastructure, you'll find future projects difficult to complete successfully. Infrastructure must meet both corporate and end-user needs and lay the foundation for improving business performance and capabilities. These decisions set the tone for lower-level-planning project decisions and implementations. Infrastructure must evolve, and there should be a plan that encourages constant renewal and improvement.

You'll need general policies on technology choices and sourcing to guide the way you implement projects. For some organizations, this may mean adopting a policy of always buying and never developing. For others, this may mean working out a mix of outsourcing, purchasing and developing. Through these policies you define the types of relationships your company seeks with its suppliers and its own internal information systems staff and the methods used for selecting products and suppliers.

Here, too, different companies with different strategies will pursue different types of infrastructure. McDonald's, a company focused on minimizing costs, has not yet been able to justify an investment in e-mail to its stores.

Projects

TigerPearl

Software projects are often selected because they make technical sense. They should be selected because they make business sense.

The first order of project planning is to determine whether the project should even go ahead. In this you should be guided by the planning decisions that preceded it: business strategy, IT strategy and investment strategy. The project should also be considered in light of the whole range of information technology projects available. Once a project has been approved, you should plan how you carry it out very carefully. No matter how large or small a project, *planning* is essential for it to succeed. At this point, managers want to make sure the process follows quality guidelines and that users are involved in the process and properly trained for its deployment.

Many managers have found, to their cost, that building software is often easier than getting employees to use it. There are many reasons for this. Users resist making changes unless they recognize a large incentive to do so. Poorly designed new systems can alter the power balance in an organization. New systems make users' jobs more difficult to perform. Users may resent systems that try to monitor them rather than empower them. Managers need a deployment and training plan for rolling out their new software applications.

The end of a project usually means the end of just one phase. Your company and you will learn many lessons from the initial phase. You will discover how to improve the design, the development process, use of the technology and interaction with users for the project's next phase. Painful as it may be, you need this feedback to achieve your goals for improving your capabilities.

Experiments with project developers reveal an interesting phenomenon. Projects are influenced by the organization's expectations of them. Project managers will, either implicitly or explicitly, optimize their projects in different directions. Some will stress the speed of processing; others will pursue low maintenance cost; others will seek flexibility. There is no such thing as a standard way of carrying out a project.

As a result, even project management, often considered a tactical issue by a strategist, can be affected by and can affect an organization's strategy. Project management demonstrates both strategy-push and strategy-pull. A project is affected by the leadership, values, mission, strategies and policies of the whole organization. Projects in turn affect the strategy and infrastructure of the organization.

Roles

As you progress through the cycle of Plan–Do–Improve, you will find that different groups of people tend to get involved along the way. Involvement, not abdication, is vital.

Making decisions in a complex area such as information technology is confusing. Many parties come in, each bringing his or her own perspective to the problem. Strategy can serve as a focal point, but having responsibilities clearly spelled out will also save your project from failure.

Results

Smart information management is not just about selecting the right technology. It is about sustainable information systems capabilities (SISC). Technology comes and goes, but capabilities allow you to grow with the changes. Capabilities encompass people, knowledge, skills and processes, and the policies and assets that support them. To have sustainable capabilities, we need processes that allow us to grow. The cycle of Plan–Do–Improve best exemplifies how to think before you jump and learn your lessons from your last move.

Section by section we will discuss how this model can work for you. And in the appendix, we have included a questionnaire to help you profile and benchmark your own organization's capabilities.

Competitive Advantage through Information Technology— The Wal-Mart Story

Sam Walton opened his first Wal-Mart store in 1962 in Bentonville, Arkansas. He believed that a discount store with a wide variety of merchandise would attract customers. Not only did Wal-Mart Stores, Inc. become the biggest company in Arkansas, it has become the world's largest retailer. Its 1995 sales were nearly $100 billion, it was number four of the Fortune 500 and it had roughly 675,000 associates, as its employees are called. Any problems today all stem from its success. To a large extent, this success has been driven by an unrelenting focus on minimizing costs and using information technology to support its strategy.

Strategic Objectives

Sam Walton had a clear idea of the guiding principle he wanted for his business. It was to give customers what they want—that is, as a *Fortune* magazine article put it in 1996, "a wide assortment of good quality merchandise; the lowest possible prices; guaranteed satisfaction with what you buy; friendly, knowledgeable service; convenient hours; free parking; a pleasant shopping experience." Sam believed it's important to exceed customers' expectations.

This is a business where the senior management has clear strategic objectives. Sam also supported investments in technology. Although he was difficult to persuade to invest in technology, he was a CEO who cared about his decisions. He listened carefully and asked many questions to make sure his people really supported their recommendations. Wal-Mart placed itself ahead of most other retailers by its investment in technology, and its IT focus consistently supported its strategy of driving down costs.

Business System Excellence

Wal-Mart could not have grown to its current size without pursuing excellent distribution of goods from its suppliers to its stores. The corporation developed distribution warehouses that gave it a great competitive advantage. The company overtook Kmart, its discount store rival, and then Sears, to make itself the largest US retailer by 1991.

Ironically, Kmart, another early entrant into discount retailing, took a very different regional strategy from Wal-Mart's. Kmart "cherry picked" the best urban markets and only later entered the sparser markets between major urban centers. Wal-Mart built up stores around the warehouses it used for supplying its stores, creating a more efficient logistical system than KMart's.

An excellent distribution process is a critical success factor for a retailer, and IT can influence its success. In developing the technology to support this process, the retailing giant has made distribution its distinguishing competitive organizational capability. There are several specific Wal-Mart innovations in this area, described in the March 1995 issue of *The Economist*:

> *The first was "cross-docking": goods were centrally ordered, delivered to one side of the distribution center, and then transferred to the other side for delivery to an individual store, along with other goods that store had ordered. This meant that one full truck would make frequent trips to each store, instead of several half-empty ones visiting less often. To make this system work well, the firm had to keep track of thousands of cases and packages, making sure they were delivered to the right store at the right time.*

That was where computers came in. By the early 1980s Wal-Mart had not only set up computer links between each store and the distribution warehouses; through a system called EDI (electronic data interchange), it had also hooked up with the computers of the firm's main suppliers. The distribution centers themselves were equipped with miles of laser-guided conveyor belts that could read the bar codes on incoming cases and direct them to the right truck for their onward journey. The final step was to buy a satellite to transmit the firm's enormous data volumes. The whole system, covering all the firm's warehouses, cost at least $700 million, but it quickly paid for itself.

The first benefit was just-in-time replenishment across hundreds of stores. This has since been refined further, using computer modeling programs to allow the firm to anticipate sales patterns. The second benefit was cost. According to Walton, Wal-Mart's distribution costs in 1992 were under 3% of sales, compared with 4.5–5% for the firm's competitors—a saving of close to $750 million in that year alone.

The average Wal-Mart distribution center ships and receives about 240,000 cases of merchandise every day. It stocks about 9,000 basic everyday items that can be ordered any day of the year. In addition, the shelves hold 2,000 seasonal items on a predetermined basis. The Douglas, Georgia, distribution center, whose floor covers 705,000 square feet, has 6 miles of rack storage space, with 12 shipping lanes and 86 doors onto the truck dock. This is fairly typical of a large Wal-Mart warehouse that can serve about 150 to 200 stores.

Information technology was successfully used to manage growth, manage the complexity of the business and reduce costs. According to Sam Walton, "the efficiencies and economies of scale we realize from our distribution system gives us one of our greatest competitive advantages."

Technology Affects Business Strategy

Information technology has in turn transformed Wal-Mart's business strategy and its relationship with its suppliers. The installation of electronic data interchange (EDI) enabled an estimated 90 percent of Wal-Mart's suppliers to receive orders and interact with Wal-Mart electronically. The program was later expanded to include forecasting, planning, replenishing and shipping applications. Wal-Mart uses electronic invoicing with more than 65 percent of its vendors, and electronic funds transfer with many. As a result, Wal-Mart and its vendors dramatically reduced their inventory costs and increased their sales.

Wal-Mart's Information Management Model

	Plan	Do	Improve
Leadership	• Wal-Mart's corporate values emphasize creating value for customers and driving down costs	• Skeptical and demanding senior managers supported use of IT where it would produce improvement	• Entering partnering relationships with suppliers and use of IT needed to drive down costs
Policies	• Stores are located close to warehouses to reduce delivery costs • Scanner data and EDI shorten ordering cycles, reducing the risk and cost of slow-selling merchandise	• Major investment made in telecom infrastructure and EDI	• Wal-Mart's ordering infrastructure benefits customers and suppliers • Inventory costs and stock-outs minimized
Projects	• Senior management paid attention to strategic objectives of information management use	• Project actually provided better data for measurement	• Rapid growth of Wal-Mart likely aided their project management abilities

SUMMARY

Information management and technology does not exist for its own sake. It must fall into one of three categories:

1. Basic operating tasks that the company must perform in order to exist—for example, the accounting system. Such tasks are usually justified on the basis of cost reduction or the impossibility of carrying out the task by hand. The risk with these basic systems is that the processes that management chooses to automate may not be the most appropriate processes to create for that organization in the first place. The strategic imperative is to SIA—simplify, improve and make information accessible.

2. Quality enhancement. Using IT to increase the company's ability to constantly improve its product or service to its customers.

3. Improved decision making. In a world of rapid change, organizations must create information systems that allow the members within that organization to operate quickly and decisively. Organizations with slow decision making will simply go out of business.

Strategy is about selectivity. All managers know that some investments of their personal time, of their department or business unit, in the business pay back more than others do. Making sure that they are investing much of their efforts in these high-payback areas almost guarantees success. Yet at the same time, managers must pay attention to the details of running the business. Balancing these two trade-offs is clearly an art.

Select the Path for the Tiger

By choosing your information management strategy you choose the path that you and your tiger will travel. Some trails will offer you options and turnoffs as you ride. Others will commit you to paths with no exits or turning back.

Along the way you will visit people, business strategies, policies, processes, infrastructure and projects. Your tiger prowls and charges through cycles of Plan–Do–Improve. You will find it a most interesting ride.

The CEO is the chief strategist in any organization. He or she chooses the path for the tiger. We turn next to the CEO's critical role.

The Bank of Glen Burnie Case Study:

Hotel meeting room several weeks later.
Strategy planning retreat, Day One.

DEVELOPING THE STRATEGY

Bill: Hello, my name is Bill Underwood. I am going to be your facilitator for the weekend. I am a professor of strategy and also teach in the information technology area at the university. I am not here to lecture, though—thank goodness! I am just here to run the meeting and help you as a group come up with a picture of your strategic situation. We're going to spend some time looking at how information technology and management are going to change the business, as well.

Ron Silver, VP, Marketing: Isn't that kind of a technical area for most of us? We're not computer specialists, after all.

Bill: That's right, Ron. But let me ask this question. What's your biggest operational frustration today?

Ron: Well, we've got two big problems. The computer software that runs our teller stations keeps breaking down on Fridays when we get a lot of traffic. And I can't launch new products as fast as I would like. Shall I go on?

Bill: No. I think you're demonstrating that your tasks pretty much depend on information technology. That's not just an operational problem anymore. It's a strategic problem. But this is not going to be an MIS department-bashing session. The whole purpose of this planning retreat is to get some agreement on where we are going as a business, and what that means for our information technology requirements.

Okay, people, I'd like you to break into groups. I'd like the left half of the room to focus on the weaknesses, and the right half to focus on the strengths of the organization. Take about 30 minutes. Then I'll ask a representative of each group to talk about your report. Try to address both the business and the information technology strengths if you have time. You may find it's a lot easier identifying weaknesses than it is strengths. That's what most companies find.

An hour later the whiteboard was filled with two lists.

Strengths	Weaknesses
• Good relations with retail customers and small businesses • Service-oriented culture • Good range of retail products • Long-term employees • Good relations with community • Low loan loss rate • Successful telephone loan banking operation	• Weak relationships with medium-sized clients because of our size • Poor penetration of car loan and mortgage market • Terrible transaction processing • Too few banking machines • Too few branches • Poor telecom links between branches • Lousy telephone system • No central place to access customer information • Weak selling efforts • Not innovating as fast as competitors because of weak systems • Weak information systems in general • Management and staff not knowledgeable about computers • Systems that don't talk to each other • Dirty data in the various systems • Front-line staff have poor product knowledge • Branch managers are order takers, not sales-oriented • Peak loading problems on Fridays with tellers • Costs are too high relative to the industry • Low average services per household

Bill: Okay. Jeremy, can you get some copies made of this? Well, as usual, it's a pretty depressing picture. Should we slit our wrists and close up shop? Or are there some opportunities here?

Aldo Moretti, Chairperson and CEO: Sure, we've got lots of opportunities. We're not doing nearly enough in the area of mortgage and car loans.

Bill: Well, why don't we try to figure out where the opportunities are and rank them. Let's put up a list and rank them in terms of effort and pay-off.

Opportunities for the Bank of Glen Burnie

	Low Effort	High Effort
High Pay-off	• Increase number of services per household • Customer profile database • Product knowledge training • Improved business planning • Improved costing, asset and liability management forecasting	• Better access to VISA and MasterCard transaction information • Internet banking • Process improvement • Fix mortgage processing
Low Pay-off	• Car loans • Add more ATMs • Debit cards	• Fix existing teller system

Bill: Any reaction, anybody?

Steve Arbeit, President and COO: I think the thing that sticks out like a sore thumb is that low-effort, high pay-off systems are actually more managerial than transactional.

Peter Schultz, VP, Information Systems and CIO: You know, I think as an organization we have this huge tendency to focus our attention and resources on the past and on our transaction-oriented systems. They seem to devour all of our energy.

Aldo: Yes, we seem to spend all our time making what we do work better, rather than asking what we should be doing.

Bill: That's a good insight. Let's extend it a bit. Before we leave today, I would like to address one final issue. This list is pretty good, but most people tend to stick a little too close the past. I'd like us to think a bit more broadly about the future.

To do this, why don't we do some scenario analysis? Now, the idea behind this is that the world is an uncertain place and that we must therefore look at our business and information management strategies with several possible futures in mind. I'm going to divide you up into three groups. I'd like you to come back with a list of the trends that you see are going to affect our business so we can evaluate our opportunities and strategies in the context of some alternative futures that we might face.

Two hours later, the group had the following scenarios in front of them:

	Key Trends
Scenario 1: Rapid deregulation	• Massive increase in competition • Consolidation of financial services marketplace • Many mergers • National competition from specialist companies • Increased importance of branding and marketing expenditures

	Key Trends
Scenario 2: **Rapid deregulation of Internet banking**	• Tremendous price competition for deposits • Sale of bank assets (e.g., mortgage portfolio) to improve the balance sheets • Increase in rate of shopping by customers • Rise of brokers and advisory services to seek services on behalf of customers on the Internet
Scenario 3: **Continued deflation**	• Real-estate loans a continuing problem for financial institutions • Customers concerned about declining equity in homes and shrinking pension funds • Customers pursue a better return and put their money in mutual funds and other high-yield investments

Bill: I think we've done a good day's work. We'll come back to these issues tomorrow.

chapter 4

RUNNING AWAY FROM THE TIGER

THE DELINQUENT CEO FAILS TO MAKE SURE THAT THE INFORMATION MANAGEMENT OF THE ORGANIZATION IS EXCELLENT

Wisdom is like electricity. There is no permanently wise man, but only men capable of wisdom, who being put into certain company or other favorable conditions become wise, as glasses rubbed acquire power for a time.

Ralph Waldo Emerson,
Natural History of Intellect, 1893

Being a CEO is never easy. There are always too many issues to think about and address, too few resources available and too little time. What makes the job even harder is that the CEO must lead the senior management of the organization, who are experts in their own narrower specialties. The CEO is the one who must make the final decision on major issues. In larger organizations, where the CEO is less hands-on, many CEOs complain that trying to influence the rest of the organization is like pushing on a string.

This problem is especially acute in information management. Most managers are frustrated by things they cannot understand, especially when the answer seems to vary every time they ask the question. Until recently, few CEOs used computers or had much interest in them. Computers were what other people used for work, not CEOs. When you became the CEO, you could breathe a sigh of relief. Somebody else would do things for you. While statistics suggest that roughly half of all CEOs use computers, we suspect that most don't use them very much.

As the cost of computing plunges and new applications for computer and information management projects open up, CEOs and their teams seem to be presented with never-ending opportunities and problems. However, there are few precedents, examples of success and models to help the senior manager in this ever-changing area. If all this wasn't bad enough, poorly thought-out investments in information technology can put a career and organization at risk.

THE DELINQUENT CEO IGNORES INFORMATION MANAGEMENT

No information technology should frighten you. If someone can't explain it to you, it's their problem—not yours.

Delegate and Avoid!

Leaders come in every size, shape and disposition.... Nevertheless they all seem to share some, if not all, of the following ingredients: ... a guiding vision ... passion ... integrity ... trust ... curiosity and daring.

Warren Bennis, *On Becoming a Leader,* 1989

Some people will say, "Computers are so complicated and the technological issues keep changing so fast that the head of information systems or chief information officer (CIO) has to be the one who pays attention to information technology." Senior management can't be expected to keep up with philosophical debates over which IT is best.

Indeed, many organizations take this view. A CIO is often appointed and put in charge of the company's information technology. This is a dangerous position. *BusinessWeek* titled one article "CIO Is Starting to Stand for 'Career Is Over.'" But why do we see such high turnover in these ranks?

Are so many CIOs incompetent? On the contrary, most of them, we have found, are intelligent, energetic and creative. They try to do excellent jobs for their employers.

Many CEOs practice "avoidance by delegation" to cope with the technology confusion. This approach invariably causes problems. In our travels, the organizations with bad information systems consistently have CEOs who ignore the role of information management. They may believe they are too old for information management or that information management and technology are too specialized and complicated. They may think information management is a narrow technical area that can, and should be, delegated.

In the pacesetting organizations, in contrast—those with good information systems and information management—the CEOs pay full attention to the role of information systems. They also make the senior IT executive part of their top management team and work hard to exploit their technology's full potential.

The technology responsibility, like other important corporate issues, rests squarely on the shoulders of the CEO. If you are a CEO, you are the one responsible for making sure that the information management of your organization is excellent. By not accepting your role in driving the information management in your organization, you make as big a mistake as a CEO who ignores the manufacturing strategy of a manufacturing organization, or the people management issues of any organization.

Organizations get good information management only if the CEO demands it.

We do not recommend that CEOs attempt to become CIOs. We urge them, instead, to pay attention to the issues and learn more about the uses and consequences of technology. They should try to raise the visibility of information management within their organizations. They should demand that investments in infrastructure and particular projects be made with business improvements always in mind.

The CEO must insist on the basic model we have proposed: Plan–Do–Improve. Strategic plans must address information management issues for all areas of the organization. The greater performance and capabilities being sought should be made explicit in the organization's management processes.

A few years ago, a large retail company was having trouble in getting one of its new computer systems to work properly. The system used new hardware technology that kept breaking down. The system's software had many flaws, as well.

The system's defects caused serious problems for the people who were serving customers.

These problems finally came to the attention of the CEO. Until that point, he had ignored information management and delegated it to his chief financial officer. When the CEO finally recognized the severity of the problem, he called in a firm of consultants to fix the problem.

After the problem was solved, the CEO decided to have the chief information officer report directly to the CEO. The CEO had decided that he had been delinquent long enough.

Signals from the CEO

We cannot emphasize enough that the most important mistake CEOs or general managers make is to ignore the importance of information management. By doing so, they manage with one arm tied behind their backs. They doom their organization. Instead, they must set an example within their organizations. They must exhibit a willingness to learn more about information management and encourage their colleagues to do the same.

A CEO's own use of computers can influence an organization, as well. This may not seem important, but it signals to the rest of the organization the importance of information management.

Mistake 1. CEOs do not use computers because they are too important and too busy. The organization gets the message that the CEO doesn't understand or care about the technology.

Mistake 2. CEOs have the most expensive machines sitting on their desks and use them only for looking at their e-mail. The rest of the organization learns that status is more important than competence, that the company does not value improvement.

Mistake 3. CEOs spend too much time on their computers, messing around on them. They demonstrate to the organization that computers actually reduce a senior manager's productivity. They do not provide any better performance or capability.

Mistake 4. CEOs use the executive information system or decision support system to micromanage and interfere with the responsibilities and accountabilities of those who report to them directly. They send the message that "Big Brother is watching you," which never motivates people greatly.

Mistake 5. CEOs are afraid to admit their ignorance of information technology. So they never develop any useful competence in important technologies and processes within the organization. These leaders illustrate that fear of technology is acceptable, even while it paralyzes the organization.

Mistake 6. CEOs love to experiment with their machines or are hackers themselves. This leads to unreliable technology. Their productivity sinks. They convey the message that playing with your computer is okay even if it interferes with your job. Employees imitating them will not try to improve their own performance or capabilities.

Mistake 7. CEOs delegate all decisions to their management teams or—worse—to the CIOs. They send the message that information technology and managing it are the responsibilities of lower-level management only.

The CEO Who Pays Attention

A little knowledge is a dangerous thing. Particularly dangerous is someone who has recently developed a little bit of knowledge about computers.

We recommend strongly that even the most enthusiastic evangelist of improved information management remember a few points. Information management is always complicated, always risky and always open to debate. There are always choices in the technology, the development process and the various improvements that you can choose.

Riding the Tiger has three authors because of the sheer complexity of addressing information management, strategic and implementation issues. This is an intrinsically difficult area to manage, let alone write about. Three minds are better than one. Any business manager can benefit from the input of both information systems professionals and users who will be affected by any project.

As with all areas of administration, listening is as important to leaders as is their ability to communicate their vision of success and to insist on the critical success factors the organization or organizational unit will concentrate on.

But once the leaders have solicited input and involved the actual users, good leaders will make their decisions and put their authority and resources firmly behind their projects.

CEOs can set the tone, pace and direction of decision making in this complex area. Their attention and influence should be felt through all the organization's strategies, policies, infrastructure, improvement goals and projects. This chapter presents a road map for wielding influence in these areas.

The activities in all areas of information technology can be grouped under either Plan, Do or Improve. Good implementation does not happen on its own. Planning must precede it. The plan must set out the *purpose* for the technology project very firmly. The technology plan and implementation will be designed to achieve the goals stated. In general, the objectives of using technology fall into two areas: improved performance or growth in organizational capabilities. Achieving these objectives will feed future technology planning and implementation. There is always a continuous cycle of Plan–Do–Improve working in a well-run organization.

	Plan	Do	Improve
Leadership	• Setting strategies and priorities • Aligning IT strategies • Developing IT strategy • Evaluating information management strategy • Process of strategy development • Planning over multiple periods • Setting investment priorities • Working smarter	• Influencing implementation	• Organizational improvement goals • Assessing the organization's capabilities
Policies	• Senior management should pay attention to policies and principles • Sample principles		• Improving infrastructure and technology
Projects			

Managers, whether they are CEOs or not, are responsible for making sure that the organization accepts this cycle. They need to make sure that the strategy and the policies are consistent, are being implemented and target specific improvements. When any element of the cycle is missing, the organization will tend to experience incomplete and unsuccessful efforts.

How far should a manager be involved? In each of the three key areas, leadership, policies and projects, the CEO's influence is felt in different ways throughout the Plan–Do–Improve cycle.

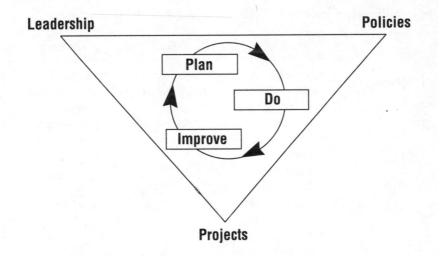

The leadership and policies of the organization combined with project management practices provide the basic framework for information management.

CEOs lead by articulating the strategy of their organizations. Without strategy, neither the overall strategies nor the information management strategies can be enacted successfully. Without specifically aiming to improve the organization in some way, managers find that information management only increases costs and benefits the organization only accidentally.

Other CEOs ensure that the *management processes* promote the production of a sound strategy for approval by senior management. In such organizations, the CEO acts more indirectly, but still needs to understand the underlying dynamic of the businesses, markets and processes on which the organization depends.

The CEO must attend to formulating policy first. Policies try to define accountabilities and responsibilities, so this definition is critical in any organization. Policies should be selected to balance customer and organization responsiveness against economies of scale and manageability that come from centralization. Implementing policies involves communication, education, central support and developing of expertise in the line functions.

Projects can be successful only with senior management's commitment to them. The role of the CEO is not to choose technology but to pay attention to how decisions regarding it are made and whether they support the organization's strategy.

In this planning, the CEO has to lead the organization in taking into account the people, policies and infrastructure issues. The principles he or she adopts will influence how future projects will be chosen and measured.

In many organizations, the absence of management leads to an information technology infrastructure that consists of one of everything. Standards are set, but changed so frequently that they are effectively useless.

The desire to continuously improve through information management is an explicit policy. It affects the capabilities of the whole organization. A CEO's vision and commitment will affect how much the organization can improve. How CEOs deal with small failures will dramatically influence the organization's risk-taking profile.

There is a famous story that in the early days of IBM, Tom Watson received in his office a manager who had just made a huge mistake that cost the company $10 million. Expecting to be fired, the manager offered his resignation. Watson tore it up, explaining that he had just spent $10 million dollars educating the manager. Now he wanted a return on this expensive education.

Setting Strategies and Priorities

	Plan	Do	Improve
Leadership	• Setting strategies and priorities • Aligning IT strategies • Developing IT strategy • Evaluating information management strategy • Process of strategy development • Planning over multiple periods • Setting investment priorities • Working smarter	• Influencing implementation	• Organizational improvement goals • Assessing the organization's capabilities
Policies			
Projects			

Adopting information technology without a coherent business strategy and purpose means you blunder blindly down a potentially dangerous path. You may end up at a dead-end or a totally irrelevant destination. While many managers can try to harness the technology tiger, the chief rider and the corporate strategy must guide their direction as a group.

First, identify the organization's priorities—its strategies, its vision of success, its mission and the critical success factors for the strategies to succeed. The CEO must insist that the strategy be constantly reviewed, updated and relevant, and, just as important, communicated to the rest of the organization. The corporate plan must be useful and practical, forming the basis upon which lower-level managers can build their plans and allocate resources.

CEOs are supposed to be smarter than everyone else in the organization. Their challenge is to share their vision with other managers in the organization so they can support that vision and in turn modify it.

The business strategy should be more than just financially driven, taking into account more than short-term financial consequences. It must involve other areas that contribute to the organization's sustainable strategic position. One way to address multiple strategic areas is to adopt a balanced score card approach to track performance. This approach helps the organization balance the many things it needs to get right to succeed. It sets objectives for, and measures the success of, the organization with respect to customers, competition, sales, marketing and operational issues.

> *Organizational commitment and perseverance are driven by the desire to make a difference in people's lives—the bigger the difference, the deeper the commitment. This suggests another difference between competing for the future and competition for the present, namely the prospect of making an impact, rather than the certitude of immediate financial returns.*

> Gary Hamel and C.K. Prahalad,
> *Competing for the Future,* 1994

Aligning Information Technology with Business Strategies

Information technology forms the backbone of today's organization. The desired direction of the organization determines its function. When the head moves, the skeletal system to which it is attached must follow. As long as strategy and information management practices are synchronized and aligned, the whole organizational body can run smoothly. When they are out of sync, the whole organization can be crippled. The effect may not show up in the short run but will be damaging and become particularly apparent in a crisis.

When organizations invest in information management badly, they suffer consequences over a long term. Organizations with bad information management miss opportunities in their customer base. They miss new opportunitites. They waste money producing the wrong products.

Without a clear direction, organizations and information systems will carry on doing what they have done in the past. It is for these reasons that typically 60 to 80 percent of the budgets of information systems departments are spent on fixing and incrementally changing existing software and supporting existing hardware. This focus on maintenance, planned or not, drains resources that should be allocated to capturing new opportunities. While maintenance and continued improvement are important, this biases organizations toward low-return projects.

Information technology is also changing

- the skills required of employees,
- the capabilities and competencies an organization must manage,
- the interfaces with customers and suppliers, and
- the production of services and products.

In industry after industry, the basis of sustainable competitive advantage, the Strategic Success Position, is being altered. No wonder managers find information management challenging.

The relatively low cost of computing tempts organizations to automate tasks simply because they *can* be automated. Some processes should be revised or even eliminated instead of being allowed to haunt the organization for another ten years! As the saying goes, "It makes no sense to invest in becoming the best manufacturer of buggy whips in a world of automobiles."

In the words of Derek Abell, a leading professor on strategy:

> In new organizations, "changing" the business is much more important than "running" the business. In the old organization, as chief executive or senior manager, you inherited the business, ran it like a custodian and then passed it on to someone else to run. In the new organization, you inherit it, you change it as much as you can to conform to the new, evolving competition, and you hand it over to someone else to change again.

Information management means

- making choices,
- choosing to support the organization's strategy and initiatives, and
- improving the performance and capabilities of the organization.

This fit between information management and strategy is often referred to as *alignment.*

Imagine that you are the CEO of IKEA, the global furniture chain. Your strategy is based on achieving huge economies of scale and shipping furniture around the world in bulk, in kits that can be assembled by highly taxed, income-poor consumers. Your greatest advantage is your unrelenting focus on cost reduction and achieving economies of scale that your competitors cannot match. As a retailer, you face numerous options:

1. You could go upmarket and start selling more expensive furniture, moving away from your low-cost production strategy.
2. You could address the time-scarcity problem of the aging and increasingly wealthy baby boomers and start to emphasize services such as delivery and assembly.
3. You could expand the geographic scope of your market and stay with your existing strategy, targeting the price-sensitive, two-career family.

Each of these strategies comes with its own set of critical requirements. Assuming you are forced to choose between them, your investment in information technology will look different.

With an *upscale* strategy, issues of quality and service will loom particularly large. Measuring customer satisfaction will be a key control issue that your organization has not previously addressed.

With the *deliver and assemble* strategy, your chief concern will be managing your delivery and assembly staff's productivity to keep costs down for the price-sensitive, busy segment of the population you serve.

For the *geographic expansion* strategy, the setting up of new stores and dealing with the problems of integrating information from many different countries, many with poor telecommunications infrastructures, poses your biggest technical challenge.

In other words, the kinds of systems you would need and the problems you would encounter would differ. The kinds of skills and investment needed will be inextricably linked to the business strategy. Those who believe that senior management can abdicate their involvement are, we believe, merely frightened.

How Organizations Develop an Information Technology Strategy

To align your various goals with your resources and policies, there should be strategies on both sides of the equation—business or operating strategy on one side and IT strategy on the other.

A group from the UK's Henley Management College has identified seven approaches organizations frequently use for developing their information management strategies:

1. **User-request driven**. The operating business plans and their projects are evaluated by the information systems department and put into a systems plan. This approach makes the most sense in a small organization, assuming that users are highly involved in the process.
2. **Business-plan driven**. The information systems department derives its strategic information systems plan from the organization's strategic plan. With this approach a company runs the risk of losing the valuable input of the technical specialists in the information systems department, and the input of front-line users.
3. Investing in information management based on **critical success factors** in IT strategy development for the particular organization. This focuses on the key performance issues that the organization must do well to succeed. It provides a good overview of the major issues but may not work well if the end-users do not participate in specifying the project and its requirements or whether there are opportunities to improve the process.

4. **Strategic analysis** underlying the competitive position of the organization. Again, this approach is extremely valuable as long as management also involves the intended end-users and applies more analysis.

5. **Information engineering**, relying primarily on the more technical issues of analyzing the organization's processes and resulting data requirements. This approach runs the risk of making the organization efficient but not effective if the application is so technocratic that strategic business changes and process reengineering are ignored.

6. The **technical architecture approach**. The focus is on developing a general framework and platform from which strategies can be supported. Seen most commonly in information warehousing projects, this approach can be so perfectionist that it drives the company into bankruptcy. However, dividing the development of the technical architecture into stages maintains the organization's strategic flexibility. It can often provide the best approach to building a strong architecture, but the sequencing of investments must be done very carefully.

7. The **organizational approach**. Widespread involvement of the management and employees contributes to greater success in implementation. The major downside is that end-users may not appreciate fully the important issues of setting standards and selecting technology architecture.

All these techniques are appropriate in varying degrees for a variety of organizations. Yet none of them works well unless the managers view the problem from all angles, seeing how their organization's elements work together. Information management is not an independent function. Like human resources management, or HRM, it is now an integral component of every part of the organization and supports most of the processes.

Developing Information Management Strategy

You can do this in three ways.

First, in the corporate planning process, identify your improvement goals and capabilities. The impact of information technology on the organization should be assessed. You can link the organization's strategy and IT as a result of this exercise.

Second, review, develop and plan your policies and infrastructure for IT. This gives your organization its corporate direction in this area.

Third, review the project initiatives and select those for implementation over a schedule of one to three years.

At every stage of this process, you should feel your senior management's leadership. Their role may change from stage to stage—from participant, to approval/veto giver, to resource provider. In addition, the *users* should play an assigned role in all these stages. A successful information management strategy is born out of the cooperation among senior management, the technical group, line managers and the users.

Evaluating Information Management Strategy

Information systems departments receive many requests for projects. They are not always in a position to determine how resources should be allocated. Senior managers need not actually allocate those resources, but they must make sure strategies and policies are in place to allow the organization to do so. Information management always involves more issues than just technology. Managers should ask themselves:

1. How does the information technology strategy support your business strategy?
2. What are the improvement goals the technology supports?
3. What is your plan for improving infrastructure? How will this improve your capabilities?
4. What are the policies and standards that support the easy exchange of information? Effective technical development? A relatively efficient computing environment?
5. What are your criteria for selecting projects? How do they relate to your organization's goals?
6. Do you have a well-defined project process for maintaining the quality of your projects?

7. Do you have a realistic way of costing technology that takes into account your full life-cycle costs as well as the impact of your whole corporate initiative (technology as part of an improvement program)?
8. Do you pay attention to timing issues related to projects?
9. What are your policies for educating people in the use of this technology? Consider your users as well as the technical group.
10. How are you planning to introduce this information technology? How does this process fit into your corporate planning cycle?
11. How can you align your corporate strategy with your information management strategy and people strategies?

Planning over Multiple Periods

In evaluating projects, consider the time value of money. You invest money in a project, typically up front, and the returns come in over an extended time. Because money in the future is worth less than money today, financial theory adjusts the flow of payments to take into account the time value of money.

There is a parallel here with information technology and management. The value of an investment in IT translates into a problem in multiperiod evaluation.

The challenge in IT planning is that any project has ongoing costs and planned performance improvement over multiple periods. It is obvious that large systems need maintenance, but this is also true for small software packages.

The authors have developed a large management simulation game to illustrate one of the important problems executives face in building an information management infrastructure. Players must commit themselves to building an information infrastructure several periods beyond their current planning. Frequently, participants have tremendous difficulty dealing with such complexity as planning simultaneously for the next period and two periods beyond that.

In the simulation, terrible planning errors emerge that can destroy the sales potential of products and services developed by the marketing department. In these cases no capacity was allocated to the new products and the players ignored the infrastructure necessary to sell them.

In real life, the same things happen time and time again. Introducing infrastructure and new information systems to your organization is like having a baby. Putting more people on the job won't speed up the process or make it easier. You still need to plan the steps. Often, the decisions made today will affect the success of the organization years down the road. If managers fail to anticipate the needs of the organization and end up resorting to crisis management, inevitably they will find it is too late to avert the crisis by the time it occurs.

Evolution is very much part of information management planning. There are very few silver bullets. Successful CEOs recognize that demanding a once-and-for-all solution to an IT problem can be shortsighted. A silver bullet is almost always unrealistic.

Setting Investment Priorities

There are always more demands for information technology than there are resources available to satisfy them. Management faces a tremendous challenge in deciding how to allocate resources and measure the consequences of its decisions.

Evaluating the payback from these decisions is always difficult. If you do your information management right but the strategy wrong, then the results will look bad. When you work out the strategy right yet your information management is poor, you'll have trouble evaluating how much better the results would have been if your information technology had been better.

When evaluating investment opportunities, remember some important questions:

1. *Is the proposed project in line with the principles and policies we have developed?*

If the project is inconsistent with traditional policies, it may force you to reevaluate your whole strategy or policies.

2. *How will the investment affect the capabilities of our people and the organization?*

If you intend the project to increase the capabilities of your organization, you may have to change the way you evaluate the project. Building capabilities to pursue a new vision of strategic success constitutes a major decision for any organization. It requires the sponsorship, support and commitment of senior management.

3. *Does the investment improve existing (information technology and other) capabilities or create new ones?*

Always analyze the improvement in a proposed project. You will be tempted to build IT capability without linking it to the organization's strategy. Exercise your self-restraint to avoid investing in an older system with little future.

4. *Is this an infrastructure decision or a business initiative decision?*

We believe that evaluation criteria for infrastructure projects should differ from those for business initiatives that are more easily tied to a particular business case. Infrastructure investments are, almost by definition, hard to evaluate. They provide a core information management capability that will benefit many future business initiatives.

For a retailer like Marks and Spencer (M&S), the quintessential British chain store, the decision in the 1970s was whether to move to electronic point-of-sale terminals to improve their tracking of inventory. Up until then they had used tags removed from the clothing at the sales counter to track their inventory. M&S had to process six million tags per year, but the accuracy of the system was only 75 percent.

Seventy-five percent accuracy was considered exceptionally good in the UK industry. M&S was the most profitable and successful retailer in Europe. Its leaders had a culture of constantly trying to improve the performance of their organization.

The board of directors had trouble justifying the investment as a major infrastructure decision, even though they considered it critical to the future of the business.

As we noted, this difficulty in evaluating the return from a major investment is typical of infrastructure decisions. Yet for a retailer, a critical success factor in the business is managing its inventory turns and minimizing its markdowns. Managing an inventory this way is like flying a plane whose compass is right only 75 percent of the time.

With accurate inventory and sales information, the board of directors decided that M&S would enjoy numerous opportunities for pay-off:

- Faster response to market trends, which translates into increased sales and profitability
- Micromarketing opportunities to exploit regional differences
- Better scheduling of staff hours
- Better tracking of more specific inventory information such as colors and sizes
- Shortened order times from linking point-of-sale data directly to suppliers
- Better marketing analysis
- Better logistics and lower warehousing costs.

With one investment in infrastructure, there should be many potential pay-offs. Ideally, these pay-offs should come from reducing the amount of investment for subsequent, business-case justified, projects. These become small or incremental costs for the organization with more rapid development times.

What we find characteristic of this type of decision is that the more successful companies aggressively pursue the high-leverage infrastructure technologies. Success gives them confidence. However, M&S managers did not introduce their new electronic point-of-sale equipment in one massive effort. They spent extensive time evaluating suppliers and learning as much about the technology as possible. When they did implement it, they chose two suppliers and customized the technology to fit their business. They also worked closely with their own people. Their disciplined approach meant that they always managed the project carefully and, therefore, reduced their risks.

Less successful organizations tend to pursue infrastructure projects with trepidation. They leave themselves less room for error and often perpetuate a history of bad practices. Without properly addressing how to acquire or develop information technology infrastructure, these organizations will continue to be unsuccessful. In contrast to M&S, a poorly managed competitor might well have forgone development of internal knowledge about electronic point-of-sale equipment, detailed supplier evaluation and testing.

M&S also did something else that good clients do. It quickly winnowed down its suppliers to two. After the initial evaluation, the retailer developed a strong partnership with the supplier that paid off in later years. There is no better supplier than a competent one, one who is committed to working with you and expects to realize a reasonable profit on your relationship.

Working Smart

Information technology can be seductively complicated. The more obscure and difficult, the better it can seem. Many people's careers are made because of their ability to master technically complicated areas. However, surrounded by complex issues, you sometimes are most practical if you take a simple approach. The following guidelines suggest several other perspectives when you need to surface and take a breath. They do not replace complex analyses.

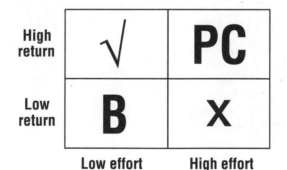

PC — The Puritan or Confucian ethic: work hard and you will be rewarded with good results.

B — The bureaucrat's choice: be seen to be working, even if the work doesn't matter.

X — The stupid choices an organization makes: high effort and low pay-off.

√ — The best kind of project: low effort and high return.

From Thomas Bonoma, *The Marketing Edge*, 1985.

Strategy involves pursuing the right mix of projects.

In a world of limited resources, there are many advantages to undertaking projects that offer high pay-off and require little effort. Organizations often fail to distinguish between working hard and working smart.

Let's take an example. Suppose you are the CEO of a financial services organization. You confront the myriad of technical choices the Internet brings to your organization. You recognize there are huge uncertainties about which technologies will turn out the most successful. You also wonder about the right timing for developing and introducing new services.

This is the problem the CEO of even a large organization such as FirstUnion, a bank with $192 billion in assets, faces. The question becomes not so much which technology will win, but rather, how can we position ourselves with investments that look beneficial no matter which technology wins? How can we be ready to jump immediately when the market takes off?

Information Management Policies and Principles

	Plan	Do	Improve
Leadership			
Policies	• Senior management should pay attention to policies and principles • Sample principles		
Projects			

It's easy to confuse information management with information technology management. Information management needs the leadership of senior management to make its IT function well. Information management aims to help management allocate resources, increase effectiveness and boost the quality of all the business' information processes, *whether or not they are automated.* It includes coordinating suppliers, employees and customers in tasks.

Information management is not a functional responsibility. It crosses functional boundaries in the organization. It spells out the policies, processes and systems requirements that frame infrastructure, project choices and the mode of technical operation. This is why it needs senior management's attention. Organizations today are run by people and procedures, and policies are implemented in software and silicon.

Elements of Information Management

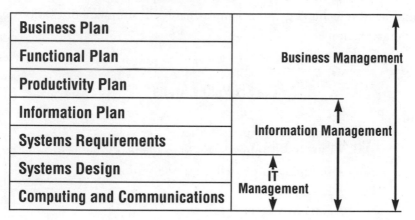

Business Plan	
Functional Plan	Business Management
Productivity Plan	
Information Plan	
Systems Requirements	Information Management
Systems Design	IT
Computing and Communications	Management

From Paul A. Strassmann, *The Politics of Information Management*, 1995.

Developing information management policies and principles really concerns how the enterprise will manage information. This makes it the responsibility of top management. These leaders should commit themselves to these principles, which they communicate to everyone, and support their adoption.

The principles should guide rather than direct information systems decision making and operations in system design and implementation. They should represent simple statements of an organization's basic beliefs about how the organization wants to manage itself, its information and information technology. If the principles are sound, business unit managers and technical experts will turn to them for guidance. People will simply ignore vague principles.

Principles simplify the lives of business unit managers who face difficult technology decisions. Principles create common ground between information systems departments and the end-users. They help the organization make decisions on information management that truly reflect the organization's priorities.

Sample Principles for an Organization

In this section, we will outline the six key areas that will benefit from information management principles and give examples of them. Your own principles will need to fit your own organization's situation, its strategy and use of information technology. Our samples here will stimulate discussions in your organization.

The Six Policy Areas

- Roles and Responsibilities
- Quality of Information Management Practices
- Infrastructure and Technical Solutions
- Processes
- Data Management
- Emergencies and Backup

Roles and Responsibilities

As with all areas of management, senior managers must first delineate clearly the roles and responsibilities of those in the organization concerned with and involved with information management. At the same time they must address the issue of centralization and decentralization.

The old planning and budgeting processes and the old model of a central information systems (IS) function reporting to a chief financial officer and guided by a steering committee have broken down. We work in an era where computing is both pervasive and distributed, and organizations are decentralizing their decision-making authority accordingly.

Power is an unfashionable word, but power needs to be properly rebalanced to promote use of IT as well as increase effectiveness and efficiency in the system. An effective and efficient organization makes use of distributed elements and core control. It is unreasonable to expect CIOs to succeed in their jobs if top management does not set policies on how to balance central control with distributed systems. The balance of information management needs to reflect the principles behind the organizational structure as a whole. Otherwise, conflicts will arise.

One of our clients had about a dozen divisions in different sectors of the publishing industry. Even though the needs of the various divisions were different, our client had a central systems development group to serve all the divisions.

Not surprisingly, the divisions didn't get good service. The developers couldn't ever have enough knowledge about each division's business. When the complaints from the divisions became loud enough, the CEO, with our help, decided to let each division find its own systems solutions.

Most were able to acquire software packages specifically designed for their businesses. Even though the initial acquisition costs for these packages appeared to be higher than the cost of an in-house solution, the profits of the divisions increased, and the complaints stopped.

We suggest the following:

- The CIO should be responsible for assessing whether the information management plans align with the approved corporate plans.
- Senior management should hold business unit managers at all levels accountable for all the benefits and costs of developing and operating their information systems.
- Business unit managers should lead the information management process. They will "own" the operating information systems that result.
- When business unit managers set the priorities for their own information systems, they should base their priorities on opportunities that provide strategic, competitive or other advantages.
- The information systems department exists to support the business units, to help them achieve their goals. They also must intervene judiciously in areas where economies of scale can be achieved through procurement, support, setting standards, say, or operating shared infrastructures, such as networks.
- The information systems department should supply applications that support the integration of the organization's processes. In

more practical terms, this means that they should set standards to make it easier to combine information from different areas of the organization.

- The information systems department should play a strong role in educating managers about the importance of using good practices in information management projects and procurement.
- The organization should manage information through centralized control over standards, security and the sharing of physical assets and information.
- The organization should insist upon a culture that expects team effort between business unit people and systems people.

As consultants, we are usually called in by the CIO to help introduce new technologies. When the CEO calls us in, we are usually asked to help deal with a systems disaster. Interestingly, in all such disasters, the systems department reported to someone other than the CEO. Without exception, our clients whose systems departments reported to the CEO had good systems and no disasters.

Quality of Information Management Practices

Information technology is a relatively young area. It is still frequently practiced with an individualistic, almost Wild West, mentality. Many organizations still behave as if there is something mysterious about developing and acquiring information management products and projects. As a result they make no attempt to control the whole process. Committing yourself to quality and adopting quality practices does not come naturally. It needs to be made an explicit part of a corporate and IT strategy. Quality does not mean slavish adherence to policies and procedures; its scope is much broader.

For example, we would want to see that

- information systems people are all dedicated to providing excellent customer service,
- a clear target is established as the achievable goal for highest quality information services,

- customer satisfaction is measured from the customer's point of view,
- software is acquired according to a formal software evaluation process that considers the total cost of ownership and its benefits to the business.

Infrastructure and Technical Solutions

Lay out your organization's principles for developing good infrastructure and projects and communicate them clearly. This will make implementation decisions easier and faster and more likely to be correct. Otherwise, you can easily become entangled and strangled in technological complexity. Information technologies always represent a network of interdependencies.

- The information systems department will maintain a short list of supported products in each technology class. Business units may purchase other products at their own discretion (subject to spending approval limits), but information systems will not support them.
- Information systems will buy rather than build business applications wherever possible. Business unit managers will control changes of purchased packages. These changes will be minimal.
- The organization will seek to develop and improve information systems with standard enterprise-wide methods to speed up such development and realize benefits quickly.
- The information systems department will make computing and communication networks natural and easy to use.

Processes

Some would argue that processes underlie all information systems. After all, technology links and supports all organizational activities in this information age. Directions and game plans for dealing with this area make implementing information technology easier for managers. Two promises we should make:

- We shall eliminate redundant tasks and simplify all information processes before we build new applications.
- Information systems and business unit managers will review process improvements to avoid frequently repeated mistakes arising from error-prone procedures, inadequacies in employees' training or mistakes in applications design.

Data Management

Data should be shared, protected and analyzed to create useful information and knowledge for the organization. This is the ultimate basis of competitive advantage. How should you set up the corporate knowledge pool? Who should contribute to it? How can it be accessed? Who should have access to it? These are all basic questions. Every time organizations push for more analysis, the answer is often "We don't have the data" or "We cannot get to the data." Those who can and do have the data make headway in the marketplace.

More promises:

- We shall adopt enterprise-wide data definitions and standards for all data.
- We shall enter data into the information system *only once*, at the point of origin.
- We shall assign to our data elements safeguards that assure nearly no errors at points of origin.
- We shall safeguard our information against unintentional or unauthorized alteration, destruction or disclosure.
- All information employees acquire or create while conducting business, except that which is specifically exempted as personal or private, is a corporate resource.
- The intellectual or property rights to all corporate information an employee produces while on the organization's payroll belong to the enterprise.

Emergencies and Backup

Emergency planning and backup of both computing facilities and data may seem like small technical issues. But more and more organizations now find that they cannot function without information technology. And with the increasing decentralization of computer use, more machines need to be backed up. Only when senior managers take an interest in guaranteeing that the organization can function in an emergency will the necessary resources come forth.

- All key databases shall be backed up to assure the data survive if the computer system fails.
- Information services support for operations related to customers shall be restored, within a specified time period, following any physical destruction.
- The organization will maintain only essential services when a specified fraction of its computer systems go down.

Organizational Improvement Goals

	Plan	Do	Improve
Leadership			• Organizational improvement goals • Assessing the organization's capabilities
Policies			• Improving infrastructure and technology
Projects			

TigerPearl

You can't improve if you don't change.

Many Japanese manufacturing companies believe that the quality or yield from a process is less important than their rate of improvement. We believe this philosophy underlies any successful organization.

Managers used to think that change was similar to the occasional white water a canoeist comes across in a stream. Today's business seems more like continuous white water. Modern management grapples with constant change.

Change is even more costly if the organization faces a major transition or crisis regularly and its managers do not manage change as part of the organization's routine tasks.

On learning, Peter Senge writes in *The Fifth Discipline:*

> *Today, systems thinking is needed more than ever because we are becoming overwhelmed by complexity. Perhaps for the first time in history, humankind has the capacity to create far more information than anyone can manage, and to accelerate change faster than anyone's ability to keep pace. . . . Organizations break down, despite individual brilliance and innovative products because they are unable to pull their diverse functions and talents into a productive whole.*
>
> *Complexity can easily undermine confidence and responsibility.*

The velocity and scope of change are even more significant in information technology. Technology needs a "succession and replacement plan," much like a management succession plan. Organizations will go through many generations of technology, considering the average life cycle of a product is no longer than five years and in some industries can be as short as six months to two years. Issues such as When should the technology be adopted? and When should it be considered obsolete? are easy to ignore but critical to address. Proceeding without a succession plan is likely to be costly.

Good organizations not only measure what they do, they provide policies that allow their managers to experiment in the interests of improvement.

Chaparral Steel, one of the most successful steel minimills in the US, has put in place roughly 100,000 performance measures for its operation. Over the past decade, its productivity has increased by 7 to 8 percent each year, which means they have almost doubled their productivity over the past decade.

Chaparral permits any managers to experiment with improving the process as long as they can get four VPs in the organization to sign off on the proposed change. The manager is not held accountable for experiments and they do not affect his performance ratios.

CEOs play an important role in guiding the organization so it can meet these unrelenting challenges. They develop the vision that will enable their organizations to acquire new capabilities and they seek continuous improvements. Senior management should determine its goals for development of employee knowledge and make sure the information management strategy supports that goal.

Assessing the Organization's Capabilities

Assessing an organization's capabilities is the first step toward establishing its performance goals. When we work with CEOs, we have them ask themselves the following questions:

1. How fast can your organization develop a new variation on a product or service today?
2. How fast can it build or acquire, set up and launch the information technology for a new product today?
3. How fast can it make and implement decisions?
4. How fast can it change its ability to manage and control rapid change?
5. Do your staff possess the capabilities and competencies appropriate for a slow-moving, bureaucratic, centralized organization, or do they have the skills and knowledge suited to a rapidly changing environment?
6. What is the organization doing today to speed up its ability to respond to changes in the environment?
7. Where is the organization putting its capital dollars? Is it investing in the past or in the future?

8. Do you blame the managers or the organization's strategy for any weaknesses? Even the most motivated and effective manager can do little if the market in which the company is competing is unattractive or the strategy is inappropriate.

9. Have the strategy, mission and values of your organization been clearly communicated to the managers?

10. To what extent are managers held responsible for their actions? Are the consequences of their actions clearly linked to personal rewards and opportunities?

11. Do the managers have the skills they need to carry out their jobs? If not, is there a plan to arm them with those skills?

12. Is the information managers need available and easily accessible to them?

13. Do managers have the time to use the information they should be using?

14. Has information management enabled managers to become more productive and effective?

15. What frustrations within the organization can be eliminated through decentralization? This would release the energy and enthusiasm of the managers and staff.

16. Do people within the organization believe that change is possible and that individual managers can contribute? Managers need to be rewarded for their individual and collective actions.

17. Has the organization considered the mix of its activities and which ones are critical to its success?

18. Are you learning as much from your failures as your successes as an organization?

Improving Infrastructure and Technology

Planning and implementing new technology can be so exhausting and costly that you may believe the new tool will serve your organization unchanged for a long time. In reality, information technology is changing and improving at breakneck speed. Take the simple example of personal computers—the market is almost guaranteed to offer a better and cheaper machine as soon as you place your order.

One of the old rules of thumb about managing continuous change is to accept it as a given and plan accordingly. This means planning for new improvement goals and new adoption as soon as you are done with the current implementation, if not before. Some smart managers plan obsolescence of the technology they use so that they are well aware how much they should invest in the technology and the time frame for doing so. Many develop their own plans to upgrade independent of their vendors' plans so they need not rely completely on one vendor's picture of reality. This allows them to take advantage of new alternatives when the market changes.

Managing technology change challenges the specialists, too. It is also frequently difficult for the lay manager to accept the specialists' advice. The interaction between senior management and technologists resembles that between parent and teenagers. The teenagers expound on the virtues of the latest gadget and ask for the money to buy it. And then they turn around moments later to ask for another gadget. The technology is often new enough that you must expect some degree of experimentation. But the risks are downplayed to senior managers who do not understand technology. These managers have to recognize that technology does change and carries risks, and that they can anticipate a continued stream of requests for new implementation. They must support efforts to develop improvement plans that suit current technology and the business requirements of their organizations.

Influencing Implementation

	Plan	Do	Improve
Leadership		• Influencing implementation	
Policies			
Projects			

Although CEOs are not involved in projects, they can exert influence to affect their outcomes. When senior managers lay out business strategies and policies, they go a long way toward shaping the type of projects to be implemented. Their attitudes toward evaluating and measuring results will affect the organization's criteria for project selection.

CEOs can affect projects in other ways:

1. By supporting redesign of the organization's processes, CEOs encourage more teams and departments to improve the way they work to take best advantage of computing technology.
2. CEOs can motivate their troops to strive for computing excellence.
3. CEOs can be exemplary team players.
4. CEOs can respect project management principles and not skew important projects in which they have personal interests.
5. CEOs can encourage interdepartmental teams.

SUMMARY

The Role of Senior Management

The one fact on which all senior managers agree is that they cannot do everything by themselves. Their job is to harness and focus the enthusiasm of the organization's employees. Senior managers possess remarkably few tools for creating an environment that will shape the behavior of their entire organization, but information management is clearly one major tool. Information technology can change the filters and feedback loops with which the organization interacts with the world.

Senior managers exert significant leverage on making sure information technology is seen as a major concern of theirs and of all managers. Senior managers should communicate that they expect and want good information management.

But this is not enough. Senior managers must see that the division of labor in the organization is appropriate. Good information management today does not result from giving all this power to a strong centralized information systems department. Nor does it come from eliminating the centralized information systems department and decentralizing to the line business units.

Most organizations require a balance between the hub of the wheel and its rim. Without the hub, the rim will distort. With the rim and spokes, the wheel becomes heavier and slower to rotate. The balance between the two is always as difficult as it is mandatory for any organization.

Strategically, you face two conflicting economic issues. On the one hand, the development of expertise (the descending of a technology learning curve) means that central control is likely to be more economical for the organization. On the other hand, in a world of rapid change, decision making should be as close to the customer as possible. Managers should be required to improve their systems as quickly as possible to gain the advantage over their competitors.

Paying Attention

CEOs who neglect computers are like CEOs who ignore financial strategy, the human beings in the organization or its manufacturing strategy. They are delinquent CEOs.

The Bank of Glen Burnie Case Study:

Hotel meeting room. Strategy planning retreat, Day Two, morning session.

THE DELINQUENT CEO

Bill Underwood, Facilitator: Well, folks, we did well yesterday. Now we need to turn to our information technology situation. Aldo, the group needs your point of view. How serious are you about this process?

Aldo Moretti, Chairperson and CEO: You have my commitment. We have to address these problems or we don't have an organization that can survive, let alone grow.

Peter Schultz, VP, Information Systems: Then in my view, we're not in good shape. Our big machine is old and unreliable. Getting support on our ten-year-old software is impossible. If it weren't for the finance department's years of experience with getting data off the system, we'd be in big trouble.

    Even worse, we're spending all this money on PCs. I don't think we're getting much value out of them. I feel as if my budget is leaking out to the end-users and yet I can't keep them happy. It's a pretty thankless task.

Aldo (*looking stunned*): Oh?

Bill: So, what do we do to fix these problems?

Peter (*pausing*): I know I have the reputation of always wanting to spend more money on computers and software, but I think we need a plan to coordinate what we *are* doing. We probably do need to spend more money, but we need priorities. We've got all these systems that don't talk to each other and each one is programmed in a different language. Each system kinda does its job, but if I were in, say, Ron's shoes and trying to market our services, I'd be awfully frustrated at how hard it is to get at information about customers.

Aldo: How much money would you need over, say, three years?

Bill: Now, hold on. Before we jump into what we want to spend, perhaps we should ask ourselves, What would success look like for us as a company? What are we trying to achieve? But first, let's pause for breakfast.

THE TIGER'S BACKBONE — BASIC ANATOMY

POLICIES AND INFRASTRUCTURE FOR THE CORPORATE INFORMATION HIGHWAY

Managing Where the Tiger Roams

Managers are often bewildered by all the opportunities to use information technology at work. Even if they have developed a business strategy to guide their information technology strategy, they still have to decide which projects to pursue first.

How can you as a manager coordinate your efforts so that your work is not duplicated unnecessarily? How can you keep your programs working with one another? How do you avoid wasting your time reinventing the wheel? How can you be sure that the hardware is sufficient to run your great software programs? How can you find the support you need in all of this?

Good information technology in an organization is built on sound infrastructure and policies. Properly constructed, this framework unleashes the power of the tiger to your end-users. It constitutes the first step toward implementing an IT strategy.

Infrastructure is a particularly difficult area in information management. For most technologists, infrastructure means the *hardware* side of computers and networks. They draw an analogy with the US interstate highway system. Build the highways and people will come (and park in traffic jams). The freeways connect the smaller existing road systems. However, as governments have found to their cost, potholes require fixing, and capacity is always a problem.

In urban planning, cities with overburdened transportation networks such as Los Angeles have been forced to change the *use* of their infrastructure. High Occupancy Vehicle (or car pool) and bus lanes give priority to those who burden the highway system less. New freeways are built with variable tolls to control transit times. Employers are forced to encourage car pooling and limit the parking available for employees.

PEOPLE AND THEIR SKILLS MAKE INFORMATION MANAGEMENT SUCCESSFUL

While working at home is one proposed solution, it turns out that even with current technologies there are many benefits to having employees work in an office. They can exchange soft information, so most people work at home only when they need an extended period of concentration, devoid of interruptions.

How the highway system is managed, how users respond to the policies that operate it, the economic and personal incentives for living close to work, urban planning, tax policy—all influence the *effectiveness* of the highway infrastructure.

The information infrastructure in an organization operates the same way. How the infrastructure functions and how people respond to the policies and practices both make an enormous difference to the success of the organization and the information infrastructure itself.

If you manage this infrastructure well, your tiger can speed along the highway. If you design and manage it poorly, your tiger will have to pick its way over narrow winding paths to reach its destinations.

The Highway for the Tiger

Most managers associate infrastructure with hardware. They generally think of 10 types:

- Personal computers, notebook computers and workstations for managers
- Point of sale and bar-coding equipment for retail staff and those involved with inventory management
- File servers for departmental computing
- Printers
- Local area networks and wireless networks for short-range communications
- Servers, minicomputers and mainframes for processing transactions, and more broadly based client-server computing
- The phone system, which is either called a key system or private branch exchange (PBX)
- The call-center hardware for routing telephone calls, such as automatic call distributors (ACDs)

- Wide area networks, telecommunication connections, fax-modems, multiplexers and other telecom equipment, often leased from the telephone company, to link different locations or to gain access to public networks and network services such as the Internet
- Process control equipment to manage the manufacturing process

What is less obvious in these tangible components is that the equipment is largely useless without competent people to operate it. Obvious as this may seem, many organizations only consider hardware in their plans. When evaluating a piece of equipment for approval, many only consider the cost of that specific acquisition explicitly. Few think of related issues of ownership over the life of the equipment: its maintenance costs and the human cost of implementing, supporting and using that infrastructure.

A simple example: One company wished to set up a fax-server—an apparently simple task. A fax-server is a piece of software put on a network to allow employees to send faxes from their desks and share a fax-modem. This particularly helps sales representatives, who can send their faxes to clients overnight, which saves money on long-distance telephone charges.

The company had received a number of faxing packages with the computers they bought. One could be upgraded for relatively little cost into a networked fax-server. Over 24 months, the company spent roughly 20 days trying to get the $1,000 piece of software to work. At an opportunity cost of, say, $500 per day for the skilled person involved, the company had spent around $10,000 to produce a solution that did not meet its needs. Management would have been wiser to buy a more industrial-strength piece of faxing software for between $1,500 to $2,500. This would have cost one day to set up. By trying to save too much money on the initial infrastructure cost, the company ended up wasting a lot of effort and money on software that wouldn't work.

In fact, some studies suggest that the cost to a company of owning a personal computer over its three-year life can range from 2.5 to five times the initial acquisition cost, taking support costs, repairs and upgrading into account. That means if your policies are right, you as just one manager can spend $12,000 to $20,000 to maintain the computer over three years. These are not small numbers. Many managers may not initially believe them until they consider the cost of wasted employee time due to computer problems.

The more important the users, the more expensive downtime is for them, particularly if they depend on the computer to do their work. And increasingly everyone is dependent upon his or her computer.

Coming up with the total costs involved, we discover many other issues related to infrastructure that should be considered when laying the foundation for implementing any information technology.

TigerPearl Infrastructure means the right people first, good policies second and the right equipment third. Most people get this backward. Having good equipment is no guarantee of success.

A Broader View of Infrastructure and Policies

Infrastructure is more than just the core physical assets of information management. It is the set of ingredients that enable and provide the foundation for successful IT management.

To test whether something should be thought of as infrastructure, ask yourself whether the benefits of a particular information management capability will prove useful for other systems to come over multiple periods.

As a general rule, we believe the infrastructure for an organization falls into four types:

1. Adequate network infrastructure and hardware
2. Excellent software
3. Competent trained and empowered people
4. Policies and procedures that help the organization respond quickly to change

In addition to the obvious physical assets, software is the other core component that drives technology. Software today can represent our business knowledge and procedures in bits and bytes.

If we accept that the purpose of IT is not merely to *automate* but *informate*—to automate and give information about the automated process—

the importance of people in its successful use becomes obvious. Technology without computer-literate people is like a car without a driver.

To make all these ingredients work smoothly together, we must add policies and standards to the recipe for infrastructure. These hold them all together. Policies will always evolve, especially in an environment of change. There are good policies and bad policies. Good ones should not spell out precise answers. Answers will change, but policies spell out flexible approaches and principles that will allow systems from different units to work together as conditions change.

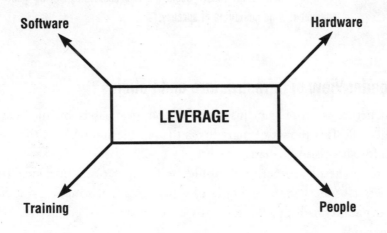

Let's see how policies and infrastructure fit into the Plan–Do–Improve cycle. Most of our discussion will concern hardware, software and policies. Since Chapter 6 is entirely devoted to people, our discussion of this topic here will be limited.

Planning Policies and Infrastructure—Expect a Moving Target

	Plan	Do	Improve
Leadership			
Policies	• Evolution of objectives • Accountability • Principles • Adequate hardware • Excellent software • Architecture • Supporting management effectiveness • Mobile and temporary computing • Managing risks • Costing infrastructure • Outsourcing decision	• Benefit from evolution • Motivating knowledge workers • Customer satisfaction • On time and on budget • Evaluating technology • Buy versus develop	• Infrastructure evolution game plan • Technical capability upgrade
Projects			

Three forces drive the need to improve infrastructure.

First, improved infrastructure may improve your effectiveness in solving current business problems. Few organizations have the luxury of not considering technology upgrades and improvements.

Second, the competitive environment often requires that you develop new ways of interacting with your customers. Gaining competitive advantage may demand that you analyze new or more information or use new technology.

Third, those who use software are transformed by the experience. As they master their programs, they inevitably discover and demand new approaches to running their businesses. This growth is healthy as long as the evolution of these needs is framed and evaluated against the strategy of the business and the return from the additional investment.

A good company must think of its information technology the way a manufacturing company thinks about its production capability. It must continuously seek to improve its capabilities and involve all its users in the process.

Rapid and continuous improvement require an IT foundation to the infrastructure that can be replaced in modules, or separate components. *Modularity* is key if an organization wants to reduce disruptions to the running of its business. There will always be transitions during which some portion of the infrastructure will be retained and reinforced while other parts are being replaced. With a good modular architecture, new capabilities can be grafted onto the foundation without destroying the overall effectiveness of the organization during the transition.

The structure is now seldom a single system running on a mainframe. Instead of one large "house" built on a foundation, organizations need many smaller structures. The applications are smaller, modular, capable of communicating with one another and can exploit the infrastructure upon which they are built.

Contrary to the belief of most people, the best way to deal with moving targets and change is to have a plan. Developing a plan forces the planners to think through the connections in their business and projects. When a new event or force is introduced they can evaluate it much more easily if the organization already has in place a systemic view of how things work and will evolve.

So you need a planning process that identifies how you can move from an inflexible foundation to a modular one for updating and meeting new challenges. This transition is one of the most challenging exercises for any organization. It requires consensus on the future and constant, careful analysis of technology choices.

	Plan	Do	Improve
Leadership			
Policies	• Expect a moving target • Accountability • Principles • Adequate hardware • Excellent software • Architecture • Supporting management effectiveness • Managing risks • Costing infrastructure • Outsourcing decision		
Projects			

Accountability

In the more traditional view of computing as the exclusive domain of experts and specialists, accountabilities are localized. A single department is deemed accountable for its own success. In today's decentralized environment, users may initiate projects themselves, have a greater say in implementing them and may not need help from the information systems department at all. Responsibilities and authority must be balanced afresh. Of course the responsibility of top management must be included in this whole.

Information management policies are about achieving economies of scale and taking advantage of the staff's learning curve. Decentralization is about empowering the manager to be entrepreneurial and effective and, above all, being responsive to the customer. Managing the balance between the two is the job of senior management.

In a well-managed company, we expect to see the following types of relationships and policies:

1. Top management should care about information technology. Senior managers are interested in, and educated about, IT. They expect to be kept informed about IT issues and to be updated regularly on technology choices. They consider information management part of their business strategy and their personal knowledge.
2. The chief information officer, or CIO, reports directly to the CEO and is part of the senior management team.
3. Responsibilities for information systems have been decentralized to business units that must justify their information technology investments strategically.
4. The central information systems group sets its policies carefully. It seeks to specify which policy items would offer the organization the most leverage.
5. IT specialists recognize business issues.
6. General managers are familiar with IT issues and priorities.
7. Where internal expertise is lacking, or where an external perspective is needed, outside consultants are used appropriately.

What CEOs Should Do

To achieve the kind of organization described above, we suggest the following:

1. You should not abdicate your responsibility for information technology management.
2. You should establish the IT policies and principles that the organization will live by and see that the organization sticks to them.
3. You should make sure everyone in the organization believes in the company's IT policies and principles.
4. You should provide opportunities for your executives to learn about IT.
5. You should support your CIO but not attempt to assume his role.

What CIOs Should Do

The CIO's role clearly remains different from the CEO's. As a CIO you must:

1. Develop means to ensure that all uses of IT contribute to overall corporate goals.

2. Put in place education programs to make sure everyone in the organization understands, believes in and follows the IT principles and policies established. This will reduce the cost of IT and give the organization more chances to integrate the information.

3. Keep your finger on your business' pulse. CIOs need to know enough about the business that the information systems area can support and add value to. To develop this business knowledge, attend trade shows related to your business' industry and make sales calls with your salespeople, for example.

4. Where senior managers are reluctant to devote attention to information management policy and infrastructure issues, build a coalition of people who can influence senior management.

5. Bear most of the reponsibility for ensuring your information systems area documents, maintains and encourages corporate standards.

6. Consider project selection and development, procedures, backup and security policies—in fact, most of the issues covered in *Riding the Tiger*.

7. As the standard bearer for IT, promote the building of a strong executive team capable of many different functions. Its concerns include the use of IT that will compete strongly with other companies.

8. Reevaluate your role in this area—often. Many CIOs see themselves as coaches who can help their organizations use information effectively in making and implementing decisions, for example.

9. Within your areas and throughout the organization, seek to improve project management skills. You must also sell your people as specialists who can help line business units. Maybe you could standardize the way corporate project management operates for non-IT as well as IT projects. This is so information technology teams and business managers can work together more smoothly.

TigerPearl

Decisions made today will haunt you for at least three years. That's the bad news. It's also the good news.

Technology Principles

For someone who has never been a CIO, the question will arise, What kind of technology policies are likely to make sense for my organization? We suggest that you should

1. develop an information management plan that describes:

   - the roles and responsibilities for information management
   - the strategies for quality improvement, both with respect to clean data and development processes
   - precise objectives for learning about and improving your employees' and your organization's capabilities
   - data strategies driven by both the business objectives of your business units and the corporate economies of scale resulting from standardization
   - principles for addressing process improvement and the role of technology that are widely promoted within the organization and with suppliers and distributors
   - specific technology architectures that link information throughout the organization to meet the needs of customers, internal stakeholders and your major external relationships
   - how policies will be developed, documented and communicated throughout the entire organization in case of emergencies
   - a multiperiod technology plan that (1) covers what will be done to maintain and improve information management and (2) plans the evolution and replacement of key technologies (it should take into account the transition costs)
   - development and monitoring of and education about processes for evaluating technology and packaged solutions

- how technical and business managers will be educated so that both have adequate knowledge about technology and business issues (this is a relatively new responsibility for CIOs)

2. develop a corporate culture that endorses information management and technology as part of a business solution;
3. tackle the difficult issue of ensuring that projects are generally done on time and close to budget. This is likely to be increasingly difficult in the future, so you will have to devote extra effort. While there may be more packaged solutions and components available, the devolution of information systems purchase and development to line units means that those with the least IT knowledge are now dealing with some of the most difficult types of projects;
4. try to encourage the purchase of packaged or already developed solutions as long as they fit with corporate standards and a decentralized architecture;
5. where you have to develop software, seek a quantum jump in productivity at the same time. This stretch goal is important. Normally created through development tool selection, the reuse of programming components does not happen naturally. It requires active management by an organization. Smaller organizations may have to pursue reuse strategies through joint ventures or partnerships with selected suppliers who are large or specialized enough to support such reuse.

Adequate Hardware

Although we have *de*emphasized the role of hardware, good hardware *is* important. As a rule of thumb, err on the high side of your hardware needs. Your need for computing power grows very quickly, generally much faster than most business managers can imagine. Managers tend to underestimate their hardware requirements because (1) vendors try to meet their price points, not their performance requirements, and (2) information technology transforms the users, making them more demanding.

People are expensive and you should invest in them. Hardware is cheap and depreciates. You should get rid of the hardware before you have to use people to compensate for its obsolescence.

You will find almost any decisions that discourage your employees from sitting around wasting time are cost-effective decisions.

You may be influenced by the common observation that upgrading hardware tends to be a labor-intensive, fairly unreliable process and hence an expensive one. For mission-critical systems, upgrading information technology always seems to be done at the most awkward moment.

Of course, the real complexity in buying hardware is its timing. With prices constantly dropping, you can find advantages to buying the merely adequate today because the state of the art is unproven or still being priced at a premium. This strategy is certainly reasonable as long as you do buy the more advanced equipment when the information technology does become available.

Many managers have entered a newer area for infrastructure investment networking. This comes in many shapes today: (1) internal local area networks to hook together PCs, printers and client-server databases, (2) wide-area networks to link different locations, and (3) internetworking, through which companies communicate with other companies or individuals over the Internet.

Networking in all its varieties is probably one of the most rapidly growing and most complex areas today. The benefits are high, and both the problems and the opportunities are evolving rapidly as the markets dramatically deregulate. For the consequences of these issues, see Chapter 2.

Excellent Software

Technology should empower people and increase their understanding of the world. It should also give employees the power to delight customers. In testing any system you are implementing, ask yourself two questions: Would I want to use it? How does it benefit our customers? If the answers are No, and Low or no benefit, then you should rethink your approach.

Excellent software is dramatically better than bad software. Remember the first time you used a painting program on the computer—such as

MacPaint? You discovered that a complex task with a keyboard could be effortless and fun with a mouse and icons.

Good usually equals expensive. But surprisingly, good software can often have dramatic cost advantages. Often, good and bad software have the same up-front cost, but over time, the cost of maintaining, evolving and improving the software can be dramatically different.

There are several important facts to remember so you obtain excellent software:

1. *Good software is easy to use.* If you find any information technology difficult to use, then no matter how powerful it is, your employees will not use it. If it is used, making it attractive to its intended users will have been very expensive and few employees will succeed with it. We call difficult-to-use software *shelfware,* because it will stay on the shelf.

2. *Good software is open in architecture.* You should be able to get at the data in the application from other vendors' applications. Good software should be able to access information from other packages. This requirement normally means that an application should write its data to a database that is easy to get at.

3. *Good software works.* This may sound obvious, but there is a great deal of software on the market that doesn't work. Often, it was launched before it was ready.

4. *Development tools should be scalable.* They have to be able to satisfy a range of needs from department to corporation. Often, the tools that work well at the departmental level do not work well at the corporate level.

5. *Good software is easy to change.* Small changes to the program should not make the software unreliable. This is easier to insist on with internally developed software or contracted-for software. Evaluating the architecture of large purchased packages is always wise because you depend on the supplier's ability to innovate. This can be dramatically restricted if the supplier has made poor choices in technology (and most have). One of our customers recently ran into serious problems when two key suppliers of mission-critical systems failed to move their

applications to a client-server architecture over the same three-year period.

6. *Good software is well documented.* This is so obvious that it is surprising that so many companies have poorly documented software. A common mistake made by small customers is to engage a consulting firm to build software, but not to authorize sufficient budget to obtain documentation on it for its maintenance.

7. *Good software is more a service than a product.* The supporting infrastructure of the supplier, value-added resellers, magazines and the availability of people are at least as important as the product itself.

8. *Software represents a commitment to a supplier, so it is important to know the supplier's prospects.* Like the father of the bride, the potential buyer must ask hard questions about the business strategy and competitive position, the technical strategy and trends, and the long-term survival of the supplier. With the shortage of skills in many software areas, purchasers should also realize that they will often have to enter into partnerships with small firms and create longer-term partnering relationships.

9. *Good software tends to be modular and layered.* Most organizations fail because their projects are too grandiose, not because they have shown restraint. It is always good practice to invest in a solid architectural design and then deliver only a small piece first.

10. *Good software can be adapted to different applications.* It is not possible to standardize always on software, so you must establish guidelines to assure that your data will not be trapped in just one application. Consider setting guidelines on the type of software language used, the databases and office application suites, including word processing, spreadsheet and presentation software.

11. *Ideally, good software should be portable.* This allows an organization to move its application to another operating system if required. If software is not portable, then it should be available on an operating system that many hardware vendors support.

Supporting Management Effectiveness

Not very long ago, information technology was a simple division between the line and staff use of computers. The data on the organization's transactions were collected, and the reports were centrally generated and distributed on paper. Computing supported production or transaction processes. The information processed focused on capturing the organization's transactions. The data was highly granular, or detailed. The transactions tended to be repetitive and often processed in batches.

The widespread availability of computers on managers' desks has transformed the demands on an organization's information technology. Instead of using the computer for record keeping—for the basic accounting, ordering and selling activities—a wide variety of managers use information to make decisions. This decision-making usage is dramatically different from the traditional line or transaction functions.

By one company's measures, the average computing power per user for a traditional application such as an accounting system is around 1 MIP (or millions of instructions per second) per user. For decision support, the requirement for computing power is likely at least 10 times higher and much more volatile. This difference explains why it is possible to run an accounting system for 20 people on a single PC, yet analysts, planners or marketers often find their own workstations inadequate.

This need for more computing power makes sense if you think about it. Entering a single order for a customer is a relatively simple task. A transaction is a simple piece of data. Once entered, little else needs to be done.

In contrast, analyzing market research or consolidating multiple spreadsheets requires a more complex graphical user interface as well as the comparison and use of numbers for multiple time periods, organizations, products, budgets versus actuals, regions, markets, competitors, channels of distribution. The sheer volume of data is far greater in magnitude and the required manipulations are computationally very intensive.

In addition to working with a variety of tools and information from a variety of sources, managers are also now looking for more detailed information for their decision making. Marketing managers, for instance, are becoming interested in finer-grained customer information so they can design marketing for ever smaller segments. *Drill down* has become a popular term among managers who use computers.

An interesting development on the other side of the user spectrum is that front-line employees are now looking for broader and sometimes more summary information so they can make a wider range of decisions to satisfy various customer needs. Customer service staff need more complete customer information to solve customer problems more intelligently and make decisions that affect their company's relationships with customers. With the flattening of the hierarchy, many line staff require the same decision-support tool that management needs.

So today's infrastructure plan is different. It has to take into account the information demands of management as well as the new demands of the front-line staff.

Information Warehousing

Production systems are designed to respond as fast as possible in handling many queues of users executing short transactions. These systems are single-minded and tuned to perform certain tasks well.

Many business managers are disappointed when they try to use these systems for other purposes, such as decision support. Decision support has totally different characteristics, and disrupts the transaction performance. A new way of storing and handling information for making decisions is crucial to new infrastructure in the 1990s.

The buzzword for getting your data easily today is via an *information warehouse* or *repository*. There are different kinds of these: (1) *information warehouses*, where you store everything; (2) *information marts*, where you store specialized and more narrowly focused information such as customer information; and (3)—amusingly—*information cupboards*, miniware-houses for information on even narrower topics, e.g., product pricing.

Layering and Modularizing

In the new architecture, the decision support data should be separate from, but fed by, transaction data. Separating the systems allows organizations to design and use them at their most effective. Since they are linked, however, you must update the information to make sure that the process is automatic, easy and logged.

By releasing the data into a decision support system, your organization takes the first step in solving the frequent complaint that "the data you need is never where you can get at it."

By the differing nature of the decisions you have to make, you need different levels of data. For some decisions you need summary information: What is our market share? For other decisions, you need more detailed information. Tactical information such as Which customers did not reorder this month? requires accessing nonsummary data.

The longer the planning time frame, the more summarized the data tend to be. So depending on the managerial and planning role, the level of summary data you'll require varies. For instance, a front-line customer service staff person needs detailed customer data most of the time and short-range summary customer data by the week or month some of the time. A marketing manager, on the other hand, is more likely to look at the same information summarized in longer time frames and analytical ratios derived from that information.

Therefore, think of management decision data in terms of layers. Layers collect and organize data at certain levels of aggregation or summary so that the computer can minimize the work of calculating and summarizing afresh from all the details every time.

Within each layer, we should see different applications or modules that work for different purposes. For instance, the summarized customer data layer may help feed the information to the marketing department as well as the finance department.

The layers of information in an organization often look like a pyramid:

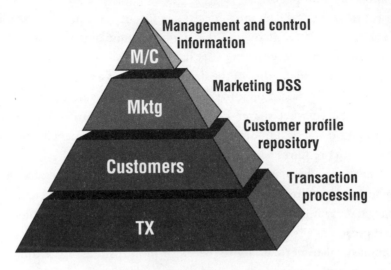

1. The bottom layer is where the operating activities take place and where transactions are documented. Different modules can represent different transaction processes within this layer.
2. The second layer is customer information. Information about individual customers and their use of products is tracked here. Customer service staff, for instance, need information at this level as well as from the transaction layer to serve their customers. Other modules can cater to other operational support departments, as well.
3. At the third layer summary information about customers is collected. The modules could be needed for marketing analysis and segmentation or for financial analysis of customer groups.
4. The top layer represents planning and control, where plans are developed, overview data are viewed and performance tracking is accessed and summarized.

The layering approach provides a way of organizing massive volumes of data that can be utilized by a wide range of users with a variety of requirements and access privileges. Explicit links between the various levels and modules can also be tracked and logged.

Mobile and Temporary Computing

TigerPearl

All technology is temporary. The only question is how soon you admit it.

With computing becoming more mobile and being included in short events (e.g., the Olympics) the "temporary" use of computers is becoming more common. Consider the following situations:

- Sales representatives set up a meeting room to present information to prospective clients. They bring in notebook computers, portable speakers and an LCD panel (that sits on top of an overhead projector) for projecting onto a screen on the wall what is on the computer for people in the room to see.
- A trainer who flies in with five computers sets up a managerial simulation for training a group of 20 managers on business strategy and teamwork under stress. They rent four laser printers and four computer monitors locally, but the heart of the network, the computers and the cabling, is transported in one case.
- At the Olympic Games, thousands of computers and dozens of minicomputers are set up for a massive temporary organization and event that lasts less than one month.
- At a booth at a trade show a vendor sets up 20 computers over a network to give booth attendees the chance to try out new software.
- A temporary head office is set up using a mix of notebook computers, cell phones and emergency power when a company's power is cut off by a natural disaster such as a flood, earthquake or fire.
- Professors at a business school arrange to set up software to introduce students to the economic data from a leading economics consulting firm.

Temporary computing situations generally involve high stress with little immediate support available. Businesspeople operating this way typically complain about having to deal with the problem of getting the software working on time or reliably. But with adequate effort and expertise, such situations are clearly possible.

These temporary systems represent in microcosm one type of situation all managers face today. These systems teach managers lessons in managing projects in all areas of business. The lessons learned through temporary computing setups apply to all systems development.

Skepticism and project management

Perhaps the most important lesson you learn from these temporary projects is to maintain a high degree of skepticism about their prospects for success. The chances are extremely good that a project will not work. It brings together so many different people and pieces. Unless there is proper project management to plan, coordinate and prepare for all possible risks, the things that are supposed to work often won't.

The general is not the specific

The skilled person quickly learns that in an open environment, you can never assume different technologies will work together. In some cases, two implementations of the same technology may not be the same. For example, it is common to buy a dozen machines from a vendor and find that they are not identical. Apparently trivial differences in motherboards, network cards, addresses of devices on the bus can cause nightmares in installation where no ordinary person would have anticipated any problems. Always test the individual equipment or software you wish to use this way. Do not assume buying or renting apparently identical technology is sufficient.

Define the testing process

With temporary computing capability you'll be tempted to do basic testing of the software. Forget it. Test everything. Run the entire system under loads and volumes as close to the real thing as possible. Higher volumes and loads than you anticipate test the system even better.

Get the right equipment

When setting up a temporary computing facility, you often face the problem of making the existing hardware work for a particular project. With the rapid decline in computing costs, you have a choice: (1) use the existing hardware and take advantage of your organization's internal expertise to fix any problems that emerge, or (2) buy new equipment that has a higher probability of working. Most organizations use existing equipment and fail to take into account the cost of making information technology work. In many situations, you may well find it cheaper to rent or purchase new equipment for this purpose.

Make contingency plans and plan for redundancy

Even with the best testing, the best people and the best equipment and software, things will go wrong. The prudent manager will anticipate alternative solutions in case of such failure.

On a recent project, one of the authors was delivering a tried-and-tested simulation exercise to a group of 16 managers. They were running the simulation on six computers. In spite of extensive testing on the specific equipment, the author had to contend with failure of the server, a network cable, the testing equipment for the cable, a client computer, two printers, another network operating system and the power supply to the entire building—all in the space of one day. He managed to run the simulation on a *third* network operating system. With other equipment and operating systems available, he was able to complete the simulation exercise successfully.

An important part of the ability to carry on with the exercise was the author's confidence that the software was absolutely sound, or robust. He had run the simulation with hundreds of managers on many networks, in several languages and in four countries. Under more normal circumstances, this type of confidence is harder to gain.

Managing Risks

Whether temporarily or for a longer term, computing technology always carries an element of risk. The reasons for this, and the forms of risk, can be traced to the nature and state of development of the discipline.

Since the Second World War, we have witnessed a rapid development of the computing market. Not only has the number of computer users increased rapidly, the number and type of products introduced to meet their needs has been phenomenal. In the past 20 years alone, the growth has been so large that some North American software tracking services, such as Softsearch in Vancouver, track 70,000 software applications.

This market is still changing a lot and fast. We are now accustomed to seeing new hardware generations in less than a year. In spite of consolidation in some segments of the market, such as word processors and spreadsheets, there are still many new applications—look at Netscape—whose speed of acceptance and adoption has astounded even the pundits. Operating systems are still developing. This young market still offers various products and standards, so it is not uncommon for users to adopt conflicting or less-than-stable technology.

To manage risks, managers first have to recognize their existence. Then they must assess the magnitude of these risks. Where are the likely sources of trouble? How likely are they to occur? How serious would the damage be? Who would be the losers?

Organizations have different risk-tolerance levels. Some are motivated by the potential rewards of competitive advantage a new technology offers. They may adopt it early. Others, more conservative, prefer to deploy the tried, more mature technologies. Managers need to understand their organization's risk-tolerance profile when deciding when and whether to adopt a new technology. They want to better the chance of adopting it successfully. It is also useful, to this end, to assess the sheer competence of your business. Will your employees be able to handle any problems that arise from that technology? Are they strongly motivated to learn and change?

Managers may find possible failures intimidating. After all, each asks, Why should I risk my career? The risk–reward equation may look different when you consider the following:

1. Adopting new technology may not depend entirely on one organization. Your competitors may force your business to adopt new technology. Always ask yourself, Can we afford to wait?
2. Reduce the risk of introducing new technology with proper support and training. In fact, treat all new technology as a new product

launch. Many of the problems of new technology adoption can be traced to the lack of a proper launch within the organization.

When managers decide to champion a new technology or new application, they should ask themselves some other questions: When is the best time for us to change to a new technology? How much risk should we take? Take into consideration your business strategy, the dynamics of the marketplace and competition and the needs of your customers. And when you do go ahead, it is again good practice to make sure that any new initiative is properly managed to reduce risks to your organization and yourself.

There is a reason that our IT model is Plan–Do–Improve. Implementation requires that you follow good practices.

Human Errors and Force Majeure

Working with computers is often humbling. Even though we can blame the technology for half of our problems, we always find that the other half of the foul-ups are caused by fallible human beings. Computing is a joint effort between human and machine. The opportunities for problems are everywhere: carelessness, misunderstanding, forgetfulness, lack of discipline, lack of procedures. And this excludes uncontrollable factors, such as burglary, flood, fire, earthquakes, hurricanes, explosions, that can destroy all corporate records and knowledge in one fell swoop.

Always have contingency plans. Also, have those action plans clearly stated and communicated, particularly in mission-critical areas. Include how to recover technically and how to deal with unhappy customers and concerned parties. This may sound like motherhood, but amazingly few organizations have proper policies and procedures for dealing with these increasingly important and probable situations.

Even if organizations do have contingency plans for disasters, they still find themselves dangerously exposed. As the departmental and personal use of computers have become more important, these uses often constitute risk for the organization. While each individual loss might not damage the overall organization, the accumulated many small problems pose a measurable, large impact upon organizational effectiveness and costs. Consider the cost in a large organization of 5 percent of the employees experiencing hard-disk failure in one year.

Organizational changes are typically caused by crises. One crisis you should plan on not having is the failure to prepare for information systems emergencies. It's not a question of whether—merely a question of when. Redundancy and backup are unglamorous tools that will allow your organization to survive.

Costing Infrastructure

Businesspeople tend to look at IT investments as merely a matter of the cost of acquisition, whether a purchase of hardware, software or both. In reality the costs are much more complex. You would do better to attempt to identify the following components explicitly:

	Costs	
	Direct and indirect costs in initial period	**Costs over subsequent periods**
Acquisition costs		
Installation and deployment costs		
Maintenance costs for routine upgrades		
Evolution costs for adding additional functionality		
Integration costs for linking with other systems		
Ongoing user training and support costs		
Exit technology costs for transitions to next technology		
Opportunity costs: revenues that not having this technology will make us miss		
Relative performance costs: impact on our market share based on the performance level our competitors can achieve with this or competitive technologies		

Analyzing Infrastructure Benefits

Peter Drucker once observed in an article in the *Wall Street Journal* that the well-managed Japanese or German organization builds its capabilities on the assumption that capabilities build shareholder value. Well-managed North American firms tend to focus on maximizing shareholder value to the detriment of their competitive positions and their growth capabilities.

When assessing infrastructure investments, managers have to consider the importance of the investment for the company's long-term capabilities and the impact of the better capabilities on the long-term value of the organization.

Individual project initiatives can eclipse infrastructure investments. It is much more exciting to build a project that will create more profits. However, wise infrastructure investments, such as a fast network, can benefit many projects and, in the long term, mean savings for the organization as a whole.

One danger in the extensive decentralizing of organizations is that so much power and budget are removed from the central information systems unit that the organization loses the big pay-off decisions. Senior management plays an important role here in making sure that the decentralized organization remembers the big picture.

Renting a Tiger—The Outsourcing Decision

Sometimes the best infrastructure is none at all. Not owning the infrastructure makes sense if (1) the area is not critical to your business; (2) you lack skills in that area and will be unable to keep up with more competent competitors; or (3) your organization is too small to become competent in that particular technology.

Outsourcing—or contracting out work—first became highly visible in 1988 when Eastman Kodak and IBM announced a service bureau arrangement. IBM would combine the operations of five Kodak data centers.

Spokespeople for Kodak said that saving money was one reason the company decided to outsource, but the main reason was to allow Kodak to devote more time, energy and financial resources to its core business. Also, Kodak was unable to transform its information systems function because of middle management resistance. Kodak had a particularly intransigent union, too, that raised its IT costs extremely high.

The photo developing giant's arrangements with its outsourcing vendor are not the traditional contractual associations between vendors and customers; they are strategic partnerships. Hundreds of Kodak employees, formerly associated with the data center, now work for IBM. They are doing the same jobs they were doing before outsourcing came in. It merely changed the source of their paychecks.

Why Do Companies Outsource?

The simple explanation is that information systems chiefs are caught in a sea of change. They once enjoyed soaring budgets but must now keep a tight lid on spending. Outsourcing is a popular solution. It allows information systems chiefs to pay greater attention to their long-term strategic issues. These managers know that running data centers is not where they should be focusing their attention. Hardware is not strategic; the way you use information technology *is*.

One point companies raise to justify outsourcing: the outsourcing vendor often enjoys greater economies of scale. Many people dispute this view because the cost of technology has declined so much. We think a stronger reason is likely to be the amortization of software development and maintenance costs over a number of customers. This amortization can also be achieved through joint ventures and entering into partnering with suppliers, as noted in *PC Week*, "A Guide to Outsourcing."

The Outsourcing Institute in New York lists seven reasons as key in deciding to outsource:

1. Improved company focus
2. Gaining access to world-class capabilities
3. Sharing of risks
4. Freeing up capital funds
5. Reducing company operating costs
6. Gaining resources not available internally
7. Managing a particularly difficult function

What to Outsource?

An organization can outsource its entire information systems function: software reengineering and renewal, maintenance, systems operations, network services, systems building and integration, education and training, to name the major components. Or it can outsource a few selected tasks.

The very nature and function of outsourcing have changed dramatically since it began seriously less than a decade ago. In the beginning, organizations used outside vendors only for those operations that were heavily data-intensive and not particularly valuable in terms of business strategy. Payroll, for instance, has always been an attractive candidate for contracting out. Today, more strategic IT functions are given to outside integrators and consultants. LAN/WAN (local area network/wide area network) management, client-server applications and software training are some of the more commonly known services being outsourced today.

What makes this shift noteworthy, according to Stanley J. Goldman's article in *Datamation*, is the mission-critical nature of these services and applications. Companies now entrust outside providers with functions necessary for their very survival and strategic growth. We even see companies outsourcing the business functions of whole departments or divisions, and this growth will likely continue. Many companies now contract out their customer-service functions. Help-desk operations are a good example of the kind of IT functions currently on the "hot list," along with desktop support.

When Not to Outsource

If an organization studies selective outsourcing carefully, it can increase both its productivity and strategic focus with it. Limiting or eliminating those activities that produce no strategic advantage, and that the best outside sources provide much better, enables a company to increase the value its information technology delivers to both its customers and its shareholders.

However, you are probably not well advised to outsource capabilities critical to the company or somehow unstable. Nor should you plan to outsource information management tasks that represent your company's core infrastructure from which you and your staff can learn rapidly and from which new projects will emerge.

Long-term outsourcing arrangements have tended to fail. More successful have been short-term and more specific relationships when both client
and supplier anticipate the need for a changing relationship.

How to Outsource

Contracting with outsourcers and system integrators has always been risky.
What if the vendor doesn't live up to service level agreements? What if he or
she cannot implement the latest in information technology? Or what if, several years into an outsourcing deal, rapid changes in technology mean your
information system could have given you better service and at lower cost?

Some information systems managers try to eliminate some of the risk
from information technology service contracts in the way they structure
their outsourcing and systems integration deals. This way the vendors
share some of the risks as well as some of the rewards. The four main types
of these information systems deals are, as Jeff Moad portrays them in his
article in *Datamation*:

1. **Shared benefit**. You pay the service vendor a percentage of the
   revenue the new system generates in exchange for reducing or
   eliminating the up-front fee you pay.
2. **Reward as a bonus**. IT service providers guarantee a specific
   business result, but their compensation does not depend entirely
   on the outcome.
3. **Information technology efficiency-based**. The service provider
   promises a range of greater IT efficiencies rather than a bottom-
   line business benefit.
4. **Reward as a shared business opportunity**. Here service vendors
   agree to business- or information technology-based performance
   levels and themselves take a related business opportunity, such as
   the right to remarket software, as their reward.

Along with the growth of outsourcing come increased customer demands.
Customers want leading-edge technology and service and productivity
gains they can measure. They also want variable pricing that is linked to
vendor performance, along with shorter, more flexible contracts. In the

recent past, customers often felt taken advantage of because of multiyear deals that locked them into outdated technology.

Out-Tasking

Managers off-load particular planning, operations or management tasks to contractors instead of simply outsourcing an entire function to a vendor. Out-tasking can be more selective and not as risky as outsourcing. In a successful out-tasking deal, an organization hires contractors with the skills or resources it needs. The organization saves on the expense of hiring new employees, but retains direct control of vital systems.

Out-tasking can make relationships between businesses and their technology suppliers smoother. The all-or-nothing style of outsourcing can be too much like a marriage. If the relationship sours, both parties suffer a lot of pain. With out-tasking, if one party finds it doesn't like the risk, it can more easily pull out.

The concept of outsourcing has changed. Information systems managers now expect more than lower IT costs. They want ways to improve business processes. Many companies now work with several outsourcing contractors rather than employ a single one to provide a total solution. Information systems managers are also changing the way they evaluate the performance of outsourcers by including business-based evaluation criteria in the contract. This enables them to evaluate the vendor's performance frequently. Information systems managers need to keep their systems up-to-date. They build periodic adjustments right into their outsourcing contracts as part of this effort.

Implementation Strategies

	Plan	Do	Improve
Leadership			
Policies		• Benefit from evolution • Motivating knowledge workers • Customer satisfaction • On time and on budget • Evaluating technology • Buy versus develop	
Projects			

Getting It Right the First Time

Experienced people know some basics about implementing information technology. Perhaps the most important is that you never get a project right the first two times.

Most honest developers will admit that it takes three attempts to get software right in the best organization. We believe that any IT task—be it setting up new hardware, implementing a purchased package, developing software or training staff—will benefit from evolution. Because technology keeps improving and we are constantly improving the way things are done—and so have to change our application requirements—few information systems can ever be described as perfect.

The hardest lesson we all learn is that it is better to build an imperfect system and refine it than to attempt to build the perfect system immediately and fail.

Knowing this requires a different mind-set in managers accustomed to other, more easily defined tasks in their organizations. They need not and cannot expect the perfect system the first time out of the box. Thinking this way also suggests that the skills for maintaining continuity—the ability to pass the baton—are very important in a manager. By extension, retaining your people is a major concern for your corporate infrastructure.

Motivating and Keeping Your Knowledge Workers

It seems out of place to discuss retaining people in a chapter that addresses abstractions like infrastructure and policies. But organizations are always vulnerable to losing their best people—especially their knowledge workers. These workers are part of our broad definition of *infrastructure*. Their attrition shrinks an organization's capabilities and affects its continuity in business. In an age of downsizing, you might overlook this factor.

Organizations often lose their people to competitors because they aren't paying attention to them themselves. From Christine Comaford in *PC Week*, here are some suggestions on how to keep your good people:

- Be generous. Don't think you can get by with paying them tiny bonuses.
- Give them good tools, interesting assignments and plenty of praise.
- Don't force them to deal with red tape.
- Give them some independence.
- Make learning fun and easy.
- Give them projects that increase their value in the marketplace to ensure that you are an employer of choice.

Customer Satisfaction

All good computing technology supports a business purpose and a business function process. You want to deliver computing that satisfies the internal customer. This is part of producing good service. Internal and external suppliers should expect to meet internal customer expectations. (What complicates this issue is that those expectations constantly change.)

Many information systems people find it difficult to buy into a customer satisfaction philosophy. From experience, they have found customers can be unreasonable, ignorant and have unrealistic expectations. Unquestionably, many customers do not appreciate the requirements of project success and the trade-offs and limitations of technology. It is to the suppliers' benefit to educate their customers in these areas.

An educated customer knows how to leverage the supplier and behaves as a better partner. As a result, this customer will likely set realistic goals and be satisfied with the results.

Customer satisfaction depends on a commitment to success from both parties and a commitment by both to increase their pool of knowledge.

On Time and on Budget

Some readers may be shocked to learn that in a recent survey of CIOs many said delivering on time and within budget is not a high priority. Delivering on time and within budget *should* be an important component of customer satisfaction. This is not a matter of hit or miss on a per-project basis but a core value in project management. It affects morale, productivity, human resources and other costs tremendously.

The reasons for late or overbudget delivery are usually

1. poor definition of the project's purpose and requirements,
2. lack of project management, and
3. lack of cooperation between the parties involved.

Choice of technology is seldom a reason for delays. Every technology has its risks and shortcomings. The project team should define and manage risks right up front. Projects go astray when people harbor unrealistic expectations. Every project requires a trade-off between features and time to deliver. To deliver projects on time and within budget means seeking and deciding upon the best trade-off at every phase of the project.

People successfully managing projects must nurture a certain mind-set. Encourage these beliefs with the right policies.

Evaluating Technology

You'll find a set of guidelines for evaluating technology useful not only for technical staff but also for end-users who may initiate or become involved in technology projects. The guidelines can incorporate the policies and standards the business has chosen as well as general educational material about computing technology. The higher the general level of computer literacy among business managers, the better customers they make and the greater the likelihood of your project's success.

When evaluating a technology choice, consider:

1. Vendors tend not to tell the whole truth (knowingly, or more likely, unknowingly). Information technology *is* complicated, so sometimes vendors are late to market or just can't keep up with competition. Unfortunately, if you are tied to their product, your business or projects are the ones that suffer. Selecting vendors is an art in itself, deserving of a great deal of attention. Even if you select the best possible vendor, be prepared to make mistakes. So plan ahead of time how you might change your suppliers if one doesn't work out.

2. Promises are cheap. Don't rely on those from a vendor. That promise is credible only if the general trends in the industry support it. Yes, we have to take into account the direction of development that a vendor confidently predicts, but there are too many promises broken in the IT industry. The reason is simple: in a world of competitive standards (remember the video Beta and VHS standards?), the losers have to drop their own standards eventually and follow the majority, no matter what they promised while trying to set the dominant standard themselves.

3. Spending too little money is more expensive than spending too much. Most customers make a simple mistake. They buy according to price. They should buy according to the total cost of ownership.

4. Most companies harm themselves more by being penny-wise and pound-foolish than they do by buying more capability than they currently think they'll ever need. In other words, as in all areas of life, quality pays in the long run.

Beware of the solution that promises everything. Remember your component stereo system. There's a reason it makes sense to have components. You can replace the turntable with the CD-player or the cassette deck with the digital audio tape recorder.

5. Another important issue for companies today is architecture. In the 1970s and 1980s, companies tended to select a top-name supplier such as IBM or DEC and rely on that company to attach other pieces of the IT as they come along. Today, with so much more IT in the organization, you need an explicit policy on your architecture.

6. Integration is a major goal for most organizations. The concept of the information warehouse—one place where you can find all the important information about your organization—is based upon this apparently simple goal. However, many organizations try to integrate too much. If you run your entire organization off one database, any small change could lead to a domino effect in other areas of your business. Follow the better strategy of a more modular, decentralized and layered storage of information that only *looks* like one database. If one component fails, then the entire organization will not collapse.

7. Managers focus on quick and easy solutions to meet their budget constraints, their time frame and their narrow departmental requirements. Frequently, they may pick solutions that do not scale—that cannot meet higher volume or sophisticated demands later on. Business managers usually need guidance here.

8. If you must choose between a product that is available on a variety of hardware platforms and operating systems, it is often preferable to choose one available on multiple operating systems. Portability generally means lower risk. If you are not locked in to one kind of hardware or operating system supplier, you can negotiate with your supplier from a stronger position. Bear in mind, however, that software vendors such as Oracle don't deliver the latest version on all platforms at the same time. You could encounter situations in which the version of the database you are working with does not work with the operating system you would like. The result: portable systems can sometimes slow your ability to keep up if you are using an unusual combination of operating system, hardware and software.

Buy versus Develop

As we have implied already, buying is nearly always a good idea. If someone develops software better than you do, you should buy it from him or her. In almost all cases it will be less expensive than sticking with your own.

 Use outsiders to help you with your information management. No one company can be expert in everything, so you should always consider purchasing an off-the-shelf solution or hiring someone who has done it many times before. Their learning will more than compensate for their profit margin.

Many companies do better to change their processes to match the processes the software provides than to build custom software to match the historical expediencies your organization has developed over the years to do its work.

Purchasing may not always be appropriate. Some companies have developed their own software because the different way they run their business is their competitive advantage. These companies are fewer in number than most managers realize.

Generally, companies purchase software packages and programming components, design databases and then need to link information contained in different formats on the different operating systems. Gluing together this information, or moving IT to a central location, is likely where most organizations will need to seek expertise.

Improving Infrastructure

Time-sharing, mainframes, dumb terminals, PCs, networks, client-server, distributed computing, Intranets. Many managers throw up their hands in horror and ask, Will this change ever stop? The answer is, No. Never.

The more an organization believes in decentralizing its computing power, the more it must make sure it actively manages the infrastructure to handle the exploding demand for it. How many client-server applications have failed because of underpowered networks and servers? How many new applications fail for lack of good training programs and support systems?

	Plan	Do	Improve
Leadership			
Policies			• Infrastructure evolution game plan • Upgrading technical capability
Projects			

Evolution Game Plan

In an age where the demand for information systems is high and budgets are not, you cannot do a good job with your information management without a plan. Plan what you will do, how you'll do it and how you will put in force and measure later improvements.

Most plans need to address

- Replacement
- Maintenance
- Upgrading
- The IT capabilities the organization requires
- Shifts in power within the company
- The balance between infrastructure and projects
- Related human resources capabilities and required training

The guiding criteria should be the organization's strategy, long-term capabilities goals and long-term shareholders' value.

Ignoring infrastructure improvement can be very costly. Like the maintenance of a house and machinery, long neglect can lead to costly replacements later on. Even more important for a business are the opportunities it loses, the revenues that slipped away, the customers that defected, the costs not saved.

Upgrading the Technical Capability of Your People

Some say that education is what you have left when you have forgotten the specifics. As result, one of the most important lessons in education is that the content and specifics taught are not as important as the set of basic skills upon which graduates can build. This is definitely true in engineering. Many electrical engineers find their knowledge out-of-date a few years after graduation and so rely on their ability to learn new things to survive.

To hire people for narrowly focused technical skills and not give them the chance to grow and acquire new skills is to waste your human capital investment. Technical skills get out-of-date. Assume constant upgrading as part of any technical job description. Include a technical training plan for both technical staff and end-users if you consider computer literacy a key part of your organization's core competence.

The only good computer is a used computer.

At Toyota in Japan, janitors receive 14 days of training a year. More complex tasks such as managing information deserve a little more extensive training and attention than North American business leaders tend to assume. Many organizations think they are training by merely providing a tool to an employee. Given the high cost of time wasted, you need training that will pay you back fast and increase employees' skills.

In some organizations, people are assigned tools and a problem to solve as part of their training. This is *training by attrition*. Those who survive end up "sort of" trained. It takes a lot more effort to create more capable staff. It requires leadership, management, measurement and objectives.

Training payback can be measured, although few organizations do it well. Trainers distinguish between four levels of measurement:

Level 1
This is the kind of measurement most of us have experienced. At the end of the training program, we are asked whether we liked different components of it.

Level 2

The trainer tries to determine whether the employees have mastered the material presented. Certification programs and college exams are examples of this level of measurement.

Level 3

This purports to measure whether the employee uses the knowledge or skills he or she has acquired. Level 3 requires that usage in the workplace be measured.

Level 4

This is the most difficult kind of measurement to take unless you run a large company. Level 4 measurement looks for differences in business results directly related to training. In effect, this is a controlled experiment—what happens if we give sales training to the West Division and not to the East Division, for example.

Since training makes for a large and important part of your overall investment, pay some attention to how you can achieve the best results in your own business.

Building a corporation without an architecture is like trying to build a house without load-bearing walls.

SUMMARY

Information infrastructure is so important that all organizations should study it in detail.

The best software applications will fail miserably if there is no adequate network and hardware support, if people are not using software or if your company doesn't have policies to deal with it. Software selected with no regard for other systems and standards will remain isolated and underused.

Good information management infrastructure does not happen by accident. It has to be planned and guided and endorsed by senior management.

The Bank of Glen Burnie Case Study:

Hotel meeting room. Strategy planning retreat, Day Two, afternoon session.

INFRASTRUCTURE

Bill Underwood, Facilitator: The question that most companies never ask themselves is, What would success look like for us as a firm? Do you have any thoughts?

Jeremy Havelock, VP, Finance, and CFO: We'd be making lots of money.

Bill: That's true. But generally, making money is something that happens because you are creating value for customers. What do you have to do to create value for your customers?

Gail Bartok, VP, Human Resources: We'd offer lower rates on loans, lower fees and higher rates on deposits and investments.

Ron Silver, VP, Marketing: We'd be so attractive that customers would want to use us for all their needs.

Martha Rodrigues, VP, Operations: Don't you think that's a bit aggressive? I'd be happy if people gave us half their business. It would be better than the 10 to15 percent we seem to get right now.

Kathy Smith, Main Branch Manager: I think success also includes doing things right. For us to be really successful, our internal procedures and processes would have to be a lot better. My people and I seem to spend half our time dealing with things that went wrong somewhere. We're very good at solving problems we shouldn't have had in the first place.

Steve Arbeit, President and COO: That's one of my pet peeves. I think we need better trained people, too.

Bill: What it sounds like to me is that you need to fix the processes *and* the people. Would we have branches? ATMs? A telephone customer-service center? Internet capabilities? Credit-card processing? What do we need to own? What do we need to rent?

I'd like you to split into groups and come back with your ranking of the importance of owning and doing all our key activities. Start with a list of what we do, and tell us what you think is critical to our business. What capabilities do we really need? Let's take half an hour or so.

The eventual chart produced looked as follows:

Time Period	Critical Capabilities
Short term	Improved selling skills and product knowledge
	Reducing costs of delivering processes and processing transactions
	Eliminating errors
	Developing a learning culture
Medium term	Knowing more about the customer
	Targeting profitable customers
	Better marketing
	Retaining customers
Long term	Developing and launching new services for customers
	Measuring customer satisfaction
	Total quality of experience of doing business with Glen Burnie

Bill: So what does this mean for our information technology decisions? Peter?

Peter Schultz, VP, Information Systems, and CIO: I think it says we have three or four important projects in the short term. First, we're going to have to improve our processes. My problem is that it's pretty hard to improve them without changing our core transaction processing system, and that's going to be expensive. We're looking at $2.2 million for the software and I figure another $2 to $3 million for new hardware and networks. And the organization is going to be disrupted if we're not careful.

Bill: What about the selling side? Martha?

Martha: I think we can do some training, but the real problem is getting information about customers and their transactions. Our system is so old that it doesn't use a database. It has proprietary file formats that take a lot of work to get at. Only the finance department can do it and they only dare do it once a month. You can't just query the data. You know, it'd be a lot easier if we had only one customer. Then we wouldn't have any problems!

Bill: Ignoring what could be a very good idea . . . So, what I hear you saying is that we need to start putting information about our customers in a place where it can be accessed easily. We call that a *repository*, or *information warehouse*.

Peter: That's not going to be enough, Bill. If we build a database with all this data, it's going to be accessible only from head office. That's a start. If we really want to let the branches at this data we've got to get it out to them. That means better telecom links to the branches, and that's expensive. We've only got these really slow leased lines that're only twice as fast as a good modem.

Bill: Good point. But for the moment, let's just note the cost issues and we'll come back to them. Costs only have meaning relative to the opportunity and the profits we're creating.

Aldo Moretti, Chairperson and CEO: What about the inconsistent procedures and processes? What do you suggest there, Bill?

Bill: Let me turn the question around. What do *you* think, Aldo?

Aldo: I think we're annoying a lot of customers here. Not easy to fix that. Gonna take a lot of effort.

Bill: No question. It's going to take commitment and perseverance. If the people in this room don't want to improve the processes and fix the information technology, it just won't happen. So we need to replace our transaction system and make sure that the data coming off that system is accessible and usable.

Steve: And if we go to more modern machines and client-server architecture, then we'll need better telecom links to the branches, Peter is saying.

Martha: What about teller machines—our ATMs?

Bill: What do you think, Martha?

Martha: I'm of two minds about them. In the short term, it would be nice to have more ATMs. Customers like them, of course. But I'm worried that ATMs will become like branches. Customers won't use them anymore when debit cards take off. They'll get cash at the supermarket and get information via the phone or their computers.

Bill: What does the rest of the group think? How many of you agree with Martha? Ten out of 12 hands. Okay, we seem to have some agreement on this topic! So our short list of priority projects is:

1. Replace the transaction system.
2. Improve the processes in the organization. (May I suggest we try to plan this one in advance? It's too late once the software is installed.)
3. Plan to develop a small information warehouse that focuses on customer information, perhaps with transaction information in another database where it can be checked.
4. Install better telecom links to the branches.
5. Freeze the number of ATMs and branches and look at our overall strategy there. Maybe we can close down some branches.
6. Kick off quality-improvement training and start getting our people to think about how to improve our processes.
7. Upgrade people's computer skills.
8. Improve our programming capability.

Peter, can you write up something about the hardware side of infrastructure for presentation at the next session? Gail, can you do something on the people side?

It looks like we need another session. Aldo? Steven? Is that all right?

Aldo: Absolutely. It seems that we as a management group—and I in particular—haven't been paying enough attention to this area. We've really fallen behind. This is a high priority for me personally. But I have one concern—the board. We're going to have to put together a very convincing case that these projects are going to help generate more revenues and profits.

Steve: Aldo's right. We're also going to have to convince the rest of the organization that these decisions are good ones so that people will want to work hard to make them successful.

Aldo: You know, I think we need to address some of the frustrations the front-line staff have. We have to make information easier for

front-line staff to get at and make planning and marketing analysis easier for the managers.

Bill: Maybe some of the front-line staff can help their managers and
become directly involved in planning the activities at the front line.

Gail: That would certainly be a change in our culture! I'd be in favor of
a more open management style. You know, if all this stuff is going
to work, we're going to have to involve everyone in the organization. We're going to have to have an organization where everyone is part of the solution.

HARNESSING THE POWER OF THE TIGER

THE PEOPLE SIDE OF TECHNOLOGY— THE CRITICAL ROLE OF PEOPLE IN INFORMATION MANAGEMENT

 TigerPearl If you want to manage information successfully, recognize that people are more important than technology.

When computing moved from a centralized, controlled environment to a decentralized, free-for-all of personal computers, everyone became a potential rider. Everyone is using and affected by the tiger.

Once free of central control, users all have biases and idiosyncrasies in how they use computers. They play by their own rules because they have different backgrounds and experience. They all learn differently. Their interests in programs and operating systems differ. Users apply different criteria for evaluating software choices.

For some technocrats, the ideal organization has as few employees as possible and the employees who do exist are absolutely disciplined in their business practices and their use of computers. Such managers want standardization everywhere.

We take the view that building an organization is about creating value for customers and building the capabilities to deliver that value, monitor the evolution of value and change the organization to deliver the new value its customers seek. If these things are done well, then the organization will prosper and grow. It will earn its reward in substantial profits.

So how much can be standardized and automated, and how much of the organization must be kept flexible so that it can monitor the changes in the marketplace?

HARNESSING THE TIGER

Any form of automation, manufacturing or management information tends to introduce rigidities into the organization. You need good users who can keep an eye on the fit of their information technology and their evolving needs. Organizations need people who can master the technology yet not be enslaved by it. *The technology tiger needs riders to guide it through the storms that all businesses experience. When there are many riders with different skills and goals, the challenge is not only riding but also coordinating with others in the midst of those storms.*

Informating People, Not Automating

With this need to monitor and manage change, people are obviously a vital asset. And yet, throughout the history of computer systems, writers have talked incessantly about replacing people with machines. We talk about automating factories, offices, information processing and even contacts with customers. In reality, computers don't "replace" people. They change what people do and how they do it. They change the skills and competencies that people must have to function effectively in fast-paced competitive environments.

TigerPearl

Computers are bad for people who can't think.

When the personal computer arrived, some thinkers predicted radical changes in the role of computers in general. They saw—and see—the idea of *leveraging,* or *amplifying,* the abilities of people with computers as IT's primary objective.

This attitude is perhaps best expressed in the title of Donald Norman's book, *Things That Make Us Smart.* There has been a growing emphasis on increasing *efficiency* as well as the *effectiveness* of individuals, work groups and organizations. Efficiency means doing things right. Effectiveness means doing the right things. To quote Peter Drucker, "There is surely nothing quite so useless as doing with great efficiency what should not be done at all."

The desire for effectiveness leads to a more productive use of computers, one that motivates. More effective organizations grow. Growing organizations don't have to lay off 25 percent of their workforces.

In her book *In the Age of the Smart Machine*, Shoshana Zuboff describes how computers can magnify the capabilities of people. She calls this the computer's capacity to *informate:*

> *Information technology is characterized by a fundamental duality that has not yet been fully appreciated. . . . On the one hand, the technology can be applied to automate operations. On the other hand, the same technology simultaneously generates information about the underlying productive and administrative processes through which an organization accomplishes its work. . . . In this way information technology supersedes the traditional logic of automation. The word that I have coined to describe this unique capacity is* informate.

In other words, the increased use of computers actually changes the availability of information *about* those tasks. Any salesperson who uses a sales contact management system primarily for scheduling and tracking addresses is delighted by the discovery that the software can also help him or her track the effectiveness of personal time.

Systems that improve effectiveness often help people do things they could not even try without that computerized help. Such systems can help locate things they need and alert them to important tasks. They can also help classify information so people can make more informed choices.

For example, decision support tools aim at improving effectiveness. Executive information systems that use graphics and color can dramatically highlight specific data. Such tools can help managers recognize and focus on problem areas or unexpected successes. Data mining tools, such as Angoss's Knowledge Seeker, can look for trends and relationships in customer and prospect data that no one human being could spot. Project management systems—another type of tool for improving effectiveness—help people identify the critical tasks in a project. Knowledge-based systems can help managers walk through a difficult decision-making *process* or actually can give them advice. Business simulations help managers understand their business better as well as test out scenarios safely.

A company can make its employees more effective in several ways—by giving them

- better information and analyses so they can quickly see what is happening in the business or with a particular client,
- more consistent data so various groups can collaborate,
- modeling tools to test various options,
- improved tools for working through a decision or a process in situations where employees are dealing with sporadic or new problems.

Insurance companies and banks have expanded their clerks' jobs through automation. With the new systems a clerk or small group of clerks can handle a complete transaction for a customer. The days of the traditional assembly line approach are over. This more integrated capability has improved the speed and quality of services to customers. The clerks could only perform these tasks with information technology.

 TigerPearl

Automating a bad process makes it more expensive. Fix it first.

Technology alone is often not enough. The new approach did not work well unless the clerks wanted to learn new skills and were able to learn them. The workers needed to understand the system on a higher theoretical level. First they had to expand their understanding of business procedures and integrate them with what was proposed. They needed to picture the complete process as they looked at the computer screen. They needed to know both the how and the why of the software's use.

You can cite similar examples in a variety of process industries, such as pulp and paper manufacturing. The pulp and paper mills now use process control computers. Plant operators no longer walk the floor. They sit in a control room where they watch computer screens.

More physically removed as they are from their traditional work, these plant operators can run the plant at its full capacity when they understand the information on their screens. They still must know how the plant processes work. Now they apply that knowledge to knowing how the computer control systems work.

It is ironic that, in many of these cases, middle management may prevent the clerks and operators from learning enough about this fairly recent technology to be effective. These higher-level managers may fear their own power will be eroded if they share this knowledge. They believe their jobs might become redundant. Nobody considered the needs of the supervisors as parties directly concerned with these changes and addressed those concerns. Yet the organization cannot benefit fully from the automation without them.

In applying technology to help people at work, most jobs appear to change by chance, not by design.

With foresight and planning, the largest gains from technology will come to those organizations who rethink their entire businesses. They will set out to redesign jobs, work-flows, functions and processes. They will recognize that the true promise of information technology is in the intelligent design of new jobs and new organizations, not IT itself.

Change, Change, Change . . .

> *Skill enhancement goals, even bold ones, will not suffice. Your personal program should [must] add up to nothing less than retooling every four to six years. Think of yourself as a machine with a four- to six-year useful life.*

> Tom Peters,
> *Crazy Times Call for Crazy Organizations,* 1994

Technology is an agent of change. To push computing widely in an organization is to sow the seeds of change.

You'll encounter barriers in initiating change. These comprise fear of uncertainty, preference for the more comfortable tried-and-true, fear of losing one's job, lack of time and lack of support. But change snowballs. Once it gains momentum, it sparks more changes and unexpected effects.

In one organization, senior management decided that all sales managers should have their own notebook computers and get used to using computers in their daily business lives. The computer skills of these sales managers were extremely low. To the information systems director, this proposed purchase appeared to be an unnecessary capital expenditure, one that would be wasted on managers who would not likely use their computers at all. Nevertheless, senior management stood firm in its belief and insisted.

As expected, the sales managers at first resisted the change. Yet over time they all found their own reasons for using their computers. A year later, when we had to take away their computers for a short time to upgrade some software, they were reluctant to give them up. Not only had they accepted them as part of their lives—they had started to demand that more information be made available through them.

In this case senior management's belief in their managers certainly paid off. They believed that, when put to the test, their managers would rise to the occasion, and the managers did. In the process, the capabilities of their sales department improved.

Our other interesting observation is that change caused by information technology does not just stop. Software changed the way these managers worked. Their new skills and knowledge made them demand further changes—in this case, more data. The sales managers eventually caused other changes in the data the company's decision support systems supplied. Once introduced, the initial change caused a cascading series of changes. Success bred more success.

Of course, the right circumstances and support systems have to be in place to make change happen. The catalysts for change differ from person to person. Some people are motivated to take up computing because their children in school are doing it. Some are fascinated by the ability to use spreadsheets to strengthen an argument. Some believe the computer could help them make better slide show presentations, and others with material downloaded from the Internet. When given variety and relevance in their tools, people do gradually work their ways to their various destinations. Some go farther and faster than others. Acknowledge people's different learning techniques and speed. Support their efforts to learn. Whenever organizations adopt software programs without building in a training program, they are wasting money.

As we've suggested before, think of introducing a new information technology project as similar to launching a new product. The process demands that the users, internal or external, adapt to a new way of doing things. Success for new products and new projects is not automatic. Success needs a careful roll-out plan. Arrange training and hand-holding for the launch of your IT projects.

Stakeholders—Fellow Riders

Information technology presents organizations with many potential conflicts of interest. It involves many people and shifts of control. Change always means surrendering certain things to allow others to gain something else.

IT usually extends through many areas of an organization and so tends to throw different people with a wide spectrum of values and experience into the cauldron of change. In a sales automation project, for instance, the background, experience and expectation of a salesperson and those of an application developer are vastly different. Conflicts can easily break out if not foreseen and managed.

Complaints about strategies that don't work, people who won't cooperate, departments run like petty fiefdoms, strategic business units that behave like independent baronies abound in any organization. In fact, similar complaints are made about external parties—the unreliable suppliers, the distributors who don't understand, the media looking for a scandal, the regulators turned into petty bureaucrats and the unreasonable public. Such complaining often rumbles informally through the organization—around the water cooler, over lunch or drinks and in the exit interview as the frustrated employee departs.

To the strategist, these are *stakeholder* issues. Not to be confused with shareholders (though they, too, are stakeholders), a stakeholder is an individual or group that can influence the success of your strategic implementation and the achievement of your objectives.

To identify yours, you answer three basic sets of questions:

- Who are your company's stakeholders? What are their needs and their "hot buttons"? What behavior, results or events will trigger the stakeholders' involvement, positively or negatively?
- How is your organization or how are your activities affecting the needs of the stakeholders? What response can you expect?

- Are you over- or underinvesting in the stakeholders? Are you spending enough, too much or too little effort in meeting their needs?

Whenever an organization tries to implement changes, the astute manager always needs to spend some time analyzing the needs of the stakeholders affected by those proposed changes. This "political" exercise alone can prevent many project failures and crises and increase the chance of success.

You can always benefit from this stakeholders analysis when planning to implement any IT project.

Stakeholder Issues at the Leadership Level

When senior management sets a new direction, employees worry about their future and their own roles. What management says it will do and, even more important, its actions will dramatically influence the success of the organization. Nothing demoralizes people more than working in a large organization that downsizes every year.

The fear this generates hits other managers, too. Reengineering is often mishandled. Managers are instructed to eliminate their own jobs, with no attractive departure program or rewards promised to the successful reengineering team.

At the Policy Level

Always examine policies with all the affected parties in mind. For instance, consider an organization that has traditionally used mainframes and now decides to move to a more modern client-server approach. It may now alienate some of its employees, who have skills only in mainframes and no clear career path with the new technology, during the difficult transition.

At the Project Management Level

Most IT projects trigger more change than their managers expect. Power shifts with the availability of information. Prepare an introduction plan for managing how to handle these changes for the various stakeholders.

Employees do not always welcome the change cycle of Plan–Do–Improve as a blessing. Remembering that change can make people nervous about losing their jobs will help you identify and avoid potential pitfalls. Only in very few organizations, such as H-P, where employee layoffs have been rare and where employees *expect* to change roles and learn new skills, will such concerns be low and employees cooperate with changes.

Kraft Foods—In Control

Kraft worldwide is the largest packaged food company in the world. Its Canadian operation has all the complexity of the US operation but on a smaller scale.

Like other packaged food marketers, Kraft realizes it must know its market and react to it promptly and intelligently. No longer is it competing with other traditional consumer marketing companies but in some cases the very chain stores through which Kraft sells. Some retailers, such as Loblaws, with its President's Choice brand, try to duplicate or even improve upon the established products that move through their stores, as do many other retailers around the world—Safeway in the US, Sainbury's in the UK or the Coop in Switzerland.

To counter this kind of competition, Kraft has developed a sophisticated information management operation worldwide. The corporation sells a huge variety of products in many countries to many different market segments and through multiple distribution channels. Thanks to how frequently consumers buy its products, it can apply sophisticated statistical approaches to analyzing its data.

Within its organization Kraft promotes the use of computers by almost all its employess. The information systems department sees itself as a consulting resource to the rest of the organization. To minimize support costs in Canada, the former CIO, Alan Brans, standardized three basic configurations of personal computers within the company. Kraft leases its desktop hardware for two and a half years, at the end of which time it replaces all of it. This eliminates a lot of hardware failures and the need for upgrades and spare parts. In terms of managing the data it collects, the information systems department monitors its data dictionaries carefully. By guarding against redundant information, it avoids confusion.

Kraft Canada's operation is a smoothly running machine. What is interesting is where the challenges arise:

1. The first area concerns business unit managers and the way software is acquired and developed. Sometimes the managers succumb to the sizzle of sales presentations rather than studying the quality of the underlying products closely enough—which is hardly surprising. Managers and users who are not computer professionals will make decisions and create mistakes different from those the information systems department would make. (Of course, the latter would probably pay less attention to customer and marketing issues.) Obviously, the corporation needs input from both to reach a balanced and suitable solution.

2. Senior management uses notebooks and e-mail, a notoriously unstable combination, resulting in the delicate political issue of what to do when the president and other senior managers complain they can't get into their e-mail. Solution: make co-op students from a local university, working at Kraft, part of Kraft's support team specifically for senior management.

3. Despite the widespread use of computers in the organization, most users lack a firm understanding of what the information systems can handle. Brans recalled that one of his colleagues came to him with an example of e-mail overkill. One manager had sent a two-page memo with 30 spreadsheets attached. He even copied it to a dozen people. The exponential growth of documents like this could threaten a company's whole network.

4. The *subterranean* development of applications can occur. One or two obsessive colleagues can fall in love with spreadsheets. They build and build and build, until the spreadsheet's creator can barely use it, let alone anyone else. These people at Kraft eventually have to come to the information systems department for help in straightening out and cleaning up their applications. Again, co-op computer students clean up these kinds of operations very well.

Kraft Canada represents a wonderful example of the new challenges of information technology. Even when the information systems department willingly gives up control, new classes of problems still emerge for internal support programs to unravel.

Alan Brans had to become an internal marketer. He had to persuade senior management of the relevance and appropriateness of the systems department policies, principles and standards he recommends. At the same time, he acted as detective and market researcher, seeking out the activities going on in the organization. He developed training programs, acquired tools on his own initiative or provided support and training to maximize the effectiveness of the managers.

The organization's strategy is to push down accountability and authority. For information technology this means dispersing responsibility for procurement and development. Decentralization complicates the job of putting all the pieces together unless the right policies support the business' strategy and its management.

The Philosophy of Decentralization

Decentralization represents a fundamental change in the way we have viewed organizations from the 1980s and on. We see it in reporting structure and information flow. Decentralization helps large organizations meet customer demands better, deliver faster responses, improve the quality of their output and help their people expand their own potential.

Kevin Kelly is the editor of *Wired* magazine, the first high-gloss magazine to focus on the implications of the Internet. In his book *Out of Control*, he summarizes his observations about the flow of information in a distributed environment. He draws parallels with the way more complex forms of organic life emerge. He offers nine rules about information management that seem to apply broadly, whether you're talking about evolution or organizations:

1. **Distribute being.** Distribute the intelligence of the organization throughout it so that if one portion experiences a catastrophe or damage, the rest can survive and grow in the new environment.
2. **Control from the bottom up.** As companies and systems become more complicated, pushing the locus of control to the front lines of the organization as far as possible will be more effective. You can't manage a global organization with micromanagement by the head office in New York. Local adaptation is always required.

3. **Cultivate increasing returns.** As the front lines experiment with new ways to function, track what works to allow you to grow the business more quickly. Reinforce your successes and deploy widely to better your organization's performance. Some, like Peter Senge, author of *The Fifth Discipline*, would call this the Learning Organization.

4. **Grow by chunking.** As organizations grow, they surpass the limits of what can be managed. Take portions of the business and spin them off as autonomously managed units with simpler roles and objectives than those of the entire organization. This approach has clearly been taken by Microsoft.

5. **Maximize the fringe.** Maintain many different types of contacts with the marketplace. Do not restrict who can learn from it.

6. **Honor your errors.** All organizations make mistakes. You can learn a lot more from these mistakes than you can by punishing the manager directly responsible. Often, change looks like a mistake. Yet it can form the basis of a new business and be rationalized as a sound strategy thereafter. Kelly's view is very similar to that of Henry Mintzberg in his writings.

7. **Pursue no optima: have multiple goals.** All organizations have multiple goals, whether they admit to them or not. As the environment changes, the importance of different goals will shift.

8. **Seek persistent disequilibrium.** Only the shortsighted believe that their organizations are stable. However, the art of information management rests in the delicate balance between using existing systems and creating or acquiring new systems that will change the organization.

9. **Change changes itself.** Change does more than merely alter an organization. It affects the very ways an organization handles the future of its own strategies, policies and infrastructure.

Decentralization in information technology supports a different technical approach. Primarily, it supports the end-user. End-users do not always need the most sophisticated technology. They need the most usable technology suited to their purposes.

Goodbye, Boss. Hello, Team Leader

Many companies can no longer choose whether or not to decentralize and empower their staff. Employees who know the how and the why of their jobs have already stepped onto the first rung of the ladder of knowledge. Computing technology has fueled their growth in numbers. More and more of us are becoming knowledge workers. If we are not, we work with people who are. Some of us even manage them.

Managing knowledge workers is not easy. They're specialists. In their respective fields, they may know more than their supervisors do. Knowledge workers are colleagues and associates rather than subordinates. You can give them an objective, but you may not be able to follow how they achieve its solution. It may take a team to determine the best solution.

Knowledge gives these workers considerable freedom. It's almost immaterial to computer specialists whether they work for a department store, university, hospital, government agency or brokerage firm. What matters — besides pay — is that their equipment is state-of-the-art and their assignments challenging and that their skills are being developed.

Challenging assignments are also of first importance for the financial analyst, physical therapist, the personnel manager, metallurgist and salesperson. As Rosabeth Moss Kanter, a professor at the Harvard Business School, argues in "The New Managerial Work," the job of being a manager has undergone such enormous change that it must be reinvented. The prescient piece, published in the *Harvard Business Review* in November/December 1989, states that change manifests itself in many ways, with one underlying cause: for organizations to succeed, employees must become increasingly knowledgeable and skillful. The more they know, however, the less easy they are to manage.

Management consultancies, advertising agencies, newspapers, research laboratories and computer software houses recruit these people precisely because they are creative, irreverent and able to come up with new and unconventional answers. In short, they hire people to break their rules.

Working with such people is often stimulating. Managing them can be exasperating. In an interview with Michael Skapinker of the *Financial Times* (UK), media baron Conrad Black, whose holdings include Great Britain's *Daily Times* and *Sunday Telegraph,* says that some of the journalists he employs are "temperamental, tiresome and nauseatingly eccentric and simply just obnoxious. They cannot, however, be treated as just another unit of production."

Kanter states that managers performed well by following set procedures in the past. Today, the rule book has vanished.

In the new corporation, managers must learn to operate without the crutch of a hierarchy. Position, title and authority are no longer adequate in a world where subordinates are encouraged to think for themselves and where managers have to work with other departments and other companies.

Competitive pressures have forced corporations to adopt new flexible strategies and structures. Many organizations have trimmed their levels of hierarchy and management positions. Horizontal relations with peers are replacing vertical channels of authority. Some organizations buy internal services from outside suppliers. Often, these external relationships can influence company policy and practice.

Kanter describes the changing picture as follows:

- A greater number and variety of channels exist for managers and companies to take action and exert influence.
- Relationships of influence are shifting from the vertical to the horizontal, from the old chain of command to peer networks.
- The distinction between managers and the managed is fading, especially in terms of information, control over assignments and access to external relationships.
- External relationships are increasingly important as sources of internal power and influence, even of career development.
- As a result of the first four changes, career development has become less intelligible and therefore less circumscribed. There are fewer assured routes to success, which causes anxiety. At the same time, career paths are more open to innovation, which provides opportunity.

Managing Knowledgeable Employees

Those managers who have tried to steer these employees point to certain basic principles:

Consistency

If you believe that employees are your biggest asset, demonstrate consistency in everything you do. Show your people that you value them. Employees still have to obey the rules and be held to performance targets. The difference is that managers should think about all the signals they send. There is no point wandering about, talking to staff, unless you are prepared to listen to what they say. If you go to talk rather than listen they will soon lose interest.

Challenging Projects

When people work on creative or problem-solving projects with firm deadlines, they come in at all hours, think about those projects in their spare time and invest vast sums of physical and emotional energy in them. Knowing they will be rewarded on the project's completion and recognized for their work encourages them to work much harder.

Reputation

Professional career people value their reputations above most other resources. By improving a person's reputation you boost his or her ego immediately with the kind of publicity that can attract other rewards, including other job offers. Managers can attract and motivate employees by creating star performers, recognizing them publicly and offering them visible rewards for their innovations. Such shared glory reflects well on these employees' managers, of course.

Charles Handy, a British management expert, believes bylines will become an important means of acknowledging an employee's contributions, just as they are for newspapers and television companies. "You don't want to know who the assistant wardrobe manager is. But he or she wants to tell you," Handy told a management conference. Some manufacturers attach notes to their products acknowledging the name or names of the workers who produced them, as Michael Skapinker reported in "The Management Environment" in the UK *Financial Times* in 1989.

Pride

Especially as other forms of certainty and security in the workplace disappear, believing in the importance of your employees' work is essential. Good leaders inspire others with the power and excitement of their visions. They give people a sense of purpose and pride in their own work. Pride often motivates people better than the traditional corporate ladder and the promotion-based reward system ever could. Technical professionals, for example, often base their decisions on their desire to contribute to an excellent final product.

Learning

In a turbulent environment, people will often take jobs as a chance to learn new skills. In a world of high technology, where people accept the uncertainty of modern employment, workers will gravitate to a company that offers to expand its employees' learning and experience. Most knowledge workers consider their own access to training, mentors and challenging projects more important than pay or benefits.

Some companies, like General Electric, have always appealed to top talent even when they could not promise any advancement to these people. The attraction stands because the company promotes itself as a good place to learn and to gain valuable mention on a résumé.

As knowledge becomes more valuable, companies must build continuing education into their offers to attract the best employees. The business may not instruct the employees itself, but it must make education available to them. It must orchestrate educational resources outside itself to lure employees into its "stable."

Freedom of Choice

As career paths lose their predictability and companies themselves grow less stable, people want to take more charge of their own working lives. More and more professionals are passing up jobs of glamour and prestige in favor of jobs that give them greater control over their own activities and direction. The wisest leaders happily encourage their subordinates to work on pet projects, and emphasize results rather than procedures. Giving workers a choice of what their next projects will be is a potent inducement for people who perform well. Everyone benefits.

Innovation

Make it easy for conscientious employees to make a difference within your organization. All managers will say they want their staff to come to them with ideas on how to increase efficiency. Not all really mean it.

The way managers talk about their employees' ideas usually tips off how they really think. Those who genuinely believe in taking their employees' suggestions seriously will immediately reel off innovations owing to staff suggestions.

Employees who take the trouble to make those suggestions in the first place should be allowed to see them tested. If the ideas are worthwhile, the managers should implement them. If not, the managers should tell them why not. The important thing is that managers should make those employees who suggest ways of improving some aspect of the business feel they have done something important. They have.

Rewards

In the past few years companies have experimented with various ways of winning their employees' commitment. They have dangled share options, profit sharing and performance-related pay in front of their people. Results have been mixed. Unfortunately, schemes of this sort are difficult to set up and easy to undermine.

Many employees are cynical about such offers, anyway. They may suspect an employee commitment program simply screens the opposite of what it purports to be—a structure determined to hang on to the old way of doing things.

An office's physical layout reveals more about what a company thinks of its employees than any number of profit-sharing schemes or corporate videos ever could. It is well nigh impossible for an organization to win its employees' loyalty when it maintains executive dining rooms and reserved parking spaces.

Akio Morita, a former chairman of Sony, has never understood the mind-set of those Western executives who believe their jobs concern anything other than their people.

Leaders today have an array of motivational tools at their disposal. These differ from those of traditional corporate bureaucrats. Rather than status, managers today offer their employees the chance to contribute. Employees consider their security not one of employment, but employability. They want their individual value recognized within their workplaces as well as outside them. While an employee's personal commitment to an organization still counts for something, smart managers build on that commitment by holding out specific project opportunities to the people they want on their teams. As Professor Kanter observes, people give their loyalty now in exchange for projects that challenge them, make them grow and will earn them personal credit for their success.

The New Manager

The ability of managers to get things done now depends more on the number of their own contacts than on their positions in a hierarchy. Access to information and the ability to get informal backing used to be confined to the official contact points between departments. Today, these barriers are disappearing, while informal networks are growing in importance.

In modern organizations, managers add value by making deals rather than presiding over their individual empires. As managers and professionals spend more time working with peers and partners over whom they have no direct control, their negotiating skills become essential assets.

The development of strategic alliances emphasizes the political side of a leader's work. Executives must be able to juggle a set of constituencies rather than control a group of subordinates. They have to bargain, negotiate and sell, instead of making unilateral decisions and issuing commands. Chester Barnard, whose works on organizational management are highly acclaimed, recognized long ago, that the leader's task is to develop a network of cooperative relationships among all the people, groups and organizations that have something to contribute to a particular economic enterprise.

The old patterns of managerial authority are eroding as new tools of leadership appear. The new managerial role relies on communication and collaboration across functions, across divisions and across companies.

Having the knowledge, skills and sensitivity to mobilize people and motivate them to do their best will outstrip rank and title.

The New Computer Literacy

In the same way that management has had to adapt itself to manage a new breed of knowledge workers, so employees must change to keep their jobs. To outsmart the computers that are after their jobs, employees must pursue what we call the New Computer Literacy.

To know the new, you have to understand the old. The rules of the Old Computer Literacy seemed rather perverse:

- It had to be difficult.
- It had to take a long time to learn.
- It had to be rational, not intuitive.
- You had to be numerically inclined.
- You had to go to school to learn it.
- You had to learn meaningless steps, which existed for reasons of historical accident rather than good design.
- You had to be a specialist.

Today, only the unfortunate must deal with computer systems that require this archaic kind of computer literacy. *Riding the Tiger* is about the *New* Computer Literacy.

The New Computer Literacy is really about the management of knowledge and information. It is about knowing your organization and striving to understand how to improve your organization's performance and capabilities.

It means understanding the connections between knowledge and information in your job and, if you are senior or aggressive enough, in the broader organization. It requires the ability to work in teams and solve problems with groups. It requires the ability to persuade and to communicate. It also requires a degree of persistence in solving problems and getting help to solve problems. It is about being selective and investing your time in activities with business pay-off.

The New Computer Literacy is as much about understanding what computers can and should do for you as it is about the "smaller skills" of composing a memo and saving it, looking up the Internet or receiving your e-mail. Knowing how to program is not the issue: most people won't, can't and shouldn't program.

Perhaps most important, the New Computer Literacy is about admitting what you don't understand so that you can get help quickly. With such help and new mastery, you can get the job done. The one sure way to get fired is to be so proud that you can't admit your ignorance of how to do something. Employees who shirk learning shrink their knowledge base and make themselves less valuable.

Since time immemorial, philosophers have said that it is the wise man who knows his own ignorance. In the New Computer Literacy, it is a cardinal sin not to know the depth of your ignorance and to repeat mistakes without trying to do something about it.

You can never know everything. You may be an expert on your IBM Thinkpad, Dell or AST notebook computer, but if you now buy a Compaq or a Hewlett-Packard notebook computer, you will inevitably find small differences and new features in which you have no experience. There will always be someone with more knowledge than you have about your new machine. As fast as old computer problems are fixed, new machines are introduced, new combinations are tried and the chances are good that something will go screwy on you.

TIGERPEARL
Educate your end-user.

Abstracting is an important skill now. Develop your knowledge about what works and draw general conclusions about it. This type of meta-knowledge will allow you to figure out new software and new problems when you must.

Along with those skills comes an additional skill. When something does not work, first you experiment to see if you can solve the problem on your own. Then over time you start to develop approaches for getting help for the intractable problems. *Learning how to get help is one of the most underrated skills of the new literacy and one that new employees almost always have to be taught.*

For firms like ours, who develop many software applications, having access to the technical support of major suppliers such as Microsoft, IBM or ParcPlace-Digitalk and learning how to exploit those resources are critical. For all three authors of this book, having access to their companies' programmers and technical specialists gives them that safety net. For the developers in their organization, having access to the suppliers and their support capabilities over the Internet and on CD-ROMs is critical.

The New Computer Literacy means that you, as a manager, must know both the business strategy of the organization and the information management practices of the organization. You also need to understand the various objectives of that organization.

In other words, the New Computer Literacy encompasses more than just computers. It is also about the knowledge and skills you need when computer technology is improving or hurting the performance of the organization. You also need to acquire the skills for planning to change and changing your organization.

Skills for the New Computer Literacy

- Formulating directions for the business
- Coordinating with internal and external suppliers
- Developing, analyzing and presenting a business case
- Implementing projects and strategies
- Managing a project
- Evaluating software
- Coordinating a project according to corporate policies and standards
- Management of, or participation in, a quality-improvement and process-improvement team
- Measuring performance
- Motivating team members and users
- Assessing and reducing project risk
- Training and transferring knowledge

Knowledge for the New Computer Literacy

- Strategy of the organization and the business unit
- Standards, architecture and technology plan of the organization
- Technology or product development process
- Identities of stakeholders for the project and their needs
- Improvement objectives
- Determination of project status

Senior Management's Computer Literacy Can Affect the Success of the Organization

Few managers, even the most senior, can afford to be illiterate about computers anymore. They must understand how information flows in their own organizations. They must also put processes in place that ensure that their people can trust the computer systems they use. Computer illiteracy can make organizations vulnerable to huge losses, embarrassment and even computer theft.

For example, on January 9, 1996, the US Securities and Exchange Commission (SEC) instituted proceedings against Joseph Jett, a former bond trader of Kidder Peabody.

The SEC alleged that from July 1991 until April 1994, Jett traded US Treasury bonds and benefited from anomalies in the broker-dealer's trading and accounting systems that generated the *appearance* of profitable trading.

These alleged improprieties began to surface in 1994. At that time, Jett was accused of booking fake profits worth an estimated $350 million over a three-year period. He denied the allegations, blaming the software used for evaluating his trades.

Eventually, more than 2,200 Kidder Peabody employees lost their jobs after General Electric, Kidder Peabody's parent, absorbed the trading losses blamed on Jett's trades. General Electric later decided to sell the firm to PaineWebber.

As a result, it appears from the public information that the management at Kidder Peabody and General Electric were delinquent because they didn't adequately check the validity of their software.

Connections between People Management and Information Management

	Plan	Do	Improve
Leadership	• Establish a corporate direction and communicate it to employees so that they can direct their technology projects toward that common goal	• Accept process redesign as a necessary part of technology adoption and lead the effort • Motivate employees to implement quality information technology processes	• Prioritize the areas of improvement and identify how IT can improve the process or the organization's capabilities
Policies	• Clearly define information management roles and accountabilities	• Lay down guidelines on adopting technology, to reduce potential conflicts	• Manage improvements in the capabilities of technical development and support staff
Projects	• Help managers develop project management skills	• Involve end-users in design • Train end-users well • Enforce a quality development process	• Try to learn from every project • Document and measure best practices

All of us who have worked in organizations have observed discrepancies between the stated goals of the organization, its capabilities and its apparent culture and values.

The great organizations try to align their capabilities with their overall strategies. Then they go one step further to make people within the organization aware that they can make a difference and that right behavior will be rewarded. Aligning strategy with the capabilities of the organization's people and IT is not optional anymore. It is what leadership and good management are all about.

SUMMARY

Organizations have many riders on many tigers. As they travel their different routes, they will learn much about the landscape they cover. By communicating, they can outpace their competition and stay ahead of storms.

Surviving on the back of the tiger requires more knowledge than ever before, whether you're a senior manager, a knowledge worker or front-line employee.

The Bank of Glen Burnie Case Study:

Hotel meeting room. Strategy planning retreat, Day Two, evening session.

PEOPLE

Bill Underwood, Facilitator: At our last meeting we focused on the basic infrastructure projects that we needed to bring our organization up to speed. I'd like to kick this meeting off with the equally important people issues. What does the group think are the critical people issues?

Gail Bartok, VP, HR: I've had a look at our personnel records, which by the way are not easy to get at. And I've interviewed some representative people in the organization. I have five pieces of feedback.

First, most of the front-line staff are extremely frustrated with the teller system. The software is difficult to use. Tellers feel embarrassed in front of customers. Their slowness is frustrating customers and causing longer line-ups. I'm a little embarrassed to admit that we've never had a formal training program. I think a low-effort, high-pay-off project would be to provide some training to tellers. It might reduce our turnover, too. I suspect we haven't been paying enough attention to this area.

Second, most middle managers are still using older computers with slower microprocessors. They're spending lots of time recalculating their spreadsheets. Several people commented to me that without good computers, this bank is not a good place to work. We seem to have fallen behind. People expect better than we are providing today.

Most of our senior managers are not very good with the computers we have. They're not setting a good example. I propose a training session for you all. I've found a good consultant with experience in this area. He can put on a seminar to upgrade your computer knowledge and give you some of the skills you need on the kinds of software you're all using.

Third, the branch managers aren't using computers at all. They can't really get access to our head office databases, so they are, in their own words, operating almost in the dark. I think this supports the need to link them into the management information systems we're proposing.

Fourth, budgeting and business planning are widely considered a waste of time. I think we'd better pay some attention to getting some value out of this process. We had a presentation recently from a firm with a business-planning, action-planning, budgeting and asset-management set of tools. It looks like these tools might save time and increase the value of our planning process. One of the problems we have in the organization is that people don't see a connection between their actions and our corporate results.

Fifth, the whole set of connections between our marketing, our customer information, and proactive selling needs to be addressed. We have very poor tracking of our customers. Ron agrees with me on this one. Our direct-mail marketing seems to consist of slipping a brochure in with the statements.

Bill to Peter Schultz, VP, Information Systems, and CIO: Peter, what have you got for us?

Peter: I've taken a look at how we're spending our time and our capabilities as an organization. I'd like to show you this chart I've developed:

Areas	Grade on Our Performance	Comment
Transaction processing	D-	• We need to replace our current system, train people on process improvement and redesign before we bring in a new system
Decision support	Nonexistent	• Three possible components: 1. Planning, budgeting and control of information 2. Marketing and customer information 3. Transaction information
Sales support and automation	Nonexistent	• We need a standard database to collect customer information that gives the sources of our transactions and other information • Automation of analysis with pattern-recognition tools is recommended • Links to direct-mail software are also important. Training is needed for people
Work flow software	Nonexistent	• Probably need to give owners of processes and participants training before we can redesign

Areas	Grade on Our Performance	Comment
Personal computers and departmental computing	C	• Easier to reform as we move to a client-server transaction system • More support staff needed for users
Programming capability and responsiveness	D	• We've been spending too much time on low-productivity maintenance and having to deal with the difficulty of creating reports from an ancient system. Need to upgrade our developers' skills. Bring in object technology expertise

Bill: Thank you, Peter. So in addition to the need for a number of important new systems, we also have a big decision to make on replacing the basic transaction system. I'd like to play devil's advocate on this one. There are essentially four choices for replacing the transaction system. Anybody like to suggest what they are?

Aldo Moretti, Chairperson and CEO: Buy a new one.

Peter: Build one from scratch.

Gail: Rent one from a bigger bank.

Kathy Smith, Branch Manager: Enter a joint venture with another small institution or vendor.

Bill: All good suggestions. So who is going to take ownership of this project? Steve?

Steve Arbeit, President and COO: Okay, it's got my name on it. But I'll need help. Peter, Gail and Kathy, I want you on the task force, too.

The three groaned, but knew they were trapped.

Bill: Now, before we wrap up today, I want to point something out about computers. Adding computers to your organization almost always reduces your productivity. Computers and new information management projects only make sense if they can improve something about your organization and its capabilities. I like to call the cycle Plan–Do–Improve.

          I would like you all to remember that this planning retreat is not a success if all we do is spend money like a drunken sailor. We also have to decide on what we are *not* going to do.

          We have to focus our efforts as a management team on making sure we have *plans* in place to guide what we are doing and share the knowledge throughout the organization. We have to *do* the projects by using the best practices available and every project must have *improvement objectives*—otherwise, why are we doing it?

Aldo: Well, that suggests we're in trouble. I don't think we do a very good job of planning. Actually, we only do budgeting. That's not going to be enough.

Gail: I agree. We need to get our people some help on thinking more than one day at a time.

Steve: We've recently been shown a very powerful system that speeds up the planning process and educates the users as they use it. It's been quite successful at helping organizations of our size and it can link to the kind of repositories we are trying to build. What's even more exciting is that we can use it to force linkage between our corporate strategies and our business strategies and projects. We can even use our action planning to drive the budgeting process and link budget to the asset and liability system.

Bill (*signaling it is time to wrap up*): Folks, I think we've got a lot of good ideas here. Your next step has to be to see what's do-able within the resources and time available.

7

ADVENTURES ON YOUR TIGER

USING INFORMATION TECHNOLOGY IS LIKE HAVING A BABY. YOU NEED TO KEEP FEEDING IT. JUST WHEN YOU THINK YOU'VE FINISHED RAISING IT, YOU HAVE TO SEND IT TO COLLEGE AND IT COSTS YOU EVEN MORE THAN YOU THOUGHT POSSIBLE.

Most managers are involved with information technology at the projects level. They either initiate, fight for, specify or manage projects. Business strategy, policies and infrastructure all affect the outcome of these and should be influenced by senior management based on the input of the rest of the organization. But it is at the level of project management that efforts can succeed or fail. Here is where the adrenaline flows fast and furious.

This chapter won't teach you everything about project management, but it will share some insights on managing IT projects from a business manager's viewpoint.

Projects—Where the Action Is

	Plan	Do	Improve
Leadership			
Policies			
Projects	• How to spot a project • Should the project proceed? • Sizing the project • Costing it • Choosing the technology • Staffing the project	• Assessing and managing project risk • Quality project process • Manage expectations • The importance of cutoff points • Deadlines • Project team • Obtaining buy-in and involving the management team • Testing and documentation • Installing new IT is a change process • Why projects fail	• Postaudits • Replacement • Success that lasts

How to Spot a Project

For most organizations, computer projects have a habit of popping up everywhere, like mushrooms in a damp forest. The job of an information systems director or chief information officer is, as a result, often not easy.

There are many different types of computer projects, each with its own special set of problems. You may have observed some of the following types in your own organization:

- Moving applications that are mission-critical, such as the accounting system, from one vendor to another
- Reengineering a process and bringing together disparate information from many sources, for example, customer service centers, on-line order entry
- Introducing complicated scheduling problems, such as manufacturing- or logistics-scheduling software;
- Implementing decision support, modeling and planning systems to assist senior managers
- Introducing a new budgeting or planning system
- Selecting hardware and a network infrastructure
- Selecting suppliers who can integrate or offer programming services
- Standardizing relations among operating systems, spreadsheets, word processors, network operating systems, hardware and service
- Managing an outsourcing project
- Buying the highly visible workstations and notebooks most managers use
- Integrating standard IT with other technologies, such as process control or telecommunications equipment

"FEATURES CREEP" IN A PROJECT

Projects typically begin with the question Why can't we . . . ? or Wouldn't it be nice if . . . ? And each question is a reasonable one. The problem is that there are always more projects than resources or dollars available permit.

TigerPearl

Don't pursue projects you are not committed to. It takes three times to get a piece of software right. If you're not in it for the long haul, don't bother.

In all organizations, one critical management decision is to set priorities. When everything can be automated, the most leveraged applications should be pursued first. What makes setting priorities difficult is that one person's leveraged application is someone else's "small potatoes." In a decentralized world, associate your budgets with the business unit. Don't manage them centrally. Each area or business should set its own priorities.

In one sense, it is not really important to an organization whether money is spent on consultants, training, computers, software, service or on people doing tasks. *What is important is that, to the greatest extent possible, the entrepreneurial spirit is not killed by centralizing bureaucracy, and the right projects, the ones that increase the capabilities of the business, are the ones the company chooses to act on.*

At the same time, the marketing, selling and promulgating standards by a central information systems area can help the line business units avoid reinventing the wheel. You can encourage economies of scale. Some statistics suggest that 60 percent of MIS expenditures fall outside the control of central MIS departments. This makes selling both capabilities and standards an important activity in the large organization's MIS department today.

What Makes a Good Project?

A good project is one that works.

A not-so-good project is a small one that fails gloriously and, you hope, inexpensively, but teaches the organization valuable lessons along the way.

A bad project is one that works erratically, destroys the faith of system users and convinces them to build their own little isolated or paper-based systems to compensate.

Planning Projects

	Plan	Do	Improve
Leadership			
Policies			
Projects	• How to spot a project • Should the project proceed? • Sizing the project • Costing the project • Choosing the technology • Staffing the project		

TIGERPEARL

Every project needs a plan, no matter how small.

Should the Project Proceed?

When selecting a project, evaluate the related issues—business direction, technical choices, people, skills, resources and competition. Of all these, the setting of your organization's strategic goals and the leadership of the CEO are most important. Senior management participation helps managers make reasonable decisions on information technology that increase, rather than reduce, the value of the business.

The business case is the usual vehicle for proposing a project. There is probably no greater cause of debate than those inspired by the "art form" of the business case. For the uninitiated, a business case is a document that justifies new investment.

The business case has six components: strategic evaluation, technical evaluation, analyzing the consequences of the proposed project, gaining support for the project, predicting the results of the budget and analyzing the project within a portfolio of competing or existing projects.

Strategic Evaluation

Frequently asked questions include: Does the project fall within the realm of our corporate strategic direction? Does it directly support a new strategic objective? If it involves improving an existing process, does it take into consideration the strategic principles and the strategic directions of our organization?

Managers often look to solve a narrow problem they face and neglect to see the problem and the solution as part of a bigger picture. Business processes tend to interconnect, and so do IT solutions. By paying attention to strategic directions, managers are more likely to take an integrated value-adding approach. Otherwise, it is likely that islands of technology and information are being created. With too many scattered systems, maintaining and linking the information can be so time-consuming that systems actually subtract value from your organization.

Technical Evaluation

Common questions: Does the system follow the technical policies and guidelines of the organization? Does it take advantage of the organization's infrastructure? Does it allow us to move the information to existing and future systems? Will it work with our existing hardware platforms? Are we using dead-end technology that no supplier will support in the future?

If this is acceptable new technology for the organization, will we have trained people to support the system? Is the new technology the best future technology direction for our organization?

Consequences of Using the System

At the outset of the project, you and your organization should have determined the direct benefits you hoped to gain by using the system. These can include simplifying a process, speeding up response time to customers and other departments, increasing useful information flow for decision making and operations—better ways to serve the customer.

One non-technical manager, Mark Weber, Director of Finance at Teachers Credit Union, describes the difficulties at the beginning of a project. "Scoping and defining a project is hard to do. Too often, when you get user involvement, their problem is that they look at their world as it is today. Just because they do it this way today does not mean it is the best way. Sometimes you need to forget the current process and start from the ground up at re-creating the process."

TIGERPEARL

"Novelty is often the result of things you would have planned for but did not know existed." —Caroline Thornton

You may not perceive the indirect benefits of the system in the beginning. You even may have to dig and calculate a little to find them. Frequently, a new process and system eliminate related and supporting processes, which translates into some significant cost savings when you consider the whole picture.

Introducing a new system also brings in its own new support and maintenance costs. Take these into consideration when measuring the effects of a new system.

As we discussed in earlier chapters, there is a clear difference between developing infrastructure and working on a specific business project. With infrastructure investments, it's much more difficult to measure the return. Specific projects, on the other hand, have often been made possible by earlier infrastructure investments.

Budget Implications

In trying to justify the costs and benefits of IT, you will look at direct costs and benefits and should examine related costs and the effects of these investments on other systems. Besides development or acquisition costs, figure on the multiple-year life cycle costs of support, upgrade and maintenance. Sixty to 80 percent of the average IT department's budget is devoted to support and maintenance costs: these hold the IT department back from adopting more cost-effective and better technological solutions.

Benefits measurements can be vague and sometimes arbitrary. One way of viewing benefits—in terms other than dollars—is to examine them strategically. Are they adding value to your business or subtracting from it? Employee knowledge, teamwork and pride, for instance, are important but not easily measured attributes. Yet these are the value-adding benefits of a good information system. Distress at nonproductive and clumsy processes and systems subtracts value and is just as difficult to gauge, but will be noticeable when your organization begins to lose sales and capable employees because of it.

A business case can simply be based on payback. We will buy this widget or invest in this project and we will recover our investment in X months. Payback is a commonsense way of looking at investments and particularly appropriate in organizations with limited surplus cash flow.

A more complex business case will look at the change in cash flow and take into account the time value of money. This approach is called *discounted cash flow,* or DCF modeling.

A more difficult kind of business case analysis addresses the impact of the project from a competitive perspective, as well. In the parcel business, for example, investments by major players such as UPS and FedEx in "tracking and tracing" have made it hard for other organizations to catch up.

If You Do Nothing . . .

Often, a system is just too costly to implement. In that case you have two alternatives—abandon the idea or solve the problem with a less expensive solution. Before abandoning or postponing a project, ask yourself what the consequences will be of your doing nothing. Doing nothing is itself an action of consequence. It can affect a business' costs, competitive position, productivity and bottom line. The business that does nothing may find its competitive position eroding and find it too late or too difficult to recover.

Portfolio of Projects

As a manager you have many projects to choose from. Here are some simple rules of thumb for choosing as intelligently as possible:

1. **Fix the basics.** Many organizations must address basic questions of infrastructure before they can advance in any direction. In recent work with a financial institution, we recommended basic upgrading of their network and training of their staff. They were equally important.

2. **Pick the high pay-off projects first—the "low hanging" fruit,** the ones that support your strategies—these projects should dangle ripe for the picking before other projects!

3. **Strategic considerations** give the business perspective of when and whether you should undertake a project. Ones offering significant long-term consequences could be funded ahead of other, less significant projects.

4. **Consider the immediacy of your company's need.** A project may not be high in priority, but if you never execute it, your inaction represents an unnecessary loss of market share. Potential competitive threat may not allow you to delay the project.

5. **Look at your limitations.** Management attention can be more of a limitation than budget. A limited number of good project managers exist in any organization and there is a limit to the amount of disruption the company's operations can handle at one time. The distribution of resources and skills affect the order in which projects can be undertaken. Changing over from one skill area to another takes time and will prevent certain projects from proceeding immediately.

Politics—or, rather, Support

Information technology without organizational support means a business process without internal support. A project may be right for all the right reasons, but if the organization is not ready for it the timing is simply wrong. There are three ways to approach this situation: work on building your internal support and championship, develop a more modest pilot project to prove the point and build support, or simply shelve the idea until the time is right.

Projects have different sets of goals and as a result they vary in the effort you'll spend to get them approved:

- The easiest to sell are those with short paybacks. Most firms get excited about a project that promises to cut costs quickly.
- More difficult to sell internally are projects that will increase revenues. There is always some risk in selling a project that proposes to increase service to customers or increase sales. Few organizations welcome the idea that they must change in order to take advantage of new information capabilities.
- The hardest projects to sell are those that must be taken on faith. Their impact will be large, but no one can measure it today. Information warehousing and customer information repository projects often fall into this category. There is no question that knowing more about your customers will be beneficial in most industries, but it may be hard to quantify all the benefits in advance.

Sizing the Project

Organizations make several common mistakes in failing to scope the size of their projects. If you cannot estimate the size of a project on the back of the envelope, you should not even embark on it. (Once you have scoped the project, you should still do detailed project planning, of course.) Take the simple example of estimating the size of a budget consolidation exercise. Assume:

10 business units
 5 products per business unit
12 months of budget income statement
25 lines of accounts per income statement
50 sales territories/branches per business unit

The basic size of the problem is 10 x 5 x 12 x 25 x 50, or 750,000 pieces of data, to document a budget or forecast. To enter actual results, the size of the data requirement would double to 1,500,000 pieces of data. If you store year-to-date information and do not calculate it, then your information increases by a factor of 12. If you want 10 years of data, your volume increases by a factor of 10. You can see how quickly and easily a simple budget can become a nightmare in a spreadsheet and require a database application to manage it.

Costing the Project

This area in software development presents tremendous challenges. Sometimes costing the purchase of an off-the-shelf application can be just as difficult.

As a general rule, the costing process is as follows:

1. Scope the project to determine how big it is likely to grow.
2. Estimate the hardware cost for using the software (network, client and server hardware).
3. Estimate the tools you'll need for development and the training costs associated with those tools.
4. Estimate the annual support costs for the software and any royalties for run-time versions of it.
5. Estimate how long it will take to debrief users on their needs and put an overview specification together.
6. Plan review meetings to present the overview.
7. Estimate how long it will take to develop a specification that programmers can use.
8. Estimate the design time.
9. Estimate programming time.
10. Estimate testing time.
11. Estimate documentation time.
12. Estimate training and roll-out time.
13. Estimate support time.
14. Estimate the time you'll need for project revisions, meetings, documentation, programming testing and roll-out
15. Estimate project management time.
16. Estimate downtime to allow for problems.
17. On top of all this, add some extra time for the unexpected!

Good practice also suggests that software should be developed in small chunks and in phases with well-delineated review points.

TigerPearl

The amazing thing about project management is that the apparently small stuff is what puts you way off budget. The devil is in the details, and probably in the meetings, too.

Of course, even with the best cost estimates, you'll have to review the project frequently to keep it on schedule. Even better, structure it so that at each checkoff point, some form of working software is produced.

Choosing the Technology

Beginnings are times of great delicacy. Accept that choosing a technology is always a gamble. Ask:

- Which technology choices do we have? How can we evaluate them efficiently?
- What are the strengths and weaknesses of each technology today? In the short term? In the medium term?
- Is the market support for this technology strong enough to make it economically viable for our organization?
- Does infrastructure exist outside the supplier to support the technology?
- Is this technology cost-competitive?
- Does the supplier have the staying power to remain in the game?
- What performance trade-offs must we accept if we go with this technology?
- What commitments are we directly and indirectly making to this supplier? (Annual maintenance, upgrade costs, training costs)

Perhaps the most important thing to remember about your choice here is that it often has longer-term consequences than you or your colleagues can foresee. Those organizations that invested in mainframes and minicomputers find it difficult today to switch because of the cost of moving to new technologies and replacing those earlier investments. You must maintain and gradually adjust every software project you build. Every package you buy will need upgrading and support. Every new standard you stand behind raises the total cost of your information systems. This is life.

Staffing the Project

Then there are the people. Staffing a project is one of the major critical success factors in any project. To the uninitiated, a programmer is a programmer is a programmer. However, the skilled manager will want to ask some fundamental questions about the team put together to carry out your programming project.

Personality

What kind of people are on the team? Introverts who avoid talking with users? Extroverts who never want to get down to programming? Problem or domain experts who understand the problem? Systems analysts who can interpret what people really want but lack the ability to program? Detail-oriented or big-picture people? Some consulting firms use the Myers-Briggs Personality Inventory to help project team members recognize their own biases and help them work with other team members who bring different ways of perceiving and solving problems to the group.

Education and Training

Does the team have staff who share a fundamental understanding of the type of programming the project requires? Programmers who are good with graphical user interfaces may not be as adept with networks. Those who enjoy networks may not be as accomplished with databases. Do you have fast learners with no experience or well-trained people or a combination?

TigerPearl

Nobody is ever available with the precise skills that you need. And this skills shortage is never going to change.

Experience

As in any discipline, programmers will be influenced by their past successes and failures. What kinds of projects have they been involved with? What was the scope of their responsibilities? Did they implement a portion of a project or did they manage it from beginning to end?

Motivation

Building good software requires commitment and leadership. Any good programming team has an inspiring leader and programmers proud to be building the best system they can.

The "Mythical Man–Month" Phenomenon

Fred Brooks describes one of the most important concepts related to managing information technology projects in his book, *The Mythical Man–Month*. He argues that beginning a software project is like being pregnant. No matter what you do, it still takes nine months to produce a baby. Adding more parents to the team does not help.

If your project team contains about seven developers and a reasonable schedule, you may be able to move up the delivery date by cutting back on portions of the project along the way. However, you probably cannot speed up the project by assigning more developers to it. If you do expand the team beyond seven people, the time each member will spend communicating with the others will increase, while the time spent developing begins to decrease. At a certain point, the more people you add, the less work will get done.

The Mythical Man–Month argues that projects have an ideal size—small groups of five to seven are more effective than larger groups. If a project is too big, then you can only make it work by breaking it up into smaller projects. Then you have to coordinate between these subprojects very carefully and efficiently. Interfaces between the components become the links between each subgroup's work.

TIGERPEARL

It takes time for a team to work well together. Preserve good teams.

Assessing and Managing Project Risk

	Plan	Do	Improve
Leadership			
Policies			
Projects		• Assessing and managing project risk • Quality project process • Manage expectations • The importance of cut-off points • Deadlines • Project team • Obtaining buy-in and involving the management team • Testing and documentation • Installing new IT is a process of change • Why projects fail	

Implementing Projects

All IT projects carry risks. An information management project can go wrong in so many ways that it can depress everyone associated with it.

The most expensive error you can make is to pursue a project that should not have been built or acquired in the first place. Check that you are seizing on the best project for your organization at the best time before you commit yourself to it.

The next most expensive error is to select technologies not yet ready for "prime time." You may never complete one of these projects.

The next most serious error is to specify and scope a project that will be impossible for you to complete because of the budget and time available. This is not a problem just for the small, the less knowledgeable and the inexperienced. Even well-known large organizations get into trouble making such fatal mistakes in estimating.

Then there are a number of results that could vary in effects. With inadequate testing a system may be deployed before it is ready. The system could end up crippled because of bugs and design flaws.

Beware, too, of inflexibility. You can complete most projects eventually, yet the rare project is designed with flexibility and expansion in mind from the outset.

In spite of the rapidly increasing power of computers and their dropping costs, performance continues to plague applications. Particularly in the newer area of client-server applications, good design can make the difference between success and failure.

Projecting performance in an application is tricky, too. The rate at which your data grow outstrips the rate at which computing power grows. This is a familiar business problem. One example of this is your information warehousing. With a relational database, a company often needs large parallel processing to keep up; more specialized tools may be more effective and require less hardware.

Actually deploying the software may also cause problems. A lack of training or involvement on the part of staff lead to unreliability or performance troubles. The hardware and software itself may be unreliable. Networking can often create a problem, as well.

Risk management should be a project manager's top priority. If the risk is too large, you should not undertake the project.

There are some key variables that need to be explicitly considered in project risk management:

Project Risks

Project Definition

Most projects start off badly because their specifications are poorly laid out. The consequences will ripple throughout the project.

However, users have this unfortunate habit of not really being able to specify exactly what they want at the beginning of a project. End-users who are learning about what is possible will almost never be able to define their specifications in advance. At the end of the project, they will be experts in doing so.

TigerPearl

Spend twice as much time on the specifications and the needs analysis as you think necessary. It will pay off in spades.

There are two ways of getting a fix on your requirements. First, spend a great deal of time with the users in the beginning to understand what they want. Consider what they say and what they imply between the lines of their comments. This approach depends very much on the analyst working with the business managers.

The second approach is to assume perfection is impossible and design the software in phases. You start with a very basic prototype. You anticipate that over time the users will understand much better the problem you are all working to solve, and will ask for more functionality after reviewing the basic prototype. If you have selected the tools with this continuous improvement or rapid prototyping in mind, you'll spend far less time than in the older approach (which is often called the "waterfall approach"). In this rapid prototyping, the project manager or system analyst feels tremendous pressure to document and confirm feedback from the end-users.

Project definition also has a nasty way of changing as the project moves along. You have to adhere to your original definitions. Put small changes into the next phase. Major changes should compel an explicit revision of the whole project. Mature project managers are often those who have learned to say no nicely, but firmly.

Scope

The single easiest way to reduce the risk of a project is to cut it down in size and complexity. While this sounds obvious, there is a natural tendency in anyone involved with a project to want to add features and capabilities.

TigerPearl

Large projects need exceptional project managers. There are very few of these exceptional people.

Resources

Inadequate development resources (quantity and quality) may not harm a project, but they certainly affect its schedule and must be allowed for. Development resources include hardware, development tools and team members with the personality, skills and experience to make it all work.

Your single most important resource in the team is its project manager. Is he or she competent and experienced enough to make the project a success?

Most projects require cooperation from their end-users. The team needs access to end-users for specification, feedback and testing. Make the end-users aware of the demands that will be made on them so they can make themselves available.

A plan soundly developed might still fall apart at deployment. Make sure the equipment for the project will serve the desired performance. Arrange for trainers and support personnel to launch the project well.

Timing

You can guarantee a bad project by setting unreasonable deadlines. Programmers are generally talented people and they can often achieve the miraculous in a short time if put under enough pressure. But tight deadlines squeeze out other important tasks the project needs to reach fulfillment—testing, validation, end-user involvement, project planning, documentation, user training, and designing for reuse.

 TigerPearl **You can't compress thinking time.**

As already noted, adding people to a project often slows it down. Adding people to a project team can benefit a project, up to a total of seven on that project. After that, more people tend to decrease the team's effectiveness.

Set a realistic schedule. Reduce the project's scope if needed. Predict the risk of the project's failure by assessing each stage of it not just in terms of time and budget but in terms of probability and time and budget. Instead of projecting that design will take two weeks, say, you could estimate the probability of the design taking one, two, three or four weeks and calculate the weighted time of completion you could expect in each case.

Novelty

As with any human activity, dealing with new technology, new hardware, new paradigms, a new problem area and new programming tools will reduce your productivity.

For example, in the new object-oriented programming, most people find it takes a programming team three to four projects to reach full operating efficiency. Client-server projects, or any project that requires mastering and integrating a new approach, demonstrate similar learning curves.

In a world where everything is changing, where vendors upgrade software once a year, expect things *not* to go according to plan. Early projects with a new technology should be short and simple. Ideally, they should build up to a larger and more complex project.

But merely having done three projects with a particular technology does not guarantee learning, either. Without measuring the success of each project and performing honest reviews and postaudits, you have no way of telling whether performance has improved.

Managers working with IS specialists should understand the extent to which novelty affects a project. It is a particularly slippery variable. Often, a project combines several different suppliers' products, and that particular combination of those versions of the software has never actually been tried on your particular hardware before. Check references on any such project, and select your supplier(s) with care.

Losing Attention and Support

For the project to succeed, the appropriate senior managers have to stand behind it and promote it. If these managers start to lose interest in the project, rescue the situation. Keep them informed and you'll keep them interested.

Prepare the users for the system. Take time to educate and support them through the stages of adoption. Otherwise, they will never accept and adopt the system. Remember the project's ultimate goal: that everyone use the system—even when the technical details seem overwhelming.

Determine the Critical Success Factors

Identify your critical success factors. These could be human, organizational and technical factors. Review your list in light of all these factors. Once identified, establish some plan to monitor how each factor is dealt with. Track the factors regularly with the other milestones set for your project plan.

Quality Project Process

Most projects involve these steps:

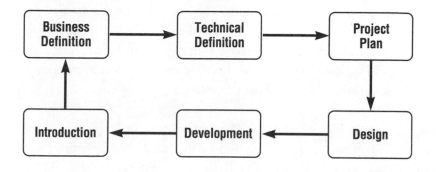

1. **Business Definition.** This gives the end-users and managers the means to communicate their needs in terms of business process, tool functionality and data requirement. Rank these clearly. Those who have to design the technical specifications will appreciate knowing the overall vision of how those needs will evolve. Spend some time on defining data.

Users and managers are really not asked to be technical. They are asked to be thoughtful and thorough. Frequently, it is difficult to nail down a company's process and data needs because business is result-oriented and fluid. However, agreed-upon assumptions, though not perfect, together with the understanding of how those assumptions might evolve, will go a long way to help the technical folks who work on the downstream side of the project.

 If you don't involve your potential users in the process of software design, you will end up with software designed for programmers. Programmers have expectations about good software that are vastly different from those of the average user.

2. **Technical Definition.** This allows the technical team to specify how it will meet the defined business requirements. This includes software

and hardware selection, and decisions on how the project can be carried out—developed internally, externally or purchased. This stage ends in high-level project specification and budget development.

3. **Project Planning.** With technical definitions in hand, you can now draw up the project plan. This includes roles, action steps, milestones and resource allocation. Most schedules conclude with system installation and delivery, which is not sufficient. The plan should include steps for user training and adoption to provide a realistic and full view of the project.

Not long ago, it was not uncommon for projects to be large and last more than one year. If business strategy and needs that drive IT change rapidly, prolonged IT projects do not match business cycle needs. So think in terms of short phases. The results of each phase should be modular, so that new ideas and changes can be added without disrupting the whole system. Each phase should produce tangible results that the project team can demonstrate to colleagues. This will generate support and interest in continuing.

4. **Design/Model.** Like any other project, time spent on design saves errors and misunderstandings down the road and creates better end-products. Here is another opportunity to verify requirements with users and managers. Sometimes you'll develop a quick prototype for verification purposes.
5. **Development.** The design is implemented in this phase. You'll test the system at the development site and at the deployment site at the end of this phase.
6. **Introduction of System.** The success of the project often depends on how this phase is planned and implemented. Think of it as a mini product launch. It will include system installation and distribution, and training of end-users and support personnel.

For large, intricate projects, these six stages are more complex, but they still address these basic issues.

Organizations can establish different points for reviews and budget allocation. You can always allocate funds in stages. You can review and even fund your business definition. If the project makes sense, proceed to the technical definition stage, which will lead to project planning and developing costs. You determine when to give the final go-ahead based on the plan and business case justification.

Manage Expectations

In any product launch, strategy counts. You time when you will promote the features and benefits of the products to their intended users. You orchestrate how often and how many and what form of communications to issue. Planning the introduction of a new system is no different. First impressions count. Be clear in your message. You want a rapid adoption curve, at least with some key users. You want to build support and get those good reviews early.

Seek out a few key users on the project team to assist you. They can help communicate with other users, adopt the new technology early and review the system for you.

Any system solution should represent a group endorsement and solution. It is no one person's silver bullet.

As in any launch, set up your distribution before advertising the product. Make sure the installation is complete and your support personnel are trained before introducing the system. This will greatly increase the confidence of end-users.

While you have to believe in the solution yourself, do not build up unrealistic expectations about the system. It is always better to have many small successes than one big failure. Limited time always restricts the delivery of full complex systems. Besides, most users are cynical about silver-bullet solutions. They'd rather see systems that respond to rapid changes than the perfect system for yesterday's needs.

The Importance of Cut-off Points

The critical rules of thumb about every project are:

- Something important will be forgotten and remembered at a late stage.
- Someone will change his or her mind about specifications.

- Some technical problems will emerge. The component everyone assumed would be easy will take more time.
- A team member will give you problems.

As a manager who specifies your business needs at the outset, you'll always find that the delivered solution is imperfect in some way. Decide what limitations you and other users can live with. Are the changes you'd like to see important? Should the project be postponed? You have to agree on a cut-off point for all changes and stick with it. Technical people are not always very good at telling users how much changes will damage the project or skew the results. They tend to oblige. Managers have to exercise the self-discipline of paying more attention in the specifications stage and restrain themselves from making changes. You have to sell the solution to users and yet not promise them the whole world—a fine line to walk.

TigerPearl

Build a prototype to discover the system's weaknesses. It's cheaper than aiming for a complete but wrong system.

Deadlines

Prize enthusiasm, commitment and persistence. These forces will drive your team and inspire them to meet their deadlines. The team members should share a sense of urgency and recognize that all delays by any party will be costly.

Delays come in two kinds—controllable and uncontrollable. A business manager can help control them by doing several things:

- ensuring that the front end of defining needs and requirements takes place as scheduled. This means pushing groups to work together and make decisions;
- making sure sufficient thinking enters into the specifications at the beginning to cut off arbitrary and unnecessary changes down the road;
- keeping in contact with the developers throughout the project. Sometimes you can avoid a technical problem or solve it easily if

you can offer a different perspective on user needs or clarify some point briefly during the team's work.

You cannot always control those delays related to technical risks and the quality of the technical team. Identify these risk factors at the start of the project.

Project Team

Any project team comprises members who are responsible for *producing* the work, people who serve as *resources,* those who *approve or veto* decisions and those who need to be *informed* of progress regularly. Identify each of these players and make them accountable for their roles.

Below are the kinds of people you need on the team and the functions they perform. These people may play one or more of the roles described above, or perform one or many of the functions.

- Those who represent users and can articulate the needs of potential users. They can describe the business process that needs to be incorporated into the system and verify how well certain innovations actually work. They also sell the project to other users.
- A member who can work with users and managers in defining the business process. This person should be able to work with existing processes or help define the new, improved ones.
- A member who works well with users and managers to define the data requirements from the business perspective.
- A member who champions the cause or has direct access to a champion for the cause.
- A technical expert who can translate the business needs into the technical specifications. He or she would also manage the technical portion of the project.
- A technical expert who knows how this project should be connected to or draw from other systems in the organization. This person brings a familiarity with the organization's technical architecture and policies to the team.

- A project manager who ensures that the project meets its deadlines and that the different resources are coordinated and approvals are obtained on time.

Obtaining Buy-In and Involving the Management Team

Involve a cross-section of managers and users in the project who will be affected by its outcome. Most people like to feel that they are in control of their lives. Involvement in the design and specification process serves several purposes:

- The design team gains valuable input.
- The management team begins to work harder on the project because they feel the project belongs to them.
- Merely participating educates the management team and users, which reduces the amount of internal selling and training you'll need later.

If users don't know very much about software, educate them about the design possibilities or choices of vendor first. Make them a part of the design or purchase process.

Every project that we have been involved in has been enriched by the involvement of users. The projects consistently achieve far more if users contribute to them. And as projects inevitably evolve, the availability of a larger pool of users speeds up future work and evolution to the benefit of all.

Testing and Documentation

Managers sometimes rush projects, leaving little time for testing and documentation. As you can imagine, inadequate testing can vary in its impact from disastrous to lethal. And while a lack of documentation does not usually show up immediately as a problem, in the longer term it can cost your business a lot of money.

Murphy's Law—If it can go wrong, it will—should be the motto of any project. If you assume that everything will go wrong, and that everything needs to be tested, you'll have a fighting chance of sponsoring a winning project.

Test all the aspects of a product on the specific configuration on which it will actually be run. You'll never regret running those tests. As applications become more complicated, you'll need more testing.

Installing New Information Technology Is a Process of Change

Many of us intuitively know this—*adopting a new information technology system is messy*. Every new IT system demands changing working habits, new knowledge and skills and different ways of relating to others. And we expect all this to happen naturally!

With constant change in the organization, some people will lose and others will gain. You will always have people who resent the new system. So develop a plan to help both users and supporters adjust.

State clearly why this system has to be installed. Offer assistance to get everyone through the rough stages. And don't forget that people learn and adjust in different ways and at different speeds. Your plan may require a variety of ways to support your staff.

Change, even for the better, is stressful. You can go a long way to make the change to a new information technology system more successful just by being considerate and helpful to those who have to adapt to it.

Why Projects Fail

Like many successful software developers, we are always amazed at the end of a project that the software is completed and is successful. The more you know about software, the more surprising it is that anything works.

When you think about it, this is an amazing industry. We have thousands of suppliers whose products must work together. So many things must go right, from the chips to the motherboards to the mechanical components to the networks.

Yet there is an even broader range of issues that need to go right to design a project right and make it work with an organization's technological and strategic decisions.

There are four policy reasons that projects fail:

1. The organization has not made the effort to develop policies that will allow individual projects to succeed and work with other projects. A simple example: an organization has not standardized its policies on the formats for data that must be exchanged by business units, or with suppliers and customers.
2. The organization sets inflexible policies. Managers become so disenchanted with the information systems staff and their rigidities that they seek and gain more autonomy. To deal with the conflicting standards that this produces takes a huge amount of extra work.
3. While the use of computers by general and line managers has increased dramatically, their understanding of what it takes to build and administer industrial-strength distributed systems has not kept up.
4. Some information systems departments have not recognized the reality that users are seeking and gaining more influence over the information technology in their offices. Information systems departments who fight this trend will lose. They must learn to pick which areas of the business they wish to exert influence over. Otherwise, they will be disliked, perhaps even hated, by end-users.

Postaudits

	Plan	Do	Improve
Leadership			
Policies			
Projects			• Postaudits • Success that lasts • Assessment

Every organization should do postaudits of its performance on different projects. Without these, the rate of performance improvement will be low. Issues include:

• Was the project delivered on time and on budget?

- Did the project give your organization the greater abilities you originally contemplated?
- What technical lessons has your company learned?
- Do the targeted users use the new technology?
- Were the users happy with the new capabilities the project gave them?
- Was there an increase in your organization's productivity, capability or quality?
- Did the project reduce your total costs?
- Did customer satisfaction increase?
- Did revenues increase?
- Did return on investment increase in the short term? In the long term?

TigerPearl

An organization should learn from its own best practices. Don't hide them. Identify yours and expand them.

The lessons you and your colleagues learn from one project or one phase of a project should be taken into account as you plan the next. The post-audit is critical in completing the Plan–Do–Improve cycle.

Success That Lasts

A project does not end with its introduction to its users. Systems never die!

To make a system successful, you want feedback so you can devise plans to improve and maintain that system. If the project progresses, you'll need feedback from the first phase before moving on to the next. Like a product, each stage of a project requires attention and ownership so the system keeps pace with your changing business needs.

Key Questions To Ask When Any IT Project Is Proposed

1. What will the up-front cost be?
2. What will its total or multi-year cost over its life cycle be?
3. What are the tangible and intangible benefits of this project?
4. Who will be using the system the project produces or modifies?
5. Have the end-users been involved in designing the project?

6. What are the review points during the project?
7. Have the deliverables in the initial stages been specified?
8. Has time been budgeted to review the specifications?
9. Have testing and documentation time been budgeted?
10. On which suppliers and standards will this project depend?
11. What is the expected evolution of the technologies the project is based on?
12. On which set of technology assumptions about the organization has this project been based?
13. Which unspecified projects will this project likely trigger?
14. How do we expect users to change their requirements of the system during the course of this project? Over the life of this project?
15. Have we mapped out how we would deal with the failure of any key technology in this project? How expensive would it be to move to another set of equipment, another database, network or operating system?
16. What will the future costs for supporting this application be?
17. What training costs must we expect to deploy this application?
18. What are the consequences of our not going ahead with this project? For us? For our customers? For our competitive position in this business?
19. How does this project rank in our portfolio of projects? Cost, risk, payback, familiarity, operational focus, strategic benefit, basic infrastructure?

Predicting Project Success

We suggest the following scoring system for predicting whether a project will succeed. Rate yourself according to how emphatically you would answer yes.

1. **Project Management.** Do we have the people with the authority, time and ability to dedicate themselves to the project? Will their careers be enhanced by the project's success? **Potential points: 15**
2. **Sizing.** Has any analysis been performed in advance to identify the size and scope of the project? Has the project design realistically

anticipated the rate of change expected on the project? **Potential points: 15**

3. **Budget Adequacy.** Is the budget adequate for a solid solution or is the strategy the thin end of a wedge? ("Once we show it works, they'll give us more money.") Has the overall life cycle cost of the project been considered? **Potential points: 12**

4. **Sponsorship.** Does senior management back this project? Are they prepared to fight to make this project successful? Does the project support a key need or strategy of the business? **Potential points: 10**

5. **Technology Risk.** Have we thoroughly investigated reference sites for the new technology in the project? Do the consultant or internal staff have experience in the technology? Is the project small or large? Is the system a critical line system that will pose problems if the project fails? **Potential points: 10**

6. **Technology Assessment and Evolution.** Has the project been analyzed to look at the likely evolution of the underlying technologies on which it depends? **Potential points: 10**

7. **User Involvement.** Have the users been involved in the design of the project? Do they like what the project will do for them? **Potential points: 10**

8. **Commitment.** Are the consultants or internal development staff totally committed to this project? Do they have a track record of success on projects? Do they have other obligations that will distract them from the project? **Potential points: 8**

9. **Planning.** Is there a project plan and adequate time set aside for testing and documentation, roll-out and support? Has the project been divided into small and manageable chunks? Are the deadlines reasonable or externally imposed to meet an arbitrary deadline? **Potential points: 8**

10. **Knowledge Transfer.** Does the project increase the capabilities of the organization or will the expertise walk out the door at the end of it? Are the consultants conveying their knowledge directly to the client staff? **Potential points: 2**

11. **Vested Interests.** Are there important parties with a vested interest in the organization and with the power and ability to prevent this project from succeeding? **Subtract maximum of 100 points**

Score Between	Assessment
(100)–(51)	If you're even looking at this project, you're going to have to make sure those vested interests leave the organization.
(50)–(1)	Time to look elsewhere in the organization for projects. Perhaps you should look into a new career.
0–20	Unless senior management makes up most of the points, go home and have a stiff drink.
21–40	A project unlikely to succeed.
41–60	The project may be built, but it may not be used.
61–80	A good project with a reasonable chance of success. Look for opportunities to improve the lower scores.
81–100	This project will likely succeed. Make sure that the project supports the organization's strategy.

The Bank of Glen Burnie Case Study:

The entire senior management group meet in Aldo's office to hear the launch of the project on the customer information repository.

PROJECT MANAGEMENT

Aldo Moretti, Chairperson and CEO: Before we begin on the customer information project, I'd like to brief you all on the board of directors meeting. I've got good news and bad news. The board approved everything except the one thing that we all assumed was a no-brainer to get approved—the replacement of the mini and the transaction processing software. They gave me specific instruction to try to prolong the life of the system for another three years. The good news is that they want us to do everything else. It's rather inconsistent, I know. I don't think we can go back to them on this for a while. Any suggestions, Peter or Steve?

Peter Schultz, VP, Information Systems, and CIO: Martha and I have come up with a transition plan that might allow us to do what they want and allow us to position ourselves for the future. We've been working on the KISS principle—Keep it simple, stupid.

Our idea is that none of the transaction systems we have been offered are very attractive. They are all older systems. We are just not impressed. It may not be a bad idea to wait for some of the newer transaction systems to get finished before we make our move. Anyway, our idea is that even at $3 billion in assets we're pretty small. We probably can't afford to develop a system by ourselves. However, it might make sense if we were able to joint-venture a system with some other small noncompetitive institutions. If we ever need to merge in order to survive the market shake-out, it might make a lot of sense to have some potential partners—firms with compatible systems that we feel we could work with.

The second and important idea is the one Bill kept on pushing at our planning retreat. That you're better off doing something small and then growing it as you understand the problem better.

So our idea is to build a really simple transaction processing system. We'll keep it generic so that it can be modified for other transactions later. We'll just use it for one type of transaction, say, checking accounts, and this will reduce the load on our minicomputer by around 30 percent so response time will improve. The board of directors has approved the new network and the customer information repository, so information about the transactions can be fed to the database and even tellers will be able to get at it.

To keep things really simple, we'll run the system on a separate computer—a separate server. If we modify the software for another product, we'll put it up on a second computer. The rule will be "One Computer, One Financial Service." We'll use the customer information repository as the link.

The real benefit of what we are proposing is that it won't cost a lot and we can innovate more quickly when we decide to launch a new product. We could even test-market a product at one branch without confusing the poor old mini.

Aldo: Sounds too good to be true. What do you think, Martha?

Martha Rodrigues, VP, Operations: It sounded a bit crazy to me at first, but I'm quite excited. It's a small project. I think it can be prototyped easily. We've got a good supplier with banking experience. By keeping the project small, we can manage the risk. I like it, because if it works, it might help us with Internet Banking. It's a modular approach and has object programming language, *SmallTalk,* one that I would like to use internally here. I'm in favor. And we get to share the risk with some other good firms.

Peter: There's a precedent for this type of relationship in the industry, so we'll be seen as a leader.

Aldo: So you're saying that the board of directors may have done us a favor.

Peter: Well, I wouldn't go that far.

Martha: However, Peter and I do think there is still risk here, so we're going to look at an outsourcing strategy. We don't think the outsourcing strategy will make sense without the customer information repository project. If we contract transactions out, we will still need superb customer information. So with any transaction approach, we still have to anticipate a need for the customer information repository. We just won't know where the information is going to come from. It may come from our systems, from outsourced transaction processors, from Internet banking suppliers. It's all going to change. That I feel sure.

Aldo (*turning to Peter*): Okay, let's start with the customer information repository project. What's the agenda here? You've got the attention of the entire management team.

Peter (*turning to Ron Silver*): Ron, as VP Marketing, this is really your project. Why don't you begin with the business problem as you see it.

Ron: Thanks, Pete. I've got five basic points that I would like to make.

First, we are not what I would call state of the art as a bank. Other banks I've worked with are doing a lot more with database marketing than we are.

Second, we are managing in the dark. How many of you have frequent flier cards for one of the airlines?

Everyone in the room puts up a hand.

How many of you belong to a warehouse outlet like our local Sam's Warehouse or Costco?

Most of the hands in the room go up again.

Well, every time you shop at one of these stores or buy an airline ticket the company is tracking your purchase decisions. What do we do?

Martha: Absolutely nothing.

Ron: That's right. We can't tell you what accounts you have with the bank. The mortgage department has their database. Checking and savings accounts are elsewhere. VISA processing is a separate system. Bottom line, it takes a huge effort even to measure services per household once a quarter.

In fact, it's even worse. If a certificate of deposit is about to expire, there is no easy way for our front-line staff to ask for the renewal. Our renewal rate is at least 15 percentage points lower than the last bank I worked at.

My business need is simple. I need to know and track everything about a customer. I want to know what services he or she has with us. I want to know the balances. I want to know expiry dates on the loans and deposits. I want to know what direct mail we sent to him or her and when. I want to know when he or she complained to us. I want all this information in one place so I can get at it easily. And I want outside information, too. I also want the credit history available easily.

Peter (*hastily scribbling on the electronic whiteboard, turns around*): So that's the business issue. Now we need to talk about when and what we should do first.

Ron: The when is easy. We needed it yesterday.

Peter: I think what Ron is saying can be translated into several pieces. First, we need to have a place we can put all the data about customers—a database repository. Second, we need to figure out how to get information into the repository and how frequently. Third, we need tools to query the database, and although you haven't said it, I am assuming you want a link to some system so that you can cue tellers, or customer service reps on the phone with dialogues or sales scripts.

Ron (*enthusiastically*): Yes, exactly, and I want to record whenever a sales attempt is made so we can track what's working and with whom. There's no point in selling the same thing time and time again to the same customer if it's not working.

Aldo: I just want to remind people. If we collect all this information, it's got to stay private. Think of the problems if this information is let out.

Gail Bartok, VP, HR: Heard loud and clear. We'll start thinking about a training program for everyone on privacy.

Steve Arbeit, President and COO: So what do we do first, Pete?

Peter: Well, we have not got the new network up between branches. We have some new servers dedicated to this project. I would like to suggest that we start off with something simple, something we can get up really quickly and something that will show us some benefits really quickly.

How about focusing on two things first—what relationships people have with us and the rollover date on their loans and deposits. We're going to need some time to iron out the wrinkles in our new network, but this would be very visible. When we've got it working, perhaps we could then turn our attention to capturing loan information on-line. There's a lot of good customer information there that can be reused. We'll need these on-line application forms for the Internet soon anyway.

Steve: So we have a limited scope for the project. That's good. What's the next stage?

Peter: My department is going to do some research and come back to the group with a more detailed technical spec. We're going to need about two weeks. Is that okay with everyone?

More generally, this is a five-stage project. The first stage is gaining commitment. With you all in the room, I think we have established the importance of this project. The second phase will be the appointing of the project team. I'm assuming that this project will be Ron's project, because he's head of marketing. The project team will be responsible for making things happen, developing a budget and a more detailed timeline.

The third stage will be the development of the system. We'll build some quick-and-dirty screens to show you. We'll need your input, but we'll be doing most of the work at this stage.

Stage four is the deployment and staff training. Gail, you'll need to have input here.

Stage five is where we track and measure the success of the system. With that information we can move successfully onto the next stage. Or we may have to revise some components.

Aldo (*rising from his chair*): Okay, ladies and gentlemen, we have kicked off this project. It has my support, and Ron is hereby appointed project owner, with approval/veto power. Peter Schultz is the "R" on the project, the one responsible for making sure it happens.

chapter 8

RIDING YOUR TIGER WITH FINESSE

GOOD CLIENTS GET EXCEPTIONAL RESULTS

Ignore Information Technology and Delegate to Experts at Your Own Risk

You cannot ignore information technology. Even if you do not hold a technical position, you will not escape the problems, rewards and challenges of computing technology. If you are not using computers today, you will be soon.

No member of management can afford to abdicate involvement in information management. Doing so leads to problems and crises. You can delegate to experts only in part. Your own reliance on technology has multiplied astronomically in the past 20 years and will continue to do so.

As you ride your tiger, so are others riding theirs. You're in a race. How each of you manages

229

and feeds your tiger will determine who wins. Some of you will fall off your tigers and be destroyed. Others will bound ahead. Some will take different routes and head off in different directions.

It's uncomfortable and disturbing on the back of the tiger, but you have to admit that the speed is thrilling. The ride is downright exhilarating. The power gives you choice. You can cover more distance than anyone on foot and your tiger can carry you to your destination first.

Everyone Is a Client

No matter what your role is in your organization, you will be a client on an information technology project. Whether you're involved in the design, project management or, potentially, using the system, you have a role to play. You can be a client to an internal information systems department, an external consultant or vendor. All organizations purchase software and information management services from external suppliers with more expertise or available staff. Most managers also need to negotiate and manage relationships with internal support staff.

As a client, you want to be a pleasure to work with. Everyone in business is a volunteer—members of the project team or the supplier—so create and keep the enthusiasm of everyone involved. Capture the enthusiasm of your suppliers, internal and external. This is no small task. If you are a project leader, you must stand firm and be a reliable source of support as you and the project weather the inevitable crises along the way.

The best clients are imaginative and competent and willing to learn. They share what is really going on in their businesses. They are professional and focused on achievement and competence. They are smart enough to appreciate extra effort put out for them.

The worst clients, on the other hand, are unwilling to put themselves solidly behind a product. They change their minds. They don't notice when anyone goes that extra mile for them.

TIGERPEARL Assume incompetence in a supplier and you won't be disappointed. When you find competence, treasure it. When you find honesty and passion, give them a long-term contract.

EFFECTIVE INFORMATION MANAGEMENT REQUIRES A PARTNERSHIP
WITH YOUR SUPPLIER

Good Clients Get Better Results

Unhappy clients always complain about the bad internal and external suppliers they have had and recite a litany of the unsuccessful projects they
have been engaged in. Because good clients rarely lose control of their projects, they have fewer unhappy experiences.

Good clients are better at figuring out why they need help in the first
place. Whether that help is internal or external, the good client always starts
by asking, What kind of help are we looking for? How big is what we're
proposing here?

Leadership

- Have a business strategy and make sure your information
  strategy supports it.
- Set business performance and capabilities goals for information
  technology.
- Aim to improve your processes with computing. Encourage and
  support redesigning processes.

Information Technology Only Looks Like Magic

Information technology can often seem to be magic, to paraphrase Arthur C. Clarke. It is not magic; it's just complicated, and so are its consequences. Understanding the role of information management means measuring and understanding its business consequences as much as the technology itself.

You will always face choices in technology and approach, and consequences from those decisions that extend over many years. Those decisions will affect everyone in any way related to your business—users, owners, regulators, the press, customers, the distributors and the suppliers.

Good clients follow a strategy that encompasses a plan, a proposed implementation approach and an improvement objective. If they have no strategy, they understand that to identify, select and implement a major information technology project they must first develop one.

Know Your Own Reasons for Using Information Technology

Many unsatisfied clients have not actually thought through the objectives of their projects. It is difficult to predict the results of many of the projects organizations undertake. It is therefore essential to have considered the consequences of the project as far as possible and whether the range of effort required can be justified by the range of results you expect. Again, the cycle for all projects should be Plan–Do–Improve.

Whether your supplier is internal or external, cultivate a healthy sense of perspective. Understand that just because a project ought to work easily does not mean that it will. Even apparently simple information management projects can take a lot of effort and run risks.

The consequences of investing even a small amount in information technology can be long-lasting in your organization's building capability. The good client will consider the longer-term consequences and the benefits of perseverance.

> **TigerPearl**
>
> Without a strategy you cannot guide your organization.
> Without leadership, you will not have policies.
> Without policies, you cannot develop good practices.
> Without strategies and policies, developing software is a blind stab in the dark.
> If strategy does not drive development, you cannot implement your project successfully.

Understand Your Competencies

A balance sheet masks the competencies and capabilities of an organization. Yet in a world of incompetent suppliers and brand-new and interesting technologies, the competencies of your people and their ability to learn quickly may be your most important investment in a short-lived technology. Fostering, measuring and rewarding such performance is never easy, but it marks the greatest organizations.

Core competence describes the ability of your organization's people to integrate skills from disparate areas within the organization into one powerful capability. For most organizations today, integrating skills in organizational change, redesign and upgrading of people will remain critical to success. What makes some organizations successful will be their skill in purchasing and installing applications. For others, it will be integrating systems or developing applications.

People

Managers who have the luxury of delegating the working out of problems to their technical staff are often brutal to these well-meaning employees. As with any management area, the best of these leaders know it is in everyone's best interest to keep enthusiasm among staff high.

Time seems to disappear when you are trying to get something to work on a computer. Demand the impossible of your suppliers and they will burn out and be less available to you for future projects. Even worse, they will make more mistakes because they're tired. Excessive overtime and "all-nighters" may end up as one of the most expensive requests you can ever make of these people.

Working on a computer often poses another risk. A team member can become so involved in developing the project that he or she forgets to *manage* the project. Most projects that wander way off schedule do so in their earliest days, when planners misjudge their scope. In the real-estate world, banks will not advance money for a project without evidence of the costs incurred to date and a third party's certification of the cost to complete it. In the equally complex world of information management, keeping your eye on the cost to complete the project is just as important.

Information Technology Is a Catalyst for Change

When computing is incorporated into business processes, you frequently end up with changes in procedures. Good clients welcome these and encourage and support change. They are the champions for the smarter way of doing things in the interests of striving for excellence.

Forward Thinking

A good client thinks ahead. You cannot, as a general rule, select and implement or develop software in a short time. Similarly, you cannot set up the policies and infrastructure overnight, either. Recognize a learning curve for using hardware and networks, and allow time to develop the capabilities of the people in your organization. Throwing more people and resources at the problem will not necessarily speed up the process. Practice foresight, not crisis management.

Policies and Infrastructure

- Set roles, accountabilities and policies that include senior management, technical departments and users.
- Set goals for improving infrastructure and technical capability.
- Take advantage of infrastructure investments.

Communicate Your Goals and Needs

Establish clear business goals and convey them to your technology partners. This will allow them to help you determine your needs. Involve the information systems department and put together a game plan. Whether or not you're comfortable with technology, ask questions. In the long run, both you and your information systems group will benefit from your greater knowledge.

Most managers complain that their ability to innovate is held back by the limitations of the information systems department. As one large financial organization put it, "Rather than the marketing department telling the information systems department what products we wish to launch, the information systems department tells the marketing department what products they can launch and when they can do it."

While information systems departments do progress slowly, it is unfair to criticize them, especially if they have received no support and commitment. Software was until recently difficult to develop, so the information systems department has had the unenviable task of maintaining awkward software and hardware. By explaining your needs and showing a game plan, you'll help them plan their transition to more powerful hardware and better software development approaches.

With Good Infrastructure, Quick-and-Dirty Projects Can Succeed

For years managers have cleverly circumvented their information systems departments by undertaking small, quick-and-dirty projects on their own. This can sometimes backfire. The small project can turn out to be much more involved than foreseen, or the wrong technology was used. Or the managers create small islands of information, making it difficult to connect to the existing applications.

This is not to say that you should never take on small projects. Do adhere to information systems policies and standards so that your project can use existing or planned infrastructure. This increases the chances that the application will communicate with other systems and that many others in the organization will be able to use it.

Software Is Always a Service

By purchasing or developing software, your organization really enters into a service relationship. Take a longer-term perspective on suppliers to help you select the best ones. Betting on Microsoft or other major suppliers may seem easy—though they, too, have their unsuccessful products and projects—but many smaller specialty firms will have to develop essential systems. They will be the ones who can give you what you need. Judging their prospects will be harder, yet making sure you help keep them in business will be important for your own organization.

One client explained several years ago, "We never actually had a successful contract with a software supplier until quite recently. We have been such good negotiators that we nickel-and-dimed them to death. The projects were never successful. It took a dramatic change in perspective—toward seeing suppliers as partners—before we had our first successful contract. Some of our managers thought we were being too easy on the supplier, but we've now been doing business with that firm over six projects and five years. In one case, we even gave the supplier a 50 percent overrun in a project, which they took advantage of. It paid off, because the supplier continued to invest in the project, and that has benefited us a great deal."

Open Systems Are Built, Not Bought

Organizations used to create information management systems that worked together by buying from one supplier. Companies were "IBM shops" or "DEC shops." Today, with the explosion of information technology, no one company alone can keep up. Organizations must identify and manage their own standards, which provide the basis for purchase and development. Instead of paying a premium to the large vendors, organizations must *create the expertise internally* that previously came as part of a vendor's solutions.

Outsourcing—Riding Others' Learning Curves

As you may recall from Chapter Five, outsourcing is more than a trend. It reflects the increasing use of information technology and the growing need to take advantage of the specialized learning curves others have descended.

As the range of tasks information technology can aid multiplies, it is impossible for any organization to be cost-effective in all uses of information. Even General Motors, the largest manufacturer in the world, needed the help of EDS and purchased it to acquire its capabilities. (Today, they have spun off their investment, taking with it much of the old information systems area formerly at GM.)

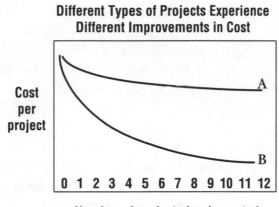

Different Types of Projects Experience Different Improvements in Cost

Cost per project

0 1 2 3 4 5 6 7 8 9 10 11 12

Number of projects implemented

Projects with steep learning curves (B) benefit from even a small number of projects. Projects with flatter learning curves (A) may require many more projects to make a company competitive.

Good clients are always looking for the value that their suppliers can provide. In addition to the experience curve with a particular technology, there may also be other sources of value added that suppliers can provide: advice on policy, business links, support, training, documentation, lower costs from a longer-term relationship or improved procurement.

The Future of Software Is in Layers and Modules

Software will increasingly be built in bits and pieces in the future. Make sure the software you purchase or develop is programmed in smaller pieces or components, and understand the technology standards that it supports. Not understanding its structure may cost you dearly.

You'll often have to be ruthless about throwing out the older technology and standards. We are not suggesting you discard technologies lightly. For many organizations, wholesale replacement is less expensive and not as risky as patching up an already unstable system.

Take, for example, General Motors' brand-new Saturn manufacturing plant in Tennessee: rather than fixing a turn-of-the-century plant, a clean-sheet design can be based upon simple modularity and designed for low maintenance. Older software may not permit strategies that minimize support and evolution costs. The development model is modular Lego, not a hand-held Gameboy that can only be used as is or replaced.

If your organization cannot replace your sytem all at once, devise your strategy on a step-by-step, piece-by-piece modular migration firmly attached to a robust architecture.

Redundancy in the support of your information management is not really redundant. Hardware is relatively cheap. Not being able to run your business threatens both the business and your career.

Murphy's Law

Murphy's Law says that if it can go wrong, it will—and probably at the most awkward moment possible. The good client will anticipate snafus by allowing for redundancy *before*—not after—the event. The good client will test the system extensively. Remember, nothing works as advertised.

In self-defense, set up arrangements to deal with failures. Keep competent people on staff. Build up more capability than you estimate you'll need. These are only sensible precautions in today's world.

Even when your information management fails, you'll have choices. Sometimes accepting a risk of failure is acceptable if the consequences are small. In some situations, imperfect software and imperfect infrastructure are acceptable and good business practice. For example, in telecommunications you can buy Frame Relay service, which guarantees you a certain amount of capacity at all times. However, if your transmission requirements suddenly jump through the roof, the telecom vendor will let you claim additional capacity at no extra cost as long as the other customers sharing your telecom "pipe" are not using all of *their* capacity. Most of the time this will be a cost-effective solution, even if occasionally you cannot get all the capacity you need.

Good clients take risks—reasonable ones—and will be rewarded many times over because they did so and then did not walk away from the process of managing those risks. They take the business initiative and make its supporting information management work for them.

Things Get Easier, but the Hurdle Is Always Being Raised

Paradoxically, the moment that something like programming becomes easier, more is demanded of it. Our knowledge of information technology improves and the business environment changes. You'll never get perfect technology.

Projects

- Set criteria for selecting projects and planning projects.
- Involve yourself in specifying projects. Insist on quality as well as reasonable deadlines and a firm budget.
- Train users.
- Always debrief your colleagues on the lessons your organization learns from projects.

Commitment

Commitment is a crucial ingredient in a good client. Information management is only partially about actual projects. It demands commitment. Important information management projects always take time to get right. The best projects take time and are implemented in phases. Good clients are prepared to rein in their expectations and reduce the scope of a project in its first generation. With restricted scope comes a higher chance of success. Generally, Pareto's Rule applies. Twenty percent of the project will account for 80 percent of the benefit. The rest of the project probably could not be accomplished even with infinite resources because it takes user feedback to finish it. Projects today are too complex to specify completely before they are built.

The good client *cares*. Good clients know that quality counts and is worth working and waiting for.

Consensus

One person's idea is someone else's calamity. Building consensus in the organization is one of your most important jobs. There is nothing more frustrating for the internal sponsor of a project than to have it shot down in flames. Good clients know what their organizations believe to be true and are clever about advancing their causes within those beliefs and preferences. They either seek a sponsor with the power to drive the organization in the correct direction or gain approval themselves to perform a test to demonstrate the value of the new approach or technology.

Champion your ideas and their implementation! Sell their benefits to end-users and pull them into solving the organization's problem as you've identified it.

KISS—Keep It Simple, Stupid!

The high priests of software design love to consider all the possible connections and features in one piece of software. If you have a choice, have a big picture, a plan, but only develop a small piece of the plan first. Get it up. Get it running. Then add another piece. You can achieve part of a larger project pretty quickly today.

Perfection will never be delivered in the time available. In fact, the data on fixing errors suggest that modularity of design is the single largest factor in making things work. The KISS principle still holds true for the most complex of information technologies. If someone can't explain it to you, it's probably not a good idea.

Good Clients in Partnership with Good Suppliers

Hire good people and manage them well. In a world short of expertise, treasure good staff and treat your suppliers like partners.

As a good client, you lead first and manage second. Establish the objectives for your project in consultation with your users and your suppliers. Then provide the resources and support to make the project happen.

Those who sell and build IT projects like to meet your needs. Be careful to ask only for what is reasonable on the project, and simultaneously design the project for its next stages.

One of our smartest clients, Peter Schueth, said to us on a business planning project, "At the end of the project, I want the managers to complain that *it was too easy*, that *they could have done more*." He knew that gaining acceptance was more important than the perfect project and that the software could be evolved in future years.

Don't hire the firm—hire the person. Just because a large consulting firm has a good reputation it doesn't mean you'll get the right and competent staff from them.

While a firm or an internal department may have the general expertise you require, the people on your project may not. It is of no help to a drowning man to know that the average depth of the water is five feet in the lake if he is sinking in 35 feet of water.

Expertise in a consulting firm or an information systems department is a mysterious commodity. Sometimes the best people are those who have just worked on the identical project elsewhere. They have descended a learning curve that will save you money. Sometimes the best people to have on a project are:

- those who ferret out the real needs of the organization best and build consensus on what is really required,
- those brash and aggressive enough to tell you that you are wrong and heading down the wrong road,
- those who have experimented with and evaluated the technologies you are considering investing in, and
- those who can understand your business strategy and can translate your aims into your IT requirements.

The Metropolitan Toronto Police Case

Good clients have a clear idea of whom they are hiring and what expertise and value their suppliers bring to the table.

An outstanding example of a good client is Roger Mahabir, who is the Director of Computing and Telecommunications for the Metropolitan Toronto Police Service. When Mahabir arrived in April 1992, he was told that the service's budget would be reduced in future years and that they needed to embark on major business initiatives such as community-based policing. His mandate was to transform an outdated and ineffective IT organization into one that would improve the efficiency and effectiveness of the service.

Mahabir believes in the value of partnerships. He has successfully gained the support of his entire staff of 200 and his top management group, members of the service, and political leaders at all levels of government. He has also gained the support of his vendors, whom he treats as partners—instead of adversaries or mere suppliers.

In 1992, Mahabir and his partners developed a comprehensive strategic plan called the Metropolitan Toronto Police Information System Project (METROPOLIS). The majority of this plan has already been implemented, and it has helped the service gain vastly improved police efficiency. Joe Pantalone, member of Metro Council's Management Committee, which is responsible for reviewing and recommending police budgets to Council, has said, "METROPOLIS has permitted the service to continue to be a leader in policing even in 1996, when their operating budget is $10 million less than last year." In fact, the police budget is approximately $70 million less than in 1992.

The METROPOLIS project has already produced many improved systems for tasks such as dispatching, mug shots and line ups. The project was expected to deliver a cumulative benefit of $90 million over a 10-year period. In fact, it delivered $92 million at the end of 1996.

Hugh Moore, the chief administrative officer, Policing, says, "Roger has made an outstanding contribution to Metro Police in effectively managing the implementation of our METROPOLIS strategy for over four years.

"My role—aside from feeling very good about hiring Roger in 1992—has been to support him, and his service computing and telecommunications colleagues, at the command, Police Services Board and Metro Council levels, given the politics and pressures of the police budget. But Roger has really achieved the results, and the service is privileged to have him leading our technology team."

When Mahabir joined the Metropolitan Toronto Police, he saw that the infrastructure for systems needed to be rebuilt. He set up a customer service group and reorganized the systems teams to fit customer needs. He also introduced client-server technology and expanded the use of desktop workstations.

A new system that was built during 1995 and 1996 is the Criminal Information Processing System (CIPS), one of 67 new applications delivered. This system automates the tracking of criminal cases. It is triggered by an arrest and includes managing prisoners, feeding them, dealing with witnesses, handling charges, etc. The main purpose of the CIPS system is to help officers in the station.

This system uses leading-edge technology based on a three-tier client-server system. The building of this system shows how Mahabir makes partnerships work. Five vendors were involved: IBM (which provided hardware, software and services), Oracle (which provided the database software), DMC (experts on implementing Oracle databases), DMB (which provided management support), and CGI Information Services and Management Consultants (which built the software for the client part).

Some of these vendors are fierce competitors, but Mahabir encouraged them to cooperate with one another.

Because the technology for the CIPS system is so new, it was inevitable that mistakes would be made and tempers would fray. However, in spite of these kinds of difficulties, Mahabir was able to keep all the teams motivated to move forward. The CIPS system was completed successfully and is now in use, with rave reviews from the users. An arrest that would have taken several hours in the past can now be accomplished in minutes, for example.

Mahabir believes it is essential to motivate his suppliers to work as partners with other suppliers to produce effective systems for the Metropolitan Toronto Police. When his team started to develop the new 911 Emergency Call System, they needed to depend on several separate vendors, such as Bell Canada, Motorola, IBM, Dictaphone and Intergraph.

Mahabir realized that the project would not succeed unless the vendors worked together as partners.

Mahabir has found that the vendors will be committed to investing in the project if they believe the project has a good chance of success. Vendors trust Mahabir because he has a good track record as a manager and as a partner. He makes a commitment that the project is going to work.

Mahabir also knows that a relationship will grow as long as there is value in it for all the people involved. Mahabir makes sure that there is value for all the vendors in the partnership. If the project is successful, each vendor will benefit from future sales to other customers. This makes the vendors go the extra mile and work beyond their own boundaries.

To increase the probability of success and to reduce risks, Mahabir divides large projects into smaller subprojects. Each smaller project has far less risk than a large project. Moreover, Mahabir believes that when team members are committed, the risk goes away. The team members will be determined to overcome obstacles.

Three Times to Get It Right

As we have already stated, most software does not work well until its third version. It is important not to take too short-term a view on the development of custom software. Having software developed is a bit like having a child. Giving birth is only the beginning of the process. Maintain your friendship with the mother. You'll need her help to raise your software right.

Whether you develop internally or hire an external supplier, you'll get what you pay for. If you place huge pressures on a supplier to meet unreasonable deadlines, you will get computer code with lots of defects. If you underpay or underbudget your supplier you'll get software that will be expensive to maintain. It's therefore very important to make sure you trust and like your supplier. Suppliers who are in it for the short term should not even make your list.

What to Look for in a Project Plan

How can you as manager predict whether a supplier is likely to keep his or her promises? Unfortunately, there are no foolproof ways to protect yourself, but there is a framework or checklist to help you improve your odds.

The Project Management Institute has published handbooks containing such checklists and guidelines. Here is a summary of the sections you should look for in your own supplier's project management plan. If some sections are missing from that particular plan, make sure your supplier explains why those sections are not appropriate for your project.

There should be processes to control a number of factors. The factors include:

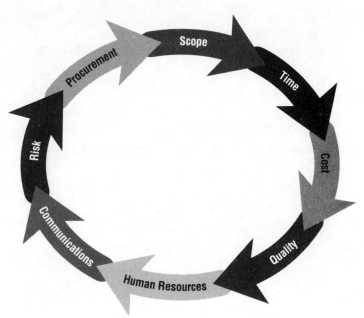

Scope

The project includes all the work required, and only the work required, to complete it successfully.

Time

The project will be completed in a reasonable length of time.

Cost

The project will be completed within the approved budget.

Quality

The project will satisfy the needs for which it was undertaken in the first place.

Human Resources

The most effective use will be made of the people involved with it.

Communications

There will be regular and appropriate generation, collection, dissemination, storage and ultimate disposition of information on the project.

Risk

The processes that identify, analyze and respond to project risks have been elaborated.

Procurement

Goods and services will be acquired from outside the organization.

The Successful Project

All successful IT projects contain 15 ingredients:

1. An internal senior management sponsor who is committed to the project.
2. A clear connection exists between the organization's strategy and the project.
3. A realistic budget and schedule are in place.
4. One person manages the budget, scope and resources.
5. Expectations are properly set.
6. Scope is well defined and constrained.
7. The need to develop the project over several generations is accepted.
8. Users are involved early on in the design of the project or selection of the package.
9. There is the sophistication to understand that there are always choices in technology and approach.
10. Analysis is done of the effects of the project on other key systems in the organization.
11. There is a desire to work with and help the developers.
12. Everyone is aware the clock is ticking—delays caused by any member of the team will cost more. There should be a healthy sense of urgency all players share.
13. Issues are dealt with as quickly as they arise.
14. All dealings are open and frank. Team members can discuss the project honestly.
15. The project's impact is measured, so that everyone can learn lessons from both success and failure.

Do not punish mistakes. On the other hand, do not tolerate "cowboys" who are irresponsible in acquiring, developing or programming solutions. Organizations learn from their mistakes. With the rapid change in information technology, this is critical. The biggest mistake you can make is to believe that making no mistakes is a good sign. If no mistakes happen, then they are not being reported. Either that or nothing is being achieved.

Remember that IT is useless without people. While technology may automate decisions and support human beings, the ultimate test of whether a project is successful is whether it helps the employees of the organization serve their customers better.

SUMMARY

Synergy does exist—demand it! Invest in people and projects that will make gradual changes to your organization's operation, that build upon a series of good decisions to make a total bigger than the sum of its individual parts. Synergy does exist in information technology and you should pursue it vigorously. Good IT solutions can solve many problems at the same time.

Business consequences are more important than project costs. People count. Short-term solutions lead to long-term costs.

When customers are delighted with you and your organization, you'll enjoy the thrill of riding your tiger and outpacing your competition.

You have no choice. You cannot climb off your tiger. Ride it well.

chapter 9

THE QUICK AND THE DEAD

THE CONCLUSION TO THE BANK OF GLEN BURNIE CASE STUDY

Report to the Board of Directors

Steve Arbeit, President and new CEO: First, I would like to thank you for appointing me CEO. I would like to begin by sharing with you where I think we stand today and where we must go in the future.

Second, the good news. Over the past five years, since our kick-off planning session with Bill Underwood, we have had, I think we would all agree, great success in changing the capabilities of our organization. I am personally very proud that we have managed to avoid downsizing by growing faster than our market. We have certainly had some turnover in staff, but our overall employment levels are up. I think my predecessor, Aldo Moretti, deserves a great deal of credit for driving the process.

Third, we have addressed the serious shortfalls in the organization. In particular, I would like to mention the following achievements:

1. We have upgraded the computer skills of everyone in the organization. Our recent surveys indicate that not only is everyone in the organization using e-mail, 100 percent of employees are accessing electronic sources of information, intranets and databases and, more important, feeling competent about the process. I take particular delight in the fact that people are now comfortable with doing complicated queries of our database and automating tasks with the latest work flow Wizards in Office 2000. With these new computer skills we have also been able to gain access to some particularly talented women working out of their homes on a part-time basis as they raise their children. This has given us a major advantage over our competitors in providing some new and flexible career paths.

2. We have improved the wait time on our teller terminals so that there is now no appreciable delay even at peak periods. Customer satisfaction, as measured by our surveys, is 25 percent higher than it is for our local competitors. However, as you all know, with fewer branches and less in-branch activity, this is a decreasingly important part of our business.

3. Our asset growth has been 35 percent per year for the past three years, outpacing our existing and new competitors typically by 25 percentage points. Our focus groups suggest that this is due to our strategy of bundled pricing on services and our rewards program for heavy users of our services.

SUCCESS IN A COMPANY IS ALWAYS TRANSITORY

4. Our customer information repository contains, as you know, information about our customers' transactions, credit history, credit card usage, housing and, for 25 percent of our customers, their financial plans. I think a lot of credit here should go to Aldo Moretti as chairperson. He insisted throughout the process that knowing everything about our customers was strategically critical. At the same time, his unwavering insistence on the privacy rights of our customers was an unsung heroic gesture that has, I think, saved us many lawsuits. We have been careful to guard our lists and not make them available to third parties. Our use of on-line questionnaires and over development of customer profiles have allowed us to avoid the junk e-mail problem that seems to have been a headline every month for the past two years. Good ethics is good business. Our competitors cannot say the same.

5. In addition, our use of positive sales incentives through our rewards program has encouraged customers to share information with us that has been very important. I personally think, also, that Aldo's decision to have a loan approval ombudsman has dramatically improved our customer relations. It has been

252 / Riding the Tiger

effective, particularly when combined with more openness about our lending policies. Customers can anticipate our loan approval policies, and we are considered a leader in this aspect of our relations with customers. This trust factor has helped us become the primary financial institution for 65 percent of our customers.

6. Over the five-year period, our average services per household has gone up from 2.5 to 3.7, based upon how we defined services five years ago. This increased share of our customers' wallets has dramatically improved both our profitability and our customer satisfaction .

  Our lower price on bundled services and our rewards program have worked very well. Ninety-two percent of our customers are participating in our rewards program. I am delighted to report that our share of our customers' wallets—in terms of financial services—has risen to the unheard of rate of 65 percent. There is some mixed news here in that the competitive environment has gotten significantly worse and we have lost 20 percent of our customers from five years ago. However, because of our use of detailed customer profiling and our customer information repository, we only regret losing half of these customers. They were not very profitable, or, predicted to be high-credit risks.

7. I am also very proud of the improvement in our capabilities as an organization. We have really upgraded our information technology staff and have developed excellent programming and client-server capability. Perhaps equally important, 70 percent of our middle managers now have a fair knowledge of project development in the information technology area from being involved in quality improvement, process improvement and new systems projects.

8. We have also switched from an adversarial role with information technology suppliers to a partnering relationship with three firms. The three provide us with specialty software in the area of transaction processing, business planning, information warehousing and Internet banking. Our initial benchmarking study suggests that we still have a long way to go relative to the

industry in terms of transaction costs. This area will be our biggest challenge in the next five years.

Now I must turn to the bad news. We have recently discovered that one of the national competitors is moving aggressively into our market. They have just signed a deal with the dominant supermarket chain in our area, as well as a chain of convenience stores. This will give them dramatic coverage of our market without the expense of ATMs or bricks and mortar.

We have updated our business plan, and our initial forecast is that we could lose 40 percent of our customers in the next three years. What worries us in particular is that 30,000 of our customers account for 80 percent of our profitability. We are particularly vulnerable to a targeted marketing program from our competitors against our heaviest users of our services.

Using our planning software, we have projected that there is only one approach. We have a short window of opportunity to defeat them. We figure around six months to set it up.

Our strategic recommendation to the board is that we must increase the value proposition that we offer our clients. Banks have historically charged customers for service. We want to put ourselves in the customers' shoes and offer them the service that we as individuals would want to experience.

We propose to combine our checking account, savings account, credit card, overdraft line and debit card with both telephone and Internet access, into one product. It will be under the HyperActive brand name. Advantages to the customer are that (1) there will be no need to manage savings and checking balances, (2) high-cost credit card balances can be transferred to a lower-cost overdraft line, and (3) clients will be able to access the account through their debit card and the Internet, in addition to traditional forms of access. Our rewards program will still be in place, though somewhat changed in format to take into account the total profitability of the customer to us.

Aldo Moretti, Chairperson: Won't this cost us a lot of money?

Steve: Our market research suggest that this combination is particularly attractive to the 40 percent of the customer base that we think is particularly at risk. We are going to gamble that the higher value proposition and the saving in time to the customer will cause us to gain accounts.

Besides, if you think about the impact of the competition we are looking at, our primary goal is retention of customers. If we don't offer the best value proposition, we are toast. But you know, there is another advantage to this approach and that's sales cost. If we sell this bundle of four products we have one sales cost versus our normal four sales costs for four products. Our projections suggest that reduced profitability is more than compensated for by our lower sales costs.

John Ho, Dean of the local business school: Why won't the competitors match this?

Steve: Well, we think that our big advantage is that we have been building, our infrastructure to permit us to change our transaction processing very quickly. We think that we have a six-month-faster implementation cycle than our competitors. We have also test-marketed this idea on a small number of customers—around 10,000—at one branch.

John: What were the results?

Steve: Obviously, we didn't have the new competitor, but average assets increased by 40 percent, so even with the loss of free checking assets and a lower rate on VISA loans, our profitability was up 12 percent. We're encouraged by the results because this is the worst case—we didn't see the sales cost reduction that we would expect in the longer term if we are attracting new customers.

John: And customer satisfaction?

Steve: We've only had two surveys, but up 35 percent.

John: Okay, so it sounds like we have a strategy that could work. What about implementation. There are a lot things to coordinate here.

Steve: Well, on that front, we have a novel proposal. If you read the Tom Clancy novels, you may have read about military war gaming at the National Training Center in California. It's also been written up in *Fast Company,* the digital age's strategic management magazine.

Our consultants who put in the strategic business planning system and our customer information warehouse have suggested the idea of *war gaming* to practice the implementation of the strategy to make sure we get it right. They have some software that they can add to our planning system so that we can war-game the implementation of these changes to minimize mistakes and time to market. They can put up a system in about one month. We'll take two weeks to plan and rehearse. We think that we can get this to market in about three to four months.

We've tried out some of this approach on a smaller scale over the past three years, so I feel confident that it will help us get HyperActive to market before our competitors can make major inroads.

Aldo: Any question or comments? It sounds like a good plan. What is the consensus of the board? . . . Okay, the ayes have it. Steve, it looks like you've got a mandate to "simulate and innovate," if I may coin a phrase. Go to it. We'd better be quick or we will be dead.

Success in a company is always transitory. But our fictional Bank of Glen Burnie seems to have built its human and technology capabilities so that its information technology provides a platform from which it can compete successfully. It has achieved about as successful a position as a company can achieve in a world of rapid change, by taking into account the Plan–Do–Improve approach and by dealing with the leadership, policy, infrastructure and project management issues that all organizations must address. It can now respond more quickly to changes. It has the tools in place to plan and anticipate. More competition and faster product innovation mean that companies that cannot decide and implement quickly will die; only the quick will survive. But even being a fast company won't work unless the infrastructure is in place from which improvement can be rolled out quickly.

Training and growing the tiger take time. Learning how to ride the tiger is a skill that can't be rushed. Knowing where to go helps if you have a map. Avoiding being consumed by the tiger takes skill. Once you have these capabilities you can dodge and weave and adjust your plan. When you reach your destination long before your competitors, it's a triumph. Ride on!

QUESTIONS FOR THE READER

Reading a book is an important activity. But it is much more effective if you articulate the lessons learned. Take the time to put down on paper what worked for the bank. It will help you think through what will work in your organization.

Go back to your answers from Chapter 1. How did you do? What did you anticipate? What did you not anticipate? More important, what did the Bank of Glen Burnie do right?

1. What leadership did the senior management of the Bank of Glen Burnie provide?
2. What was the nature of the planning process that the bank used?
3. Who was involved in the planning process? Initially? Eventually?
4. Who were the key stakeholders in the decisions made by the bank?
5. How successful was the bank in its project management?
6. What was the relationship between infrastructure investment and particular business projects?
7. What policies were developed by the bank?
8. How did the policies get implemented?
9. What mistakes did the bank make?
10. What project management approach did the bank use?
11. What improvements did the bank focus on?
12. How did the bank select projects? What seemed to be important criteria?
13. Could this transformation have occurred in other ways?

Your Own Next Steps

You may now be wondering how you can communicate these issues to the rest of your organization. In the back of the book, you will find a diagnostic questionnaire for taking a look at your own organization and its approach to information management. You will also find information on how to keep up-to-date on the kind of information we have addressed in *Riding the Tiger*. You may also want to visit one of our web sites: **www.alacrity.com** or **www.tigerpearls.com**.

APPENDIX I

DIAGNOSTIC QUESTIONNAIRE

100 Questions for diagnosing your information management effectiveness and policies

This general set of diagnostic questions will help you understand how well your organization exploits information management successfully. This questionnaire may not reflect your view, but it is an *objective* one. It is not influenced by our knowledge of your organization, so there is no attempt to slant the questions to make someone look good or bad. You may find it useful to have several different people rate your organization, including suppliers.

Before you fill out these 100 questions yourself, we suggest you predict
what your assessment will be with the following 20 factors:

ID#	Section Name	Very Bad	Bad	Average	Good	Very Good
1.	How demanding is your industry? (Very demanding =1)	1	2	3	4	5
2.	How good is your strategy?	1	2	3	4	5
3.	How strong is your leadership?	1	2	3	4	5
4.	How good is your planning process?	1	2	3	4	5
5.	Rate your infrastructure.	1	2	3	4	5
6.	Rate your policies.	1	2	3	4	5
7.	Rate your project philosophy.	1	2	3	4	5
8.	Rate your project guidelines.	1	2	3	4	5
9.	Rate your project management.	1	2	3	4	5
10.	Rate your organization's pursuit of strategic improvement.	1	2	3	4	5
11.	Rate your organization's ability to implement policy change and policy improvements.	1	2	3	4	5
12.	Rate your organization's ability to improve its processes.	1	2	3	4	5
13.	Rate the quality of your organization's people.	1	2	3	4	5
14.	Rate your organization's allocation of its resources to various activities.	1	2	3	4	5

ID#	Section Name	Very Bad	Bad	Average	Good	Very Good
15.	Rate your organization's success in creating value for customers.	1	2	3	4	5
16.	Rate the strength of your organization's operations.	1	2	3	4	5
17.	Rate your organization's ability to deal with crises and implement changes.	1	2	3	4	5
18.	Is your organization a good consulting client for the information systems area?	1	2	3	4	5
19.	How good are the capabilities of your information systems area?	1	2	3	4	5
20.	Is your organization receiving excellent value from its information systems area?	1	2	3	4	5
	Total Score					

Scoring the Next Section

We suggest that you answer the next 100 questions with a ✓ or "yes" and not bother writing anything if the answer is no. Count the number of checkmarks to find the score. There are 20 sections of five questions each, so the total possible score is 100.

For more information, contact Alacrity Inc. at 1-416-362-5099.

SECTION 1: OUR INDUSTRY

ID#	Question	Answer Yes or No
1.	Is the rate of change in our industry pretty slow?	
2.	Are we facing an increasing number of competitors?	
3.	Are new technologies not important to the way our company creates value?	
4.	Is our market protected from new competitors by high barriers to entry?	
5.	Are there large or small competitors or potential competitors taking advantage of information technology more effectively than we are?	
	Score	

SECTION 2: OUR STRATEGY

ID#	Question	Answer Yes or No
1.	Do we have a clearly articulated mission that our employees understand?	
2.	Have we defined what a position of success would look like for us as an organization and communicated that information to our employees?	
3.	Have we identified the key values and critical success factors in our business and ensured that the entire organization understands these issues?	
4.	Are our proprietary capabilities unaffected by the wider availability of information technology?	
5.	Are we trying to involve every member of our organization in making our business a success?	
	Score	

SECTION 3: LEADERSHIP

ID#	Question	Answer Yes or No
1.	Are the business managers in our business seen as involved, enthusiastic contributors to the organization?	
2.	Does the CEO have a strategic vision and know how IT contributes to strategy?	
3.	Has the organization visibly demonstrated to employees that it cares about their careers and skills?	
4.	Does the organization hold employees accountable and delegate responsibility and authority as much as possible?	
5.	Does the CEO pay attention to how IT is implemented?	
	Score	

SECTION 4: PLANNING PROCESS

ID#	Question	Answer Yes or No
1.	Do we have a planning process that is disciplined and that the organization listens to?	
2.	Is IT an integrated part of planning?	
3.	Do we try to plan the growth of skills and capabilities?	
4.	Can we make decisions faster that we could three years ago?	
5.	Does IT enable us to respond to changes in the environment?	
	Score	

SECTION 5: INFRASTRUCTURE

ID#	Question	Answer Yes or No
1.	Does our organization distinguish between *infrastructure development and innovation,* and *projects that support particular business initiatives,* in its evaluation process?	
2.	Does senior management pay attention to information management issues?	
3.	Is management prepared to be selective in order to ensure successful infrastructure deployment?	
4.	Do we permit experimentation and encourage a learning organization?	
5.	Have we established useful policies for infrastructure and empowered our business units?	
	Score	

SECTION 6: POLICIES

ID#	Question	Answer Yes or No
1.	Have we articulated the importance of good information management?	
2.	Have we clearly articulated the division of roles between the information systems area and the line units?	
3.	Have we developed hardware and software guidlines to guide decisions on projects?	
4.	Have we developed emergency policies?	
5.	Have we improved the quality of our data and the ease of its use?	
	Score	

SECTION 7: PROJECT PHILOSOPHY

ID#	Question	Answer Yes or No
1.	Have we made clear our policies on the standards for and use of purchased packaged software?	
2.	Have we developed process and criteria for selecting projects?	
3.	Do our business units and departments have good relationships with the information systems department?	
4.	Do we have a good project tracking and management process?	
5.	Do we have goals for project quality?	
	Score	

SECTION 8: PROJECT GUIDELINES

ID#	Question	Answer Yes or No
1.	Are our end-users involved in project teams?	
2.	Does the information systems area see managers as clients to be served?	
3.	Do we insist on specification and scoping discipline?	
4.	Are the best practices documented and identified throughout our organization?	
5.	Are improvement goals and benefits documented?	
	Score	

SECTION 9: PROJECT MANAGEMENT

ID#	Question	Answer Yes or No
1.	Are projects being developed on time and on budget? Is our performance improving?	
2.	Are we pursuing development strategies that will reduce risk?	
3.	Do our projects have checkpoints and milestones?	
4.	Are we giving our projects enough resources so that their quality is high?	
5.	Do we perform postaudits of project performance?	
	Score	

SECTION 10: STRATEGIC IMPROVEMENT

ID#	Question	Answer Yes or No
1.	Does our whole organization see information management as a key competitive weapon?	
2.	Are our business managers actively considering the role of information management as we develop strategies and tactics?	
3.	Are we selecting projects based on our organization's strategic initiatives?	
4.	Are we measuring our activities so that we can review and encourage improvements in information management and business activities?	
5.	Are our people's capabilities being improved by the software we're putting in place?	
	Score	

SECTION 11: POLICY CHANGE AND IMPROVEMENT

ID#	Question	Answer Yes or No
1.	Does our organization constantly seek to improve its information management?	
2.	Do we constantly seek to improve our business performance?	
3.	Are we prepared to back experimental projects?	
4.	Do we consciously avoid punishing any of our people for failed experimental projects?	
5.	Do we involve a wide range of people in task forces and projects to maximize the quality of our input and implementation?	
	Score	

SECTION 12: IMPROVING PROCESSES

ID#	Question	Answer Yes or No
1.	Does our organization discourage waste (time, resources)?	
2.	Is the quality of information available to employees exceptionally good?	
3.	Is our organization prepared to empower our front-line staff?	
4.	Do processes in our organization have clear owners who act with authority to improve them?	
5.	Do we devote enough resources to those who must improve our processes?	
	Score	

SECTION 13: OUR PEOPLE

ID#	Question	Answer Yes or No
1.	Do we find it easy to attract excellent information systems staff?	
2.	Do we have a high turnover of information systems staff?	
3.	Do most of our people feel comfortable with computers or have the interest to learn more about them?	
4.	Are our business managers knowledgeable about information management?	
5.	Are our key information systems staff knowledgeable about our business (nonsystems issues)?	
	Score	

SECTION 14: ALLOCATING RESOURCES

ID#	Question	Answer Yes or No
1.	Do we make sure that our strategies state what we will and will not do?	
2.	Are we selective in our strategies because we recognize that we cannot do everything?	
3.	Does our whole organization understand which of our customers are the most profitable?	
4.	Do we understand where leverage exists in the organization?	
5.	Do we anticipate the consequences of our decisions well?	
	Score	

SECTION 15: CREATING VALUE

ID#	Question	Answer Yes or No
1.	Do we focus on customer satisfaction by measuring the satisfaction of our current and prospective customers?	
2.	Do we systematically track and understand the needs of our customers?	
3.	Do we try to imitate or improve upon our customers' best products and services?	
4.	Do we try to systematically understand and improve our own processes so we can improve the value our customer receives?	
5.	Do we try to delight our customers?	
	Score	

SECTION 16: OPERATIONS

ID#	Question	Answer Yes or No
1.	Does procurement run smoothly and effectively relative to best practices in the area?	
2.	Are operations well run and monitored with good data?	
3.	Does our organization manage its relationships with suppliers well?	
4.	Do we manage our relationships with wholesalers, retailers and customers well?	
5.	Can we call up information about business performance easily?	
	Score	

SECTION 17: MANAGING CRISES AND CHANGE

ID#	Question	Answer Yes or No
1.	Does management have enough time to think about our organization's future?	
2.	Do we deal well with the emotional side of organizational change?	
3.	Is change considered the norm in our organization?	
4.	Are both employees and managers comfortable dealing with change?	
5.	Is decision making both well informed and rapid within our organization?	
	Score	

SECTION 18: BEING A GOOD CLIENT

ID#	Question	Answer Yes or No
1.	Are we open and honest with our internal information systems areas?	
2.	Is our organization skilled in dealing with our external suppliers?	
3.	Have we explicitly decided which information activities are key to the future of our business?	
4.	Do we motivate rather than punish the people who work on a project?	
5.	Are we persistent and disciplined in our attempts to make our projects work?	
	Score	

SECTION 19: INFORMATION SYSTEMS CAPABILITY

ID#	Question	Answer Yes or No
1.	Do we have an information systems department that can assess software, hardware and networks and provide programming services?	
2.	Do we follow the process of Plan–Do–Improve?	
3.	Are we good at selecting, purchasing and installing application packages and planning, and dealing with the resulting impact of them on the whole organization?	
4.	Are we good at developing new software?	
5.	Do we have good project management?	
	Score	

SECTION 20: INFORMATION SYSTEMS VALUE

ID#	Question	Answer Yes or No
1.	Do we have better information management systems than our competitors do?	
2.	Do we spend less than 50 percent of our information systems budget on maintaining our existing software?	
3.	Does our IT improve the capabilities of the organization?	
4.	Do our IT infrastructure and projects help meet our business goals?	
5.	Are our systems generally portable and easily upgradable so that we do not depend upon one supplier?	
	Score	

SUMMARY PROFILE

Riding the Tiger Information Management Assessment

Sections	Section Name	Number of Yes Answers	Predicted Score	Difference: Yes minus Predicted
1	Our Industry			
2	Our Strategy			
3	Leadership			
4	Planning Process			
5	Infrastructure			
6	Policies			
7	Project Philosophy			
8	Project Guidelines			
9	Project Management			
10	Strategic Improvement			
11	Policy Change and Policy Improvement			
12	Improving Processes			
13	Our People			
14	Allocating Resources			
15	Creating Value			
16	Operations			
17	Managing Crises and Change			
18	Being a Good Client			
19	Information Systems Capability			
20	Information Systems Value			
Total score out of 100	Totals			*

* For the difference between the Yes column and the Predicted column, add up the absolute numbers (ignore the sign of the difference). In other words, add up all the differences as if they were positive.

RIDING THE TIGER BENCHMARKING REQUEST

Date of assessment: YEAR MONTH DAY	
Name of contact:	
Title:	
Organization:	
Address 1:	
Address 2:	
State/Province:	
Country:	
ZIP/Postal Code	
Phone and fax:	
E-mail:	
Total assets for the most recently reported full fiscal year:	
Revenues for the most recently reported full fiscal year:	
Currency revenues reported in:	
Organization profits:	
Organization net worth:	
Number of full-time employees:	
Number of part-time employees:	
Most recent full financial year end as of:	
Industry SIC code:	
Description of business:	

You may compare your responses against those of other organizations by sending us a copy of your answers. We will mail you a comparison against other organizations for a nominal fee. Individual names of organizations will be kept confidential Please contact us for details.

Alacrity Inc.
50 Wellington Street East, Suite 301, Toronto, ON, Canada M5E 1C8
Phone: 1-416-362-5099
Fax: 1-416-362-0133
E-mail: alacrity@alacrity.com

APPENDIX II

HOW ONE LARGE ORGANIZATION EVALUATES ITS PROJECTS

The Bank of Nova Scotia is one of Canada's largest banks. The following rating scheme is what it uses for evaluating several hundred projects a year. We are grateful to Tom Russell, Vice-President, Planning, Administration and Project Management, for giving us permission to publish the Bank of Nova Scotia's copyrighted approach, which in Tom's own words is a "work in progress." Tom is obviously a fervent believer in Plan–Do–Improve. We have slightly edited the text and format to simplify presentation to readers.

Project Name: _____

Plan ID #   _____

Approved by   _____

                              Area Executive Vice-President

SECTION 1: BUSINESS FACTORS
(to be completed by the user department)

Business Need (select one category)
- Score 10 points for a mandatory project
- Score 4 points for a strategic project
- Score 3 points for a vital/critical project
- Score 2 points for a project that is important to do

Return on Investment (pick one from each of the two set of choices)
- Score 2 points for greater than 30 percent ROI
- Score 1 point from 20 to 30 percent
- Score 0 for less than 20 percent

and
- Score 3 points for greater than $1,000,000
- Score 2 points for returns from $500,000 to $1,000,000
- Score 1 point for less than $500,000 of return

Timing
- Score 2 points for projects to be completed within the next 6 months
- Score 1 point for projects within the next 7 to 12 months
- Score 0 for projects longer than 12 months

Summary of Business Factors and Weighting

1	2	3	4
Category	Points	Weighting	Weighted Score
			4 = 3 X 2
Business Need		50%	
Return on Investment		30%	
Timing		20%	
Total Business Factors	N/A	N/A	

SECTION 2: PROBABILITY OF SUCCESS FACTORS

(to be completed by the user department in consultation with the development group)

Problem Definition (select one category)
- Very good understanding – score 4 points
- Good understanding – score 3 points
- Fair understanding – score 2 points
- Vague understanding – score 1 point
- No understanding – score no points

Problem Resolution (select one category)
- Very good understanding – score 4 points
- Good understanding – score 3 points
- Fair understanding – score 2 points
- Vague understanding – score 1 point
- No understanding – score no points

User Identification and Commitment (select one category)
- Identified and committed – score 4 points
- Identified and interested – score 3 points
- Identified and uninvolved – score 2 points
- Unavailable and interested – score 1 point
- Unavailable and uninterested – score 0 points

Note that the next two sections, Size/Workdays and Functional Complexity, produce negative points. In other words, the larger and more complex the project, the more difficult it is likely to be. For organizations smaller than a major bank, the size criteria should be altered to reflect the capabilities of the organization.

Size/Workdays (select one category)
- 5,001 plus workdays – score negative 4 points
- 1,001 to 5,000 workdays – score negative 3 points
- 501 to 1,000 workdays – score negative 2 points
- 251 to 500 workdays – score negative 1 point
- 0 to 250 workdays – score 0 points.

Functional Complexity (select one category)
- Bank-wide span and high complexity – score negative 4 points
- Multidivisional and high complexity – score negative 3 points
- Multidivisional and medium complexity – score negative 2 points
- Unidivisional and medium complexity – score negative 1 point
- Unidivisional and low complexity – score 0 points

Summary of Probability of Success Factors

1	2	3	4
Category	Points	Weighting	Weighted Score 4 = 3 X 2
Problem Definition		40%	
Problem Resolution		40%	
User Identification and Commitment		20%	
Size/Number of Workdays (*note: points are negative for this category*)		20%	
Functional Complexity (*note: points are negative for this category*)		20%	
Total Success Factor Score	N/A	N/A	

Mapping a Portfolio of Projects

The Bank of Nova Scotia uses the following grid to map out the project candidates and to present information about the mix of projects that the organization is tackling:

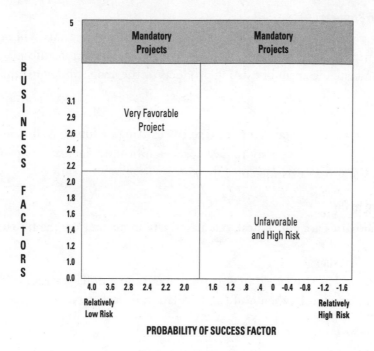

PROBABILITY OF SUCCESS FACTOR

Size of project commitment can be introduced as a third dimension. Circles can be used to represent projects, with the diameter of the circle showing the dollar size of the project commitment in terms of up-front dollars or total life cycle dollars. The center of the circle indicates the two scores—the Probability of Success and the Business Factor scores.

EXPLANATION OF BANK OF NOVA SCOTIA EVALUATION APPROACH

SECTION 1: BUSINESS FACTORS

Business Need

Mandatory projects

These are projects that must be done to comply with government legislation or key relationships. In the case of the Bank of Nova Scotia, this could include the Bank of Canada as a regulator, legislation passed under the Bank Act or other changes required by key suppliers such as Visa International, Interac (the automated teller network), SWIFT (funds transfer), etc.

Strategic Projects

These activities must not be delayed; otherwise, adverse results will occur in the area of new products offerings, competitive position, the maintenance and enhancement of existing products or the image of the institution.

Vital/Critical Projects

These activities are vital and critical to the existing or future well-being of the organization. They may reduce costs significantly, increase or protect revenues, improve existing controls.

Important to Do

These activities are not critical, but are clearly important for the future.

Return on Investment

This section has two categories—a percentage and a dollar category. If the project is mandatory, then no ROI calculation is necessary.

Timing

The timing of the project is the period of time required to complete the project.

SECTION 2: PROBABILITY OF SUCCESS FACTORS

These factors should be scored based upon the information systems department's understanding of the business problem, the technology for resolving the business problem, their assessment of the client's commitment and involvement, its estimate of the project size and complexity.

TOTAL SCORING

After the Total Business Factors and Probability of Success Factors have been calculated, all projects will be ranked as
- High Priority
- Medium Priority
- Low Priority, or
- Questionable as Presented

Mandatory projects automatically receive the High Priority Ranking.

GLOSSARY OF KEY INFORMATION AND TECHNOLOGY JARGON

Here are some examples of jargon, acronyms and buzzwords that consultants and IS departments may lob at you.

Active matrix — The best kind of color screens on a notebook, particularly appropriate for high visual demands, where you want a wider angle or view. The major alternative is known as dual scan, or DSTN.

AIX — IBM's version of UNIX.

Alpha test — An in-house test of a piece of software, before it is tested with clients or end-users.

API — Application Programming Interface. A way of interacting with a program designed to enable another developer to write applications that can communicate with a specific program.

Architecture — A system's framework.

ATM — A network protocol particularly appropriate for video and traffic that mixes video, audio and data.

Bandwidth — The width of the information highway—the amount of information a network can carry. Local area networks typically run at 10 megabits or 10 million bits per second, but will be moving to 100 megabits per second in the future. Think of it as the number of lanes in the information highway.

Baud — Bits per second transmitted by a modem. Just to confuse you, modem makers talk about their ability to send bits, yet programs and data are measured in bytes, which are eight time bigger. As a result, a 28.8 kilobaud modem can send only one-eighth of the number of bytes, or around 4 kilobytes per second.

Beta test — A software test with customers. The industry joke is that Version 1.0 is typically a beta test.

Bit — A one or a zero. Eight bits make a byte.

Bug — Often known as design defect. Something that doesn't work in the software.

Bus — The connection in a computer (its spine) over which the components of the computer talk to each other—the hard drive to the processor, the CD-ROM to the floppy.

Byte — A collection of eight bits. Also, a good computer magazine for the more technically inclined.

C — A popular programming language developed at Bell Labs.

C++ — An object-oriented version of C++, popular with commercial software developers.

Cache — A typically fast memory into which data are loaded so they can be found quickly. Operating systems often set aside a piece of RAM and preload data off the hard disk, guessing what you will want next. This speeds up the machine's operation.

CAD — Computer Aided Design. Think of it as a high-end drawing tool for engineers. It is usually linked to other software to save having to do things by hand.

CASE — Computer Aided Software Engineering. Software that is used to speed up the system's development process.

CBT — Computer Based Training.

CD-ROM — The computer equivalent of the CD, generally Read Only, though writable CD-ROMs are appearing. Basically the same technology as Magneto Optical Drives, which you can rewrite.

CISC — Complex Instruction Set Computing. A computer chip with a big vocabulary of instructions. Because it is a more complex type of microprocessor, it is harder to design. The alternative design philosophy is RISC (Reduced Instruction Set Computing). RISC allows for simpler and faster chips. Ironically, Intel, which dominates the microprocessor business, uses CISC. However, it will move toward RISC in the future in a joint venture with Hewlett-Packard.

CIT — Computer Integrated Telephony. Controlling your phone system with your computer.

Client-server — An application for which the client computer and the server computer are both intelligent, rather than traditional dumb terminals talking to a mini or mainframe.

Clustering — Combining the computing power of several computers or servers to create a more powerful overall computer. Because designing better microprocessors is very expensive, it is far cheaper to use several processors than to design new microprocessor factories. The future is parallel computing.

Coaxial cable — Used for local area networks or for cable transmission , generally at a speed of 10 megabits per second.

COBOL — A commonly used language in the 1960s. There are still millions of line of COBOL code around, but it is not a language of choice for modern programming.

CORBA — Common Object Request Broker Architecture. A server designed to allow objects in one programming language to communicate with objects in other programming languages, a standard by the Object Management Group. This is an attempt to allow programmers to build programs in small pieces developed in one computer language, such as C++, to be able to take advantage of and use pieces developed in other programming languages, say, SmallTalk.

CTI — Computer Telephony Integration (also known as CIT). Allowing computers to manipulate data and telephone activities, typically used in call centers.

Database, flat file — A simple table for storing data, like a spreadsheet, to sort and manipulate them.

Database, hierarchical — A database organized by hierarchy.

Database, object — A database in which all data are stored as an object.

Database, relational — A database in which data are stored in related tables for efficiency.

Desktop — What you see on your computer screen. The "desk" usually contains some images or icons representing programs and data. You store your data in folders or directories, as you would in a filing cabinet.

DLL — Dynamic Linked Library. A piece of programming packaged and accessed by applications using the functions as in a library. For example, the spelling checker in a suite of programs might be shared by all the software applications.

DOS — Microsoft's Disk Operating System. The software that runs the computer and permits programs to run on it. The most popular operating systems today are the Windows family of operating systems, Macintosh, OS/2 and UNIX on personal computers and workstations.

DSS — Decision Support System. Software for accessing information through one or more databases. Sometimes describes specific software for ranking and selecting decisions.

Dual scan — A pretty good passive matrix screen for a notebook. Typically not quite as fast or as crisp or with as good an angle of view as an active matrix screen.

DVD — A 1996 standard that increases the capacity of CD-ROMs to permit them to handle movies.

EDI — Electronic Data Interchange. An approach that speeds up the transfer of information.

EIS — Executive Information System. Generally icon-driven, easy-to-use software for requesting information from various information sources, most commonly databases.

EISA bus — A bus architecture most commonly used in Intel computers.

E-mail — The ability to send documents across your local area network, wide area network or the Internet.

Ethernet — The most popular standard for local area networks, first developed by Xerox and DEC.

Expert system — Software that manipulates knowledge about a narrow area of expertise—a domain—or provides a means for looking at a problem. Now more fashionably referred to as knowledge-based software.

Floppy drive — The removable 3.5-inch or 5.25-inch disk on which you can store data. Confusingly, the 3.5-inch floppy, the one that fits in your shirt pocket, is quite rigid.

4GL — Fourth Generation Language, a productivity tool from the 1970s for creating screens and database interactions typically on a terminal now generally replaced by more productive and capable tools.

Frame relay — An emerging standard for creating a virtual network. A virtual network gives you the illusion of having a private network, which you actually share with other businesses across the telephone company wires. With frame relay you are guaranteed a minimum capacity, but you can grab more if nobody is using it in your telecommunications "pipe" at the same time.

Hacker — Historically, a term of respect for a sophisticated computer user. It now tends to refer to unethical programmers who create viruses and break into other people's systems.

Hard drive — The place inside the computer where your data are stored.

Hardware — The heavy physical part of the computer, as opposed to its software, the instructions that run computers.

HP-UX — Hewlett Packard's version of UNIX.

Hypertext — Software that works like a file card. The unique idea was that there should be "hot buttons" on each card to allow you to jump around to related material as you wished. Today, this idea is taken for granted. Also, these are the basic ideas behind the World Wide Web, which takes the idea one step further. It allows the connections between these windows of material on other machines connected by one network.

IDE — The most common standard for controlling hard drives.

Informate — To provide information about an automated process.

Inheritance — The concept of a piece of software inheriting the characteristics of a parent piece of software so that programming can be minimized; characteristic of object-oriented programming languages such as C++ and Smalltalk.

Intel 8086 — Twice as fast as the original IBM PC, used by the competition such as Compaq and Olivetti.

Intel 8088 — The chip behind the original IBM PC.

Intel 80286 — The chip IBM used for upping the ante, the second generation used in the IBM AT.

Intel 80386 — The chip Compaq used to outperform IBM, the third generation.

Intel 80486 — The most common chip in the early 1990s, the fourth generation.

Intel Pentium — The state of the art in mid 1995, the fifth generation.

Intel Pentium Pro — Specialized chip for workstations, Intel's entry into the workstation market, the sixth generation.

Internet — A collection of linked networks, first funded by the military as ARPANET and now the data equivalent of the telephone system.

Internet computer — A terminal for accessing the Internet.

Intranet — An internal web server for delivering pages of information within an organization. An internal equivalent of the World Wide Web.

IS — Abbreviation for information systems.

ISA bus — The most common but obsolete bus on Intel computers, now generally replaced by the PCI bus.

ISDN — A digital networking standard consisting of two 64-kilobit channels and one 16-kilobit channel, typically used for linking two LANs or for video conferencing.

IT — Information technology.

Knowledge-based system — A more fashionable term for expert system.

LAN — Local area network, typically using the Ethernet protocol.

LCD Panel — Projection display device connected to a computer to display graphics generated on the computer.

Legacy system — Not to be confused with the car. A legacy system is generally thought to be an older technology computer such as a mini or mainframe. However, the concept is often used to describe older software systems that are difficult and expensive to maintain.

Life cycle costs — The total cost of owning a piece of information technology over its life, the most important cost issue for evaluation purposes.

Lotus Notes — The forerunner of the Intranet, a proprietary information server for handling and replicating documents that were not well handled by traditional databases.

Macintosh — The first really friendly computer, whose concepts were "stolen" from Xerox PARC (Palo Alto Research Center), generally more popular with home users and niche markets such as desktop publishing. Its predecessor was the LISA.

Macro — A series of keystrokes and commands that have been recorded and assigned a name or key combination.

Magneto-optical drive — Similar to a CD-ROM, but with more capacity and offering the ability to write once and read many times (WORM) or rewriteable.

Mainframe — A large computer, a segment dominated by IBM, with modest competition from Hitachi and Fujitsu/Amdahl.

Megahertz — The speed measure used for processors, meaning millions of times per second.

Microprocessor — A computer on a chip, the heart of the computer, by market share typically an Intel microprocessor (8086, 8088, 80286, 80386, 80486, Pentium, Pentium Pro). Macintosh uses chips from Motorola or an IBM/Motorola/Apple combination, and workstation vendors often have their own proprietary chips (DEC Alpha, Sun Sparc or Ultrasparc, etc.).

Middleware — Software that specializes in grabbing data from different data sources.

Minicomputer — The hottest thing in computers in the 1960s and 1970s, now considered to be expensive relative to client-server applications using workstations.

Minitower — A computer stood up on its end in a smaller case than a full tower.

MIS — Management information systems.

Modem — The device used for sending e-mail or dialing into another network, often combined with a fax and called a fax-modem.

MPEG — A current standard for video on computers.

Multimedia — Sound and video along with your computer, normally requires a fast machine, good speakers and a fast CD-ROM.

Mouse — A device first invented by Xerox at PARC for pointing at buttons and areas of your screen. Variants on the mouse include the trackball, the Glidepad™ and the IBM Track Point pointing device. We are old-fashioned and like mice best, though the Glidepad is not a bad backup device on a notebook computer.

MS-DOS — Microsoft's Disk Operating System for personal computers.

Multidimensional spreadsheet — A spreadsheet that allows you to rotate and pivot different views of your data.

Notebook — Notebook computers are not surprisingly about the size of a notebook and weigh about six to eight pounds. Not to be confused with the four- to five-pound subnotebook category.

Object oriented — A Lego blocks approach to developing software that promises to dramatically speed up software development. Its advantage is that you can replace a piece without crashing the entire software. In addition, if well designed, the software should be both less expensive to modify and more robust.

ODBMS — Object database management system such as Gemstone or POET.

OLAP — On-line analytical processing; an abbreviation used to describe multidimensional software products that are a specialized type of database, similar to multidimensional spreadsheets. Essentially, this means you can rotate and pivot your spreadsheet to look at it from various points of view. If you have a three-dimensional spreadsheet with the three dimensions being Time, Products and Income Statement, you would be able to easily rotate the spreadsheet to show a view of the data that used two out of three of the dimensions—in other words different slices of a cube.

OLE — Object linking and embedding; a Microsoft standard for embedding, for example, an Excel spreadsheet in your word-processing document that allows you to work on the spreadsheet while in the document.

Operating system — The traffic cop in the computer that runs the computer and allocates resources to the various tasks.

OS/2 — IBM's competitive product to Microsoft Windows NT.

Parallel port — Generally used for hooking up your printer.

Parallel processing — Hooking up lots of computers in parallel, or several processors in a multiprocessor computer to get more speed. Operating systems such as Windows NT and various versions of UNIX are increasingly available on hardware with multiple processors.

Pascal — A popular programming language for small computers.

Passive matrix — An older color screen for notebooks, generally rather dim and hard to see.

PBX — Private branch exchange, or large telephone system.

PC-Card — The new name for the PCMCIA card because no one could remember PCMCIA as an acronym.

PCI bus — The current standard in buses

PCMCIA card — The credit-card-sized devices, typically in notebooks, that allow a user to stick in a network or modem capability.

Pentium — Intel's brand name for its fifth and sixth generations of microprocessors.

Pentium Pro — The sixth generation of Intel microprocessor.

Personal computer — Originally a brand name for an IBM PC; now a generic term for a small computer used by an individual.

Programming language — The instructions used for creating a program, e.g., Basic, Pascal, C, C++, SmallTalk.

Prototyping — A development strategy for difficult-to-describe applications, where a prototype is built to allow users to evaluate the functionality of the software. Several iterations lead to a better system.

RAID — Redundant array of inexpensive disks. An inexpensive way of creating redundancy for computers. If one drive fails, another kicks in. Data are layered across various hard drives. There are six common ways of laying out your data on RAID drives, referred to as RAID 0 through RAID 5.

RAM — Random Access Memory. The part of the computer where programs get run. The name is confusing because it implies data are "memorized." Many people confuse RAM with the hard disk, where information is stored or memorized.

RDBMS — Relational database management system.

Real Soon Now — The release date of late software.

RISC processor — Reduced instruction set computing processor. An approach to simplifying microprocessor design so that processors can run faster. Typically used in workstations. Likely in the future to be used in successors to the Pentium.

ROM — Read Only Memory. This is a type of memory in which programs can be permanently stored. In PCs, the ROM tends to store proprietary information about the hardware and is rarely touched by users.

SCSI — Small Computer Serial Interface, a faster way of talking to your hard disk than the standard IDE on a personal computer. SCSI is faster than IDE and is a more elegant design that permits the daisy chaining or linking up in serial of six devices off the same SCSI controller. You could, for example, run your floppy drive, hard drive, tape backup and CD-ROM off the same SCSI controller. It would be a much more complex process with a traditional PC.

Serial port — Normally, what you connect a modem or mouse to. However, just to confuse everything, there is also a PS/2 (an IBM standard) port on many machines to which the keyboard and/or the mouse may be connected.

Server — A computer that provides a service to other client computers, e.g., file service, printing service, database service, faxing and e-mail service, etc. Servers are typically used for servicing departmental computing requirements. Increasingly, servers are powerful enough to substitute for minis and mainframes, particularly when there are several servers on a network. Servers are increasingly placed between the PCs and the legacy or older systems as the connection between the two.

Shelfware — Software that after being bought, sits on the shelf. Generally not a compliment.

Software — The instructions that make the computer do something.

Solaris — Sun Microsystems' version of UNIX.

SmallTalk — A popular object-oriented language that is particularly portable and efficient. It makes custom software almost as inexpensive as packages.

Speed — A critical issue in microprocessor, CD-ROM, hard drive and printer performance.

Spreadsheet — The software that made personal computers a success.

SQL — Standard query language, the current standard in interfaces for relational databases; used, for example, in DB/2, Oracle, Informix, Sybase and MS NT Advanced Server.

Supercomputer — A high-powered computer for complex calculations.

Surfing the net — Exploring sites on the Internet, typically visiting servers on the World Wide Web.

Switching costs — The cost of switching from one vendor to another, e.g., software conversion costs, training costs, mistakes, replacement of ancillary equipment, etc.

TCP/IP — A communications protocol that is used on UNIX networks for linking computers and is also the basis for the Internet. Competes with IPX from Novell, which historically dominated the market for local area networks.

Terminal — A computer screen whose intelligence sits on a shared computer, now being marketed under the name Internet Computer.

Tower — A personal computer on its side, sitting on the floor.

Twisted pair (UTP or unshielded twisted pair) — Wiring that is like two telephone cords that is used for LANs operating at 20 megabits per second.

UNIX — The generic operating system, typically used for servers and engineering workstations, developed at Bell Labs.

Usability testing — Testing to see how people actually use their software.

Vaporware — Nonexistent but announced software.

Version 1 — The version of software that should be avoided.

Video — As in video card, video driver, video display, full motion video.

Video conferencing — Voice plus small, slow pictures on your computer, but it's getting better.

Video RAM — Special RAM for speeding up the painting of video screens, typically at least two megabytes are required.

Voice recognition — The ability of your computer to take dictation or at least recognize commands.

WAN — Wide area network or network spread over multiple sites, often consisting of several linked local area networks, linked though the telephone company's connections or private phone lines.

Warp — A funky brand name for OS/2.

Window — The concept of a manipulatable square region on your computer screen.

Windows for Workgroups — A peer-to-peer networking and windowing interface for DOS.

Windows 95 — The successor to Windows for Workgroups, with features like Plug and Play and networking.

Windows NT — A more robust version of Windows 95, with both client and server versions.

World Wide Web — the software that made the Internet accessible for mere mortals. A way of delivering hypertext over the Internet. Hypertext is a page of data with hot buttons that allow you to navigate to other pages.

Windows 3.1 — A windowing interface for DOS.

Word processor — Software for emulating a typewriter.

Workstation — A high-end personal computer or a non-Intel-based engineering workstation targeted typically at engineers and computational intensive applications (video, number crunching in money markets, Computer Aided Design, etc.).

BIBLIOGRAPHY

A. INSTITUTIONS

The Outsourcing Institute, 353 Lexington Avenue, New York, NY 10016 (1-800-421–6767).

Project Management Institute, 130 South State Road, Upper Darby, PA 19082.

B. BOOKS AND OTHER WRITTEN SOURCES

Abell, Derek. *Managing with Dual Strategies*. New York: Free Press, 1993.

"Administrative Proceedings and Cease and Desist Proceedings Instituted Against Orlando Joseph Jett." Administrative Proceeding File 3–8919, January 9, 1996.

Bennis, Warren. *On Becoming a Leader*. Reading, MA: Addison-Wesley, 1989.

Bonoma, Thomas. *The Marketing Edge*. New York: Free Press/Macmillan, 1985.

Bresnahan, Jennifer. "Mixed Messages." *CIO Magazine*, May 15, 1996, 72.

Brooks, Frederick P., Jr. *The Mythical Man-Month,*—20th anniv. ed. New York: Addison-Wesley, 1995.

Chandler, Alfred. *The Visible Hand: The Managerial Revolution in American Business.* Cambridge, MA: Harvard University Press, 1979.

Collins, James C., and Jerry I. Porras. *Built to Last*. New York: HarperCollins, 1994.

Drucker, Peter F. *Managing for Results*. 1964. Reprinted in *The Executive in Action*. New York: HarperCollins, 1986.

Emerson, Ralph Waldo. 1893. Reprint, *Natural History of Intellect*, Solar Press, 1995.

"Fraud Charges Taint Career of Bond Trader Jett." CNNfn, New York, January 9, 1996.

Goldman, Stanley J. "Creative Outsourcing," *Datamation*. July 15, 1995, 84.

"A Guide to Outsourcing." *PC Week Executive*. September 18, 1995, E7.

Hamel, Gary, and C.K. Prahalad. *Competing for the Future*. Boston: Harvard Business School Press, 1994.

Kalish, David E. "Jett Taking Stand in First Courtroom Defense Against Bond-Fraud Charges." Associated Press, May 23, 1996.

Kanter, Rosabeth Moss. "The New Managerial Work," *Harvard Business Review* (November 1988–December 1989) 85.

Kelly, Kevin. *Out of Control: The Rise of Neo-Biological Civilization*. Reading, MA: Addison-Wesley, 1994.

Mintzberg, Henry. *Mintzberg on Management*. New York: Free Press/Macmillan, 1989.

Moad, Jeff. "Outsourcing? Go Out on a Limb Together," *Datamation*. Feburary 1, 1995, 58.

Myers, Isabel Briggs, and Mary H. McCauley. *Manual: A Guide to the Development and Use of the Myers-Briggs Type Indicator*. Palo Alto, CA: Consulting Psychologist Press, 1994.

Norman, Donald. *Things That Make Us Smart*. Reading, MA: Addison-Wesley, 1993.

Peters, Tom. *Crazy Times Call for Crazy Orgnizations*. New York: Random House, 1994.

"SEC Seeks Maximum Penalty for Jett." CNNfn, New York, June 20, 1996.

Sellers, Patricia. "Can Wal-Mart Get Back the Magic?" *Fortune*. April 29, 1996: 130–136.

Senge, Peter. *The Fifth Discipline*. New York: Doubleday, 1990.

Skapinker, Michael. "The Management Environment," *Financial Times (UK)*, December 18, 1989.

Strassmann, Paul A. *Information Payoff*. New York: Free Press, 1985.

———. *The Politics of Information Management*. New Canaan, CT: Information Economics Press, 1995.

"A Survey of Retailing." *The Economist*. March 2, 1995, 6.

Trimble, Vince H. *Sam Walton*. New York: Dutton, 1990.

Wal-Mart Stores, Inc. Case Number 9–794–024. Boston: Harvard Business School, 1995–7.

Warr, Alan, Martin Whitefield, Kaye Loveridge, Stephen Chen, Tev Dalgik, and Maggie Gray. *Managing Strategic Information*. United Kingdom: Henley Management College, 1995.

Zuboff, Shoshana. *In the Age of the Smart Machine*. New York: Basic Books, 1988.

INDEX

and capabilities, 55, 184
and information technology, 43–77
and project selection, 64–65
revising, 90–92
setting, 88–89
supporting with technology, 68–71
business systems, 55–57, 69–70
BusinessWeek magazine, 81

C

Canada Post, 35
capabilities
of organizations
assessing, 68, 109–10
improving, 29, 62, 122, 141
of people
aligning with business strategy,
184–85
improving, 153–54, 163–66
understanding, 233
capacity utilization, 52
cash flow, 57–58
CEOs. *See* chief executive officers
Chandler, Alfred, 55–56
change
catalysts for, 167, 234
initiating, 166–68
managing, 4, 108–9, 110–11
senior management and, 166–68
overcoming resistance to, 166–70
changing the business, 90–92
Chaparral Steel, 108–9
chief executive officers (CEOs)
and change management, 109
the "delinquent CEO", 79–88, 104,
113–14
effective
characteristics of, 84–87, 96, 124
influence over projects, 111–12
and information management
common mistakes, 83–84
dodging responsibility for, 79–88
role of, 3, 72, 79–113
and information technology, 124
and policies, 87
See also senior management

A

Abell, Derek, 90
abstracting, 181
accountability
and decentralization, 123–25
activity systems. *See* business systems
alignment, 60–61, 89–92, 184–85
American Airlines, 33
American Express, 33
Angoss's Knowledge Seeker, 164
automation
of bad processes, 3
and inflexibility, 163
versus "informating", 163
of the wrong processes, 72, 90
avoidance by delegation, 81–83

B

Bank of Glen Burnie, 7–13, 39–41, 73–77,
114, 155–59, 186–90, 223–27, 249–55
cast of characters, 9
Bank of Nova Scotia, 273–78
Barnard, Chester, 179
Bassett, Paul, 5
Bennis, Warren, 81
Black, Conrad, 174–75
Boeing, 33
Bonoma, Tom, 56
Brans, Alan, 170–72
Brooks, Fred, 204
Built to Last (Collins and Porras), 60–61
business case, 195–99
business strategies, 47–48
aligning with technology, 3, 88–92,
93–94

chief information officers (CIOs)
  accountability to CEO, 124
  information management planning
    and, 103
  information technology and, 125–27
  in senior management, 81–82
  pressures faced by, 81
CIOs. *See* chief information officers
Citibank, 50
Clarke, Arthur C., 232
Collins, James C., 60–61
Comaford, Christine, 147
Competing for the Future (Hamel and
  Prahalad), 89
competitive advantage
  data and, 106
  gaining, 53
  infrastructure and, 121
  technology and, 36, 68–71
competitive position
  improving, 53–56
  maintaining, 59–61
  technology planning and, 62–63
complexity
  dangers of, 108
computer-aided design (CAD), 33–34
computer illiteracy, 183
computerization
  typical cycle, 45
computer literacy
  and project success, 149
  senior management and, 183
  See also New Computer Literacy
computers, 34
  changing uses of, 3, 17, 20–22, 27–29, 44
  as decision support, 131–34
  hazards of ignoring, 35–38
  misconceptions about, 24–26
  unplanned buying of, 44–45
computing
  mobile, 135–37
  temporary, 135–37
computing power
  varying needs for, 131–34
consensus, 240
contingency plans, 107, 137, 139, 238–39

Coop, the, 35, 170
core competence, 55, 233
corporate mission, 48–50
cost drivers, 51–53
*Crazy Times Call for Crazy
  Organizations* (Peters), 166
Criminal Information Processing System,
  243
crises
  avoiding, 95–96
  preparing for, 139–40
critical risk factors, 57
critical success factors, 57, 210
customer satisfaction
  internal, 147–48
customer service
  improving, 32–33
customer service staff
  data requirements of, 132, 133
customers
  tracking, 30–34, 36, 50, 64
cycle time, 52–53

D

data
  backing up of, 107
  layering of, 132–34
  policies on, 106
  retrieval, 34, 131, 132
  varying needs for, 50, 131–34
data mining, 50, 164
data warehousing, 34–35, 50, 132
database marketing, 50
Datamation, 144
decentralization, 172–73
decision-support systems, 35, 58, 132–33,
  164
delays, controlling, 214–15
Dell Computer, 32
diagnostic questionnaire, 257–70
differentiation, 53–55
Dow Jones, 33
downtime, costs of, 118–19
drilling down, 34, 132
Drucker, Peter F., 43, 141, 163

E

Eastman Kodak, 141–42
economies of scale, 51, 55, 194
    outsourcing and, 142
economies of scope, 52
Economist, The (magazine), 69–70
EDS. *See* General Motors
education, continuing, 177
effectiveness, 16, 163, 164
efficiency
    compared with effectiveness, 163
Electronic Data Interchange (EDI), 33,
    70–71
Emerson, Ralph Waldo, 79
enabling technologies, 46–47, 55
expectations
    managing, 213
    unrealistic, 148

F

Fifth Discipline, The (Senge), 108
Financial Times (UK), 174, 176
flexibility, 206
    of policies, 218
    versus standardization, 162
Ford Motor Co., 35, 60–61
Fortune magazine, 69

G

Gates, Bill, 44
Gateway (computer company), 32
General Electric, 177, 183
General Motors, 46, 237, 238
Glen Burnie, Bank of. *See* Bank of Glen
    Burnie
good clients
    characteristics of, 230–46

H

Hamel, Gary, 89
Handy, Charles, 176
hardware
    adequate, 127–28
    benefits of leasing, 170

and temporary computing, 137
types, 117–18
hardware vendors
    pressures experienced by, 19
Harvard Business Review, 174
Harvard Business School, 56, 174
Henley Management College, 92
Hewlett-Packard, 170
hierarchies
    managing without, 175, 179
high perceived value (HPV), 53, 54, 59, 64
human resources. *See* people

I

IBM. *See* International Business
    Machines
IKEA, 54–55, 91
implementation, 146–47, 205–6, 217
    critical success factors and, 57
    senior management and, 65, 111–12
In the Age of the Smart Machine
    (Zuboff), 164
incentives, 178–79
informating, 117, 163–66
information. *See* data
information issues, 17
information management
    consequences of, 232
    costs of, 24–26
    defined, 100–102
    models, 63–68
    non-technology issues, 94–95
    people management and, 184–85
    planning, 92–96, 126–27, 152
    policies and principles, 100–107, 123
    quality of, 104–5
    redesigning and improving, 17–41
    roles and responsibilities, 102–4
    rules about, 172–73
    senior management and, 102–4
    See also information technology;
        technology
information management projects. *See*
    projects
Information Payoff (Strassman), 24

information repositories. *See* data warehousing
information systems (IS)
  decentralization of, 65–66, 102–3, 124, 141
  disconnects in, 55
  fragmentation of, 55
  strategic, 49
information systems departments
  changing role of, 65–66, 170
  danger of circumventing, 235
  policies and, 124
  pressures faced by, 235
  purpose of, 103
  responsibility of, 104–5
information technology (IT)
  aligning with business strategy, 89–92
  benefits of, 35–37
  and business strategy, 58–59
  choosing, 202–3
  and differentiation, 56
  effect on competitive position, 54
  guidelines for evaluating, 149–50
  improving, 110–11
  investments
    risks, 46
    senior management's role in, 64–65
    setting priorities for, 96–99
  opportunities created by, 46–47
  people and, 161–89
  planning, 62, 85
  principles, 126–27
  replacement of, 108, 237–38
  strategies, 92–95
  See also computers; infrastructure; technology
information warehousing. *See* data warehousing
infrastructure, 115–59
  analyzing benefits of, 141
  components of, 119–20
  costing, 140
  defined, 119
  hidden costs of, 118
  improving, 110–11, 121–22, 151–52, 199

investment
  assessing, 141
  priorities, 96–99
  outsourcing and, 141–45
  planning, 93–94, 121–22
  policies and, 66, 117, 119–22, 234
  types, 119–20
innovation, 29–35, 54–55, 178
integration, 150
Intel, 22
International Business Machines (IBM), 56–57, 87, 141–42
Internet, 46–47
islands of information, 45, 196, 235

J
Jett, Joseph, 183
Jobs, Steven, 44

K
Kanter, Rosabeth, 174, 175, 179
Kelly, Kevin, 172–73
Kidder Peabody, 183
KISS principle (Keep It Simple, Stupid), 240
Kmart, 69
knowledge workers
  keeping, 147
  managing
    challenges of, 174–75
    principles of, 175–80
Kodak, 141–42
Kraft Foods, 170–72

L
layering of data, 132–34
leadership, 62–65
  absence of, 79–89
  business strategy and, 47–48, 84–89
  information technology and, 79–113
  and stakeholder issues, 169
learning curves, 52
Levi Strauss, 32
LISA (personal computer), 27
L.L. Bean, 33
Loblaws, 35, 170

Lotus Notes, 32
low delivered cost (LDC), 53, 54, 59, 64

M
Machiavelli, 17
Macintosh (personal computer), 27
MacPaint, 128–29
Mahabir, Roger, 242–44
managers
  changing responsibilities of, 174–75, 179–80
  as impediments to training, 166
  and information management, 17, 102–4
  and infrastructure, 115–59
  involving in design process, 216
  and New Computer Literacy, 180–83
  and Plan–Do–Improve cycle, 84–87
  projects and, 191–227
  tools of, 38
Managing for Results (Drucker), 43
market segmentation, 50
marketing
  improving, 32, 50
marketing position, 53–55
Marks & Spencer, 97–99
McDonald's, 64–66
Mercedes-Benz, 37
Metropolitan Toronto Police, 242–44
Microsoft, 173
Mintzberg, Henry, 173
Mintzberg on Management (Mintzberg), 173
missions, corporate, 48–50
mission statement, 48
Moad, Jeff, 144
mobile computing, 135–37
modularity, 122, 130
Moore, Hugh, 242–43
Morita, Akio, 178–79
multi-period planning, 95–96, 126
Murphy's Law, 216, 238–39
Myers-Briggs Personality Inventory, 203
Mythical Man-Month, The (Brooks), 204

N
Natural History of Intellect (Emerson), 79
Netscape, 138
networks
  uses of, 30, 128
New Computer Literacy, 22, 180–83
Norman, Donald, 163
Northrop, 33–34
Nova Scotia, Bank of. *See* Bank of Nova Scotia

O
object databases, 201
objectives
  setting, 48
  strategic, 69
object-oriented programming, 210
obsolescence
  preparing for, 108, 111
On Becoming a Leader (Bennis), 81
open systems, 236
organizations
  improvement goals, 107–9
  influence of technology on, 30–35
Out of Control, 172–73
outside suppliers. *See* suppliers
outsourcing, 236–37
  methods, 144–45
  minimizing risks, 144
  reasons for, 142
  as strategic partnership, 141–42
  when not to outsource, 143–44
  See also suppliers
Outsourcing Institute (New York), 142
out-tasking, 145

P
Pareto's Rule, 239–40
payback
  evaluating, 26, 96–98
PC Week, 142, 147
people
  improving technical capabilities of, 153–54
  as part of infrastructure, 119–20, 153–54

people issues, 161–89
Peters, Tom, 166
Plan–Do–Improve cycle, 3, 62–63, 67, 82, 139
  managers and, 85–86
  post-audits and, 219
  and setting project goals, 232
policies, 65–66
  CEOs and, 87
  dangers of circumventing, 44
  and infrastructure, 234
  planning, 121–23
  project failure and, 217–18
  stakeholder issues and, 169
Politics of Information Management (Strassman), 101
Porras, Jerry, 60–61
portability, 130
portfolio analysis, 57–58
postaudits, 218–19
Prahalad, C.K., 89
Prince, The (Machiavelli), 17
processes
  adapting to packaged software, 151
  policies on, 105–6
  redesigning and improving, 30–35
  simulating, 33–34
product development
  improving, 35
production
  improving, 33–34
project development
  ideal situation, 17–18
  inadequate resources and, 208–9
  reality of, 18
project management, 169–70, 191–227
  See also projects
project process, 211–13
projects, 20, 239–40
  commitment to, 239–40
  common types, 192–95
  computer literacy and, 149
  costing, 201–2
  cut-off points, 213–14
  deadlines, 214–15
  defining, 207–8

  evaluating, 94–96, 192–95, 219–20, 273–78
  and expectations, 67
  failure of, 217–18
  improving, 218–19
  life cycle of, 212
  planning, 66–67, 95–96, 212, 244–46
  portfolio of, 199
  predicting results of, 220–22
  risks, 57, 205–10
  selecting, 195–200
  sizing, 200–201
  staffing, 203–4
  successful, components of, 247–48
  timing of, 209
project teams, 203–4, 215–16
  ideal size of, 204
prototypes, 208, 212

Q
quality
  managing for, 53
quality project process, 211–13

R
redundancy, 137
requirements. *See* specifications
risk
  assessing and managing, 57, 137–39, 205–10
  rewards of taking, 238–39
risk-tolerance levels, 138

S
Sainsbury's, 35, 170
Safeway, 35, 170
sales processes
  automation of, 30–32
  improving through technology, 30–32
Saturn (division of General Motors), 46, 238
selective extravagance, 56–57
Senge, Peter, 108
senior management
  and change, 166–68

and decentralization, 123
information management and, 102–4
information technology and, 79–89,
  111–12, 124–25
technology investments and, 64–65
See also chief executive officer
shelfware, 129
Skapinker, Michael, 174, 176
Softsearch, 138
software, 17–18
  buying versus developing, 151
  documentation, 216–17
  and effect on users, 121, 167
  excellent, characteristics of, 128–30
  layered, 237–38
  life cycle of, 18
  modularity, 237–38
  packaged, 151, 236
Sony, 178–79
specifications, 207–8
  problems setting, 18, 19
stakeholders, 168–70
standardization, 162
stealth bomber, 33–34
Strassman, Paul, 24, 101
strategic alliances, 179
strategic concepts, 48–58
strategic thinking, 38
Sunday Telegraph, 174
suppliers, 25
  coordinating different, 243
  developing partnerships with, 99, 130,
    141–42, 236, 240–44
  involving in project planning, 241
  negotiating effectively with, 148
  what to look for in, 230–41
sustainable information systems
  capabilities, 63, 68
sustainable success positions (SSPs), 59–63
systems. See information systems

T
technical specialists, hazards of
  overworking, 233
technology
  betting on, 27–28, 59

five major waves of, 20–21
  life cycle of, 108
temporary computing, 135–37
testing, 216–17
Things That Make Us Smart (Norman),
  163
Times, The (London), 174
Toyota, 153
training, 153–54
  by attrition, 151
  managers as impediments to, 166

U
users
  and resistance to new software, 19, 67
  effect of software on, 121, 167
  involving in project planning, 67, 207–8,
    211, 216

V
value
  creating for customers, 162
  relativity of, 53
value chain, 60
vendors. See hardware vendors; suppliers
Visible Hand, The (Chandler), 55–56

W
Wall Street Journal, 141
Wal-Mart, 68–71
Walton, Sam, 68–71
war gaming, 254–55
"waterfall approach", 208
Watson, Tom, 87
Wired magazine, 172
"working smart", 99–100

X
Xerox Star (personal computer), 27

Z
Zuboff, Shoshana, 164

THE TIGERPEARLS™ NEWSLETTER

If you enjoyed *Riding the Tiger,* you can now receive regular updates on the latest trends and topics in information management and strategy. You will receive four issues a year of the three authors' newsletter, which is written for the business manager. A newsletter format will allow us to update *Riding the Tiger* with topical and timely commentary on the strategic use of information management as new developments come along. We will extend the themes of the book and respond to selected subscribers' questions. We offer a money-back guarantee—you may cancel your subscription at any time and recover the unused portion of your subscription.

Sent via	One-year subscription	Three-year subscription
• E-mail	$20	$40
• Regular mail	$80	$160

Pricing is in US dollars, except in Canada, where it is in Canadian dollars.

To subscribe, please reproduce this page and send it by mail or fax to:
Alacrity Inc., 50 Wellington Street East, Suite 301, Toronto, ON, Canada M5E 1C8.
Phone: 1-416-362-5099. Fax: 1-416-362-0133.
E-mail: tigerpearls@alacrity.com

Circle choices on right	E-mail / Fax / Regular Mail	1-year / 3-years
	Contact me about site-licensing the newsletter for our organization. Yes ___ No ___	
Name		
Title		
Organization		
Type of business		
Your experience with IT	Noncomputer user / Light computer user / Heavy computer user / PC programmer / Mainframe programmer / IT management	
Address		
State/Province/ Country		
Zip/Postal Code		
Phone		
Fax		
E-mail address		

Check enclosed for $ _____   Purchase order enclosed for $_____
VISA Card Number _____

                    Exp. Date _____

Signature _____

Canadian residents please include 7% GST.
Ontario residents please include 8% PST.
(All subscriptions require signature
of subscriber)

Riding the Tiger FEEDBACK, NEWSLETTER QUESTION OR ANECDOTE SUBMISSION

If you would like to share an information technology horror or success story or pithy saying with us, or submit a strategic, technology or information management problem, we will review and select questions and respond to those we believe are of most interest to our readers.

Please indicate whether you wish to be identified as the author of the material if we use your material. No question will be reviewed unless contact information has been provided on this form or the subscription form.

Questions will be accepted from subscribers only. However, we welcome all feedback, sayings and anecdotes from all readers of *Riding the Tiger*.

Circle choices on right	Anonymous. I have enclosed contact information only if you need to contact me for clarification.	Use information on subscription page.	Use information below. Please use my name and/or company info.
Name			
Title			
Organization			
Type of business			
Address			
State/Province/ Country			
Zip/Postal Code			
Phone			
Fax			
E-mail address			

Send e-mail to Alacrity Inc. at tigerpearls@alacrity.com, or fax us at 1-416-362-0133. Our mail address is 50 Wellington Street East, Suite 301, Toronto, ON, Canada M5E 1C8.

Phone: 1-416-362-5099.

Please attach your feedback about the *Riding the Tiger*, or enclose your anecdote, horror story, pithy saying or question with this form.

NOTES

NOTES

NOTES

NOTES

NOTES

NOTES

NOTES